TEACH YOURSELF BOOKS

WHO'S WHO IN THE BIBLE
Including the Apocrypha

Some Other Teach Yourself Books

TEACH YOURSELF

WHO'S WHO
IN THE BIBLE
Including the Apocrypha

G. HENTON DAVIES
Principal, Regent's Park College, Oxford

Mrs A. B. DAVIES

TEACH YOURSELF BOOKS
ST. PAUL'S HOUSE WARWICK LANE LONDON EC4

First Printed 1970

Copyright © 1970
The English Universities Press Ltd.

SBN 340 05935 4

Printed and bound for The English Universities Press Ltd.
by T. & A. Constable Ltd., Hopetoun St., Edinburgh

FOREWORD

This book aims to refer to every person mentioned in the Bible, including the Apocrypha. Many persons mentioned, such as Cain's wife, David's mother and Peter's wife's mother are mentioned but not named. Very few children are mentioned by name.

Something is said, and at least one reference is given, for every person named, and longer notes are attached to the more prominent people. More information may be found in either Hastings *Dictionary of the Bible*, or in *The Interpreters' Bible Dictionary*, though the lists in these works do not always coincide. Many Biblical names of persons are omitted from *The New Bible Dictionary*. Reference to the genealogies in the Appendix will also be of some assistance. Nevertheless, the population of the Bible cannot be exactly numbered. Ambiguities in the Hebrew text, and some corruptions in the text; the lack sometimes of cross references between the O.T. and the Apocrypha, and the occasionally conflicting evidence of the Septuagint, the Greek translation of the Old Testament, make an exact census impossible.

We estimate accordingly that about 2,870 persons are named in the O.T., about 332 in the Apocrypha but not named in the O.T., and about 287 in the N.T.

Finally we thank Mrs M. Phillips, Secretary at Regent's Park College, who in her spare time faithfully and accurately typed this detailed manuscript.

A. B. DAVIES.
G. HENTON DAVIES.

GLOSSARY

A.	Apocrypha
Anc.	Ancestor
AV.	Authorised Version
AVm.	Authorised Version margin
b.	Brother
cp.	Compare
d.	Daughter
desc.	Descendant
f.	Father
grandd.	Granddaughter
grandf.	Grandfather
grandm.	Grandmother
grands.	Grandson
Gk.	Greek
Gt.	Great
h.	Husband
k. or K.	King
m.	Mother
n.	Nephew
N.T.	New Testament
O.T.	Old Testament
Q.	Queen
RSV.	Revised Standard Version
RV.	Revised Version
RVm.	Revised Version margin
s.	Son
S.	See
u.	Uncle
w.	Wife
Zerub.	Zerubbabel

THE BOOKS OF THE OLD TESTAMENT

Genesis	Gn.	Ecclesiastes	Eccl.
Exodus	Ex.	Solomon	Sol.
Leviticus	Lv.	Isaiah	Is.
Numbers	Nu.	Jeremiah	Jer.
Deuteronomy	Deut.	Lamentations	Lam.
Joshua	Jos.	Ezekiel	Ezk.
Judges	Jg.	Daniel	Dan.
Ruth	Ru.	Hosea	Hos.
I Samuel	1 S.	Joel	Jl.
II Samuel	2 S.	Amos	Amos
I Kings	1 K.	Obadiah	Obad.
II Kings	2 K.	Jonah	Jonah
I Chronicles	1 Ch.	Micah	Micah
II Chronicles	2 Ch.	Nahum	Nah.
Ezra	Ezr.	Habakkuk	Hab.
Nehemiah	Neh.	Zephaniah	Zeph.
Esther	Est.	Haggai	Hag.
Job	Job	Zechariah	Zec.
Psalms	Ps.	Malachi	Malachi
Proverbs	Pr.		

THE BOOKS OF THE NEW TESTAMENT

Matthew	Mt.	II Thessalonians	2 Thess.
Mark	Mk.	I Timothy	1 Ti.
Luke	Lk.	II Timothy	2 Ti.
John	Jn.	Titus	Tit.
The Acts	Ac.	Philemon	Philem.
Epistle to the		Hebrews	Heb.
Romans	Ro.	Epistle of James	James
I Corinthians	1 Cor.	I Peter	1 P.
II Corinthians	2 Cor.	II Peter	2 P.
Galatians	Gal.	I John	1 Jn.
Ephesians	Eph.	II John	2 Jn.
Philippians	Ph.	III John	3 Jn.
Colossians	Col.	Jude	Jude
I Thessalonians	1 Thess.	Revelation	Rev.

THE BOOKS CALLED APOCRYPHA

1 Esdras	1 Es.	Song of the	
2 Esdras	2 Es.	three holy children.	
Tobit	To.	Story of Susanna	Sus.
Judith	Jth.	The Idol Bel, and	
The rest of		the Dragon	
Esther	Ad. Est	Prayer of Manasses	Man.
Wisdom		1 Maccabees	1 Mac.
Ecclesiasticus	Sir.	2 Maccabees	2 Mac.
Baruch	Bar.		

INDEX OF ALL PERSONS MENTIONED IN THE BIBLE INCLUDING THE APOCRYPHA

(A glossary and list of abbreviations is to be found on p. vi)

Aaron	G.-grands. of Levi the s. of Jacob (Leah) and s. of Amram, b. of Miriam and elder b. of Moses (Ex. 6:16-20). Moses and Aaron shared in the deliverance of Israel from Egypt, Aaron being Moses' mouthpiece (7:1). They convinced the Israelites (4:27-31), but after increasing hardship sought interviews with Pharaoh before whom Aaron (83 years of age) was to perform miracles. Next Aaron helped Moses to defeat the Amalekites (17:8), and later with his sons and 70 elders of Israel dined in God's presence and saw God's glory (24:1, 9, 10). Later Aaron organised the idolatrous occasion of the Golden Calf (Ex. 32). In spite of all this Aaron was said to be appointed and inducted as first High Priest (Ex. 39; Lv. 8), and ancestor of all legitimate priests. With Miriam Aaron revolted against Moses' position (Nu. 12), and with Moses was the object of a rebellion, but Aaron was confirmed as High Priest by the miracle of his rod budding (Nu. 16, 17). He died aged 123, having passed on his regalia to his son and successor Eleazar (Nu. 20), a secondary figure of shadowy significance.	
A. Abacuc	is Habbakuk the prophet.	2 Es. 1:40
A. Abadias	s. of Jezelus, returned with Ezra from exile.	1 Es. 8:35
	is Obadiah, s. of Jehiel.	Ezr. 8:9
Abagtha	Persian chamberlain of k. Ahasuerus.	Est. 1:10
Abda	1. f. of Adoniram.	1 K. 4:6
	2. Levite.	Neh. 11:17
	is Obadiah.	1 Ch. 9:16

1

Abdeel	f. of Shelemiah.	Jer. 36:26
Abdi	1. Grandf. of Ethan.	1 Ch. 6:44
	2. f. of Kish.	2 Ch. 29:12
	3. Married foreign wife.	Ezr. 10:26
	is Aedias.	1 Ezr. 9:27
A. Abdias	is Obadiah the prophet.	2 Es. 1:39
Abdiel	s. of Guni	1 Ch. 5:15
Abdon	1. s. of Hillel, Ephraimite.	Jg. 12:13
	2. (s. of Shashak) Benjamite living in Jerusalem.	1 Ch. 8:23
	3. s. of Jehiel, Gibeonite.	1 Ch. 8:30
	4. Jerusalem courtier in k. Josiah's reign.	2 Ch. 34:20
	is Achbor.	2 K. 22:12
Abednego	S. Shadrach.	
Abel	Second s. of Adam and Eve (Gn. 4:2). Name means 'breath' or more probably 'son': keeper of sheep and first righteous (Mt. 23:35) innocent martyr, for he was slain by his elder brother Cain (Gn. 4; Lk. 11:51; Heb. 11:4, 12:24).	
Abi	d. of Zechariah.	2 K. 18:2
	is Abijah 7.	2 Ch. 29:1
Abia, Abiah	S. Abijah 6.	
Abi-Albon	One of David's 'Thirty'.	2 S. 23:31
	is Abiel.	1 Ch. 11:32
Abiasaph	Levite.	Ex. 6:24
	is Ebiasaph.	1 Ch. 6:23
Abiathar	lit: father (God) of abundance, s. of Ahimelek (1 K. 2:26). Sole survivor of Saul's massacre of priests of Nob he fled with Ephod to David to become his oracular priest in David's outlaw days (1 S. 23:6). Abiathar and Zadok were David's chief priests at Jerusalem (2 S. 20:25), and were sent back to Jerusalem with the ark during Absalom's revolt (2 S. 15:24-36). At the end of David's life he supported Adonijah the rightful heir to the throne, and was exiled	

	to Anathoth by king Solomon (1 K. 1:2; Jer. 1:1).	
Abida,	Fourth s. of Midian.	Gn. 25:4
AV. Abidah	is Abidah.	1 Ch. 1:33
Abidan	s. of Gideoni, Benjamite.	Nu. 1:11
Abiel	1. s. of Zeror, grandf. of Saul.	1 S. 9:1
	2. The Arbathite, one of David's 'Thirty'.	1 Ch. 11:32
	is Abi-albon.	2 S. 23:31
Abiezer	1. Manassite, s. of Gilead.	1 Ch. 7:18
	is Jeazer.	Nu. 26:30
	2. Davidic Hero, a Benjamite.	2 S. 23:27
Abigail	lit: my father rejoices.	
	1. Sister of Zeruiah and of David. m. of Joab.	1 Ch. 2:16
	2. w. of Nabal a wealthy Carmelite. Whereas he failed in hospitality to David and unwisely refused to give protection gifts to the outlaw, she gave David a handsome present. The incident caused Nabal's death, and she became David's wife and mother of his second son. A sensible, a beautiful and an astute lady.	
		1 S. 25
Abihail	1. f. of Zuriel.	Nu. 3:35
	2. w. of Abishur.	1 Ch. 2:29
	3. d. of Eliab, s. of Jesse.	2 Ch. 11:18
	4. s. of Huri, Gadite.	1 Ch. 5:14
	5. f. of Esther.	Est. 2:15
Abihu	Second s. of Aaron.	Ex. 6:23, 24:1
Abihud	Benjamite.	1 Ch. 8:3
Abijah	1. K. of Judah, s. of Rehoboam.	2 Ch. 13:20
	is Abijam.	1 K. 14:31
RV. Abiah	2. Second s. of Samuel.	1 S. 8:2
	3. s. of Jeroboam the first.	1 K. 14:1
	4. Priest.	1 Ch. 24:10
	5. grands. of Benjamin.	1 Ch. 7:8
RV. Abiah	6. w. of Hezron, Judahite.	1 Ch. 2:24
	7. w. of Ahaz, m. of Hezekiah.	2 Ch. 29:1
	is Abi.	2 K. 18:2

	8. Covenanting Priest.	Neh. 10:7
	9. Priest companion of Zerubbabel.	Neh. 12:4
Abijam	S. Abijah 1.	
Abimael	s. of Joktan descendant of Shem.	Gn. 10:28
Abimelech	1. K. of Gerar.	Gn. 20:2f.
	2. K. of Gath (presumably is Achish cf. 1 S. 21:11).	Ps. 34 title
	3. s. of Gideon became k. of Shechem.	Jg. 8:31ff.
	4. s. of Abiathar, priest. is Ahimelech.	1 Ch. 18:16 2 S. 8:17
Abinadab	1. of Kirjath-jearim.	1 S. 7:1
	2. Second s. of Jesse.	1 S. 16:8
	3. s. of Saul.	1 S. 31:2
	4. S. Ben-Abinadab.	
Abinoam	f. of Barak.	Jg. 4:6
Abiram	1. s. of Eliab, Reubenite.	Nu. 16:1f.
	2. s. of Hiel of Bethel.	1 K. 16:34
Abishag	Shunammitess.	1 K. 1:2
Abishai	s. of Zeruiah, b. of Joab, Commander of David's Thirty mighty men.	2 S. 23:18-19
Abishalom	S. Absalom	
Abishua	1. s. of Phineas.	1 Ch. 6:4
	2. Benjamite.	1 Ch. 8:4
Abishur	s. of Shammai.	1 Ch. 2:28
A. Abissei AV. Abisei	Ancestor of Ezra. is Abisue. is Abishua I.	2 Es. 1:2 1 Es. 8:2 1 Ch. 6:4
A. Abisue	S. Abissei.	
A. Abisum	is Abishua 1.	
Abital	w. of David.	2 S. 3:4
Abitub	s. of Shaharaim, Benjamite.	1 Ch. 8:11
Abiud	Anc. of Jesus Christ.	Mt. 1:13

4

Abner Lit. Father is Ner (lamp). Cousin or u. of Saul
and captain of his army and his right hand man
(1 S. 14:47, 17:55-58, 20-25). After Saul's
death Abner became the support of his son
Ishbaal and attached the allegiance of all the
tribes except Judah to the king. After a skir-
mish between the rival forces of Ishbaal and
David, Abner was compelled in self-defence to
kill Asahel, brother of Joab, David's general
(2 S. 2:18-23). In Ishbaal's second year Abner
took Saul's concubine. In spite of his known
loyalty, this was interpreted as treachery, and
Abner began to negotiate the transfer of the
kingdom to David (3:7-10). Whilst on a
mission to this end to David he was suddenly
slain by Joab (3:22-27). David disavowed
responsibility and composed a lament for
Abner (2 S. 3:33-34). He gave generous gifts
to maintain the future temple (1 Ch. 26:27-28).

Abraham Abram (the father is exalted) or Abraham, (popu-
larly but uncertainly, Father of nations) was
the s. of Terah, desc. of Shem, f. of Isaac,
grandf. of Jacob=Israel. He was h. of Sarah
(Isaac); Hagar (Ishmael, Gn. 16. 25:12-16);
Keturah (Midian and N. Arabian peoples,
Gn. 25:1-4). With his father's family Abraham
journey from Ur to Haran and thence with his
own family journeyed into Canaan (Gn. 11-12).
He was probably a merchant prince trading
along the caravan routes and in the commercial
centres. Although a visitor in many cities he
probably became a resident alien at Gerar,
where he must have spent many years (Gn.
20:1-15). Eventually Sarah and then he, aged
175 years, were buried at the cave of Machpelah
in Hebron (Gn. 23). He was the recipient of
great promises (Gn. 12:1-3, 13:14-17, 17:1-8),
and was traditionally the head of the three
great monotheistic religions, Judaism, Christianity and Mohammedanism. He was the

	father of all the faithful and figured prominently in the N.T. The phrase Abraham's bosom typified the eternal dwelling place of the righteous (Lk. 16:22f.).	
Absalom Abishalom	1. (Father of peace.) Third s. of David by Maacah, d. of k. of Geshur. A handsome but spoilt prince, who was banished from his father's court for five years. He returned only to plan and bring about an open rebellion against his father, but he was defeated and slain (2 S. 3:3, 15:1-15, 18:9-17).	
	A. 2. f. of Mattathias.	1 Mac. 11:70
	A. 3. Envoy.	2 Mac. 11:17
A. Abubus	f. of Ptolemy.	1 Mac. 16:11
A. Accaba AV. Agaba	Returned from exile with Zerubbabel.	1 Es. 5:30
	is Hagab.	Ezr. 2:46
	is Hagaba.	Neh. 7:48
A. Accos	Priestly grandf. of an envoy in Rome.	1 Mac. 8:17
Achaicus	Visited Paul at Ephesus.	1 Cor. 16:17
Achan	Man of Judah.	Jos. 7:1
	is Achar.	1 Ch. 2:7
Achar	S. Achan.	
Achbor	1 Edomite.	Gn. 36:38
	2. Courtier.	2 K. 22:12
	is Abdon 4.	2 Ch. 34:20
A. Achiacharus	n. of Tobit.	To. 1:21
A. Achias	Anc. of Ezra.	2 Es. 1:2
Achim	Anc. of Jesus Christ.	Mt. 1:14
Achior	Ammonite general.	Jth. 5:5
A. Achipha AV. Acipha	His children returned with Zerubbabel.	1 Es. 5:31
	is Hakupha.	Ezr. 2:51
Achish	k. of Gath.	1 S. 21:10

Achsah AV. Achsa	d. of Caleb.	Jos. 15:16-19
A. Acub	His sons returned with Zerubbabel.	1 Es. 5:31
	is Bakbuk.	Neh. 7:53
Acud AV. Acua	is Akkub.	1 Es. 5:30 / Ezr. 2:45
Adah	1. w. of Lamech.	Gn. 4:19, 20
	2. w. of Esau.	Gn. 36:2
Adiah	1. grandf. of Josiah.	2 K. 22:1
	2. Levite.	1 Ch. 6:41
	is Iddo.	1 Ch. 6:21
	3. s. of Shimei.	1 Ch. 8:21
	4. s. of Jeroham, a priest S 9.	1 Ch. 9:12
	5. captain.	2 Ch. 23:1
	6. of the family of Bani.	Ezr. 10:29
	7. also of the family of Bani.	Ezr. 10:39
	8. desc. of Judah.	Neh. 11:5
	9. Levite.	Neh. 11:12
A. Adaliah	Fifth s. of Haman.	Est. 9:8

Adam — (Man, mankind). First man and father of all human beings. Created on the sixth day, he was the goal and end of creation. He was created in the image of God and was to have dominion over all life and nature (Gn. 1.). He was mentioned over 500 times in O.T.; and in the N.T. he was the representative of mankind and the type and antitype of Jesus Christ (1 Cor. 15:45-9; Ro. 5:12-19).

Adbeel	Third s. of Ishmael.	Gn. 25:13
Addar	S. Ard.	
Addi	1. Anc. of Jesus Christ.	Lk. 3:28
	A. 2. Sons returned with Zerubbabel.	1 Es. 9:31
A. Addo	grandf. of Zechariah. S. Iddo.	1 Es. 6:1
A. Addus	1. His sons returned with Zerubbabel	1 Es. 5:34

	2. S. Jaddus.	
Adiel	1. Simeonite prince.	1 Ch. 4:36
	2. priest.	1 Ch. 9:12
	3. f. of Azmaveth.	1 Ch. 27:25
Adin	1. Head of Jewish family.	Ezr. 2:15
	2. Covenanting chief	Neh. 10:16
Adina	Davidic hero, Reubenite.	1 Ch. 11:42
Adino	One of David's 'Thirty'.	2 S. 23:8
A. Adinu AV. Adin	is Adin	1 Es. 8:32
Adlai	f. of Shaphat.	1 Ch. 27:29
Admatha	Wise man of Ahasuerus.	Est. 1:14
Admin	Anc. of Jesus Christ.	Lk. 3:33
Adna	1. Contemporary of Ezra.	Ezr. 10:30
	2. Priest.	Neh. 12:15
Adnah	1. Tribal Officer under Saul.	1 Ch. 12:20
	2. Military Officer under Jehoshaphat.	2 Ch. 17:14
Adonibezek	K. of Bezek.	Jg. 1:5-7
Adonijah	1. (My Lord is Yah.) Fourth s. of David (2 S. 3:4). After the death of his three eldest brothers he regarded himself as heir presumptive to David's throne, but was deposed by a palace plot in favour of Solomon, Bathsheba's son.	1 K. 1
	2. Levite.	2 Ch. 17:8
	3. Chief who sealed the covenant.	Neh. 10:16
	is Adonikam.	Ezr. 2:13
Adonikam	Post exilic Jew.	Ezr. 2:13
	is Adonijah 2.	Neh. 10:16
Adoniram	Superintendent of public works.	1 K. 4:6
	is Adoram.	2 S. 20:24
	is Hadoram.	2 Ch. 10:18

Adoni zedek AV. Adoni-Zedec	K. of Jerusalem.	Jos. 10:1-27
Adoram	S. Adoniram.	
Adrammelech	Sennacherib's s. and assassin.	2 K. 19:37
Adriel	s. of Barzillai.	1 S. 18:19
A. Aduel	Anc. of Tobit.	To. 1:1
A. Aedias	Put away his foreign wife. is Elijah.	1 Es. 9:27 Ezr. 10:26
Aeneas	Cured by Peter.	Ac. 9:33f.
Agabus	A christian prophet in Jerusalem, who predicted a 'great dearth' (Ac. 11:27-28), and presented dramatically a prediction of the binding of Paul at Jerusalem (Ac. 21:10-11).	
Agag	K. of Amalekites.	Num. 24:7
A. Agar	Head of family.	Bar. 3:23
Agee	f. of Shammah.	2 S. 23:11
A. Aggaba AV. Graba	His sons returned with Zerubbabel. S. Hagabah. S. Hagaba.	1 Es. 5:29
A. Aggaeus AV. Aggeus	is Haggai the Prophet.	1 Es. 6:1
A. Agia AV. Hagia	His family returned from captivity. is Hattil.	1 Es. 5:34 Ezr. 2:57
Agrippa	S. Herod.	
Agur	Wise Man. s. of Jakeh.	Pr. 30:1
Ahab	1. (the brother is father) k. of Israel (c. 869-850), s. of Omri and h. of Jezebel. A warrior king who fortified his cities (1 K. 16:34), and his own capital (16:32). He fought against Syria and Assyria and eventually died in battle (22:28-40). He was opposed by Elijah on religious	

	(1 K. 18) and humanitarian grounds (1 K. 21:1-16).	
	2. False Prophet, s. of Kolaiah.	Jer. 29:21f.
Aharah	s. of Benjamin. S. Ahiram.	1 Ch. 8:1
Aharhel	Judahite.	1 Ch. 4:8
Ahasbai	f. of Eliphelet.	2 S. 23:34
Ahasuerus	1. k. of Persia. is Xerxes.	Ezr. 4:6
	2. f. of Darius.	Dan. 9:1
Ahaz	1. (he has grasped), k. of Judah (c. 735-720). He appealed against Isaiah's advice (Is. 7:1-12), to Assyria for help against the alliance of the kings of Syria and Israel (2 K. 16:5). He was judged a bad king because of his idolatrous practices (2 K. 16:10-16).	
	2. S. of Micah	1 Ch. 8:35
Ahaziah	1. k. of Israel, s. of Ahab.	1 K. 22:51
	2. k. of Judah, s. of Jehoram.	2 K. 8:25
	is Jehoahaz.	2 Ch. 21:17
	is Azariah.	2 Ch. 22:6
Ahban	s. of Abishur.	1 Ch. 2:29
Aher	Benjamite.	1 Ch. 7:12
	is Ahiram.	Nu. 26:38
Ahi	1. Gadite.	1 Ch. 5:15
	2. Asherite.	1 Ch. 7:34
Ahiah	S. Ahijah 9.	
Ahiam	Davidic hero.	2 S. 23:33
Ahian	Manassite.	1 Ch. 7:19
Ahiezer	1. s. of Amishaddai.	Nu. 1:12
	2. Benjamite archer.	1 Ch. 12:1-3
Ahihud	1. Asherite prince.	Nu. 34:27
	2. Benjamite.	1 Ch. 8:6, 7
Ahijah	1. High Priest. (S. Ahimelech I.)	1 S. 14:3
	2. Prophet from Shiloh and one of Solomon's historians	1 K. 11:29f.
	3. Scribe under Solomon.	1 K. 4:3

	4. f. of King Baasha.	1 K. 15:27
	5. s. of Jerahmeel.	1 Ch. 2:25
	6. s. of Ehud.	1 Ch. 8:7
	7. Davidic hero.	1 Ch. 11:36
	8. Levite.	1 Ch. 26:20
RV. Ahiah	9. Chief who sealed the covenant. is Ahoah.	Neh. 10:26
A.	10. Ancestor of Ezra	2 Es. 1:1
Ahikam	s. of Shaphan, f. of Gedaliah.	2 K. 22:12
A. Ahikar	n. of Tobit	To. 1:21
Ahilud	1. f. of Jehoshaphat.	2 S. 8:16
	2. f. of Baana.	1 K. 4:12
Ahimaaz	1. s. of Zadok, and a swift runner.	2 S. 18:27
	2. f. of Ahinoam.	1 S. 14:50
	3. Officer under Solomon.	1 K. 4:15
Ahiman	1. s. of Anak.	Nu. 13:22
	2. Doorkeeper.	1 Ch. 9:17
Ahimelech	1. s. of Ahitub. S. Ahijah 1.	1 S. 21:1-9
	2. Hittite, one of David's captains.	1 S. 26:6
Ahimoth	s. of Elkanah.	1 Ch. 6:25
Ahinadab	Officer under Solomon.	1 K. 4:14
Ahinoam	1. w. of Saul.	1 S. 14:50
	2. w. of David.	1 S. 25:43
Ahio	1. s. of Abinadab.	2 S. 6:3f.
	2. s. of Jeiel, and u. of Saul.	1 Ch. 8:31
	3. Benjamite.	1 Ch. 8:14
Ahira	s. of Enan.	Nu. 1:15
Ahiram	Benjamite, head of family.	Nu. 26:38
	is Ehi.	Gn. 46:21
	is Aharah.	1 Ch. 8:1
Ahisamach	Danite.	Ex. 31:6
Ahishahar	s. of Bilham, Benjamite.	1 Ch. 7:10
Ahishar	Superintendent under Solomon.	1 K. 4:6
Ahithophel	Courtier under David, joined the rebellion of Absalom.	2 S. 15-17:23

A. Ahitob AV. Achitob	Anc. of Ezra.	1 Es. 8:12
Ahitub	1. grands. of Eli. 2. Relation of Zadok. 3. f. of Zadok. A. 4. Anc. of Judith (AV. Acitho).	1 S. 14:3 2 S. 8:17 1 Ch. 6:11 Jth. 8:1
Ahlai	1. d. of Sheshan. 2. f. of Zabad.	1 Ch. 2:31 1 Ch. 11:41
Ahoah	Benjamite, S. Ahijah 6.	1 Ch. 8:4
Ahohi	f. of Dodo.	2 S. 23:9
Ahumai	desc. of Judah.	1 Ch. 4:2
Ahuzzam AV. Ahuzam	Judahite.	1 Ch. 4:6
Ahuzzath	Friend of Abimelech the Philistine.	Gn. 26:26
Ahzai AV. Ahasia	Priest. is Jahzerah.	Neh. 11:13 1 Ch. 9:12
Aiah AV. Ajah	1. desc. of Esau. 2. f. of Rizpah.	Gn. 36:24 2 S. 3:7
Akan	desc. of Esau. is Jakan (AV.).	Gn. 36:27
A. Akatan AV. Acatan	f. of Joannes. is Hakkatan.	1 Es. 8:38 Ezr. 8:12
Akkos	S. Hakkoz.	
Akkub	1. s. of Elioenai. 2. Levitical Gatekeeper. A. is Dacubi 3. Levite expounder of the Law. A. is Jacubus. 4. f. of family of porters. A. is Acud.	1 Ch. 3:24 Ezr. 2:42 1 Es. 5:28 Neh. 8:7 1 Es. 9:48 1 Ch. 9:17 1 Es. 5:30
Alcimus	Leader of Hellenizing party.	1 Mac. 7:5
Alemeth	1. Benjamite (AV. Alameth). 2. desc. of Saul.	1 Ch. 7:8 1 Ch. 8:36
Alexander	1. s. of Simon of Cyrene. 2. Relation of High Priest.	Mk. 15:21 Ac. 4:6

12

	3. Jew at Ephesus.	Ac. 19:33
	4. Unconscientious teacher.	1 Ti. 1:20
	5. Metal worker.	2 Ti. 4:14
A. Alexander the Great		1 Mac. 1:1-7
A. Alexander Balas	Pretended s. of Antiochus Epiphanes.	1 Mac. 11:17
	is Alexander Epiphanes.	1 Mac. 10:1
Aliah	Duke of Edom.	1 Ch. 1:51
	is Alvah.	Gn. 36:40
Alian	desc. of Esau.	1 Ch. 1:40
	is Alvan.	Gn. 36:23
A. Allar AV. Aalar	Post-exilic leader.	1 Es. 5:36
A. Allon AV. Allom	1. desc. returned with Zerubbabel.	1 Es. 5:34
	2. Simeonite prince.	1 Ch. 4:37
Al Modad	s. of Joktan.	Gn. 10:26
Alphaeus	1. f. of Matthew.	Mk. 2:14
	2. f. of James the Apostle.	Mt. 10:3
Alvah	S. Alvan.	
Alvan	Hurrian (Horite).	Gn. 36:23
	is Alvah.	Gn. 36:40
	is Alian.	1 Ch. 1:40
	is Aliah.	1 Ch. 1:51
Amadathus	S. Hammedatha.	
Amal	Asherite.	1 Ch. 7:35
Amalek	grands. of Esau.	Gn. 36:12
Aman	A. 1. cruel man.	To. 14:10
	2. is Haman.	Est. 12:6
Amariah	1. High Priest.	2 Ch. 19:11
	2. High Priest grandf. of Zadok.	1 Ch. 6:7
	3. s. of Azariah.	1 Ch. 6:11
	4. Priest.	Neh. 10:3
	5. Levite in David's reign.	1 Ch. 23:19
	6. Levite in time of Hezekiah.	2 Ch. 31:15

13

	7. Judahite who had taken a foreign wife.	Ezr. 10:42
	8. Judahite.	Neh. 11:4
	9. Gt. grandf. of Zephaniah.	Zeph. 1:1
	10. Priest who returned with Zerubbabel.	Neh. 12:2
	11. Priest.	Neh. 12:13
	12. S. Amarias.	
A. Amarias	Anc. of Ezra.	1 Es. 8:2
	is Amariah 10.	Ezr. 7:3
Amasa	1. n. of David.	2 S. 17:25
	2. Ephraimite.	2 Ch. 28:12
Amasai	1. Levite: Kohathite.	1 Ch. 6:25
	2. Priest in the reign of David.	1 Ch. 15:24
	3. Officer under David.	1 Ch. 12:18
	4. Priest: Kohathite.	2 Ch. 29:12
Amashsai	Priest.	Neh. 11:13
AV. Amashai	is Maasai,	1 Ch. 9:12
Amasiah	Military Commander.	2 Ch. 17:16
Amaziah	1. k. of Judah.	2 K. 14:1
	2. Priest of Bethel.	Am. 7:10-17
	3. Simeonite.	1 Ch. 4:34
	4. Levite: Merarite.	1 Ch. 6:45
Ami	Head of family of temple servants.	Ezr. 2:57
Amittai	f. of Jonah the prophet.	2 K. 14:25
Ammiel	1. Spy.	Nu. 13:12
	2. f. of Machir.	2 S. 9:4f
	3. Sixth s. of Obededom.	1 Ch. 26:5
	4. f. of Bathshua.	1 Ch. 3:5
	is Eliam	2 S. 11:3
Ammihud	1. Ephraimite.	Nu. 1:10
	2. Simeonite f. of Shemuel.	Nu. 34:20
	3. Naphtalite f. of Pedahel.	Nu. 34:28
RV. Ammihur	4. f. of Talmai, k. of Geshur.	2 S. 13:37
	5. s. of Omri.	1 Ch. 9:4
Ammihur	S. Ammihud 4.	

Amminadab	1. Anc. of David, f. of Nahshon.	Ru. 4:19, Mt. 1:4
	2. s. of Kohath.	1 Ch. 6:22
	3. Levite chief of sons of Uzziel.	1 Ch. 15:10
Ammishaddai	Danite.	Nu. 1:12
Ammizabad	s. of Benaiah.	1 Ch. 27:6
Amnon	1. Eldest s. of David.	2 S. 3:2
	2. s. of Shimon.	1 Ch. 4:20
Amok	Priestly Chief.	Neh. 12:7
Amon	1. k. of Judah.	2 K. 21:18-26
	2. Governor of Samaria.	1 K. 22:26
	3. Sons returned with Zerubbabel.	Neh. 7:59
	is Ami.	Ezr. 2:57

Amos — Herdsman and sheep farmer from Tekoa, S.E. of Jerusalem. He was a great believer in the importance of Jerusalem (Amos 1:2), but ministered almost exclusively to the northern kingdom of Israel. For a time at least he became a prophet preaching in northern centres. After a quarrel with Amaziah, the head priest of Bethel, (7:10-17) he presumably retired to the south. His sermons and teaching blending, ethical demands with compassion for the poor, are contained in his book.

Amoz	f. of Isaiah the prophet.	2 K. 19:2; Is. 1:1
Ampliatus AV. Amplias	Christian.	Ro. 16:8
Amram	1. Levite, f. of Moses.	Nu. 3:17-19
	2. s. of Bani.	Ezr. 10:34
Amraphel	K. of Shinar.	Gn. 14:1
Amzi	1. Levite.	1 Ch. 6:46
	2. Priest in 2nd Temple.	Neh. 11:12
A. Anael	b. of Tobit.	To. 1:21
Anah	1. d. of Zibeon.	Gn. 36:2

	2. s. of Zibeon.	Gn. 36:24
	3. duke, b. of Zibeon.	Gn. 36:20
Anaiah	1. Levite.	Neh. 8:4
	A. is Ananias.	1 Es. 9:43
	2. Jew who sealed Nehemiah's covenant.	Neh. 10:22
Anan	1. Chief of the people who sealed the covenant.	Neh. 10:26
	A. 2. Returned from captivity.	1 Es. 5:30
	is Hanan.	Ezr. 2:46
Anani	s. of Elioenai desc. of David.	1 Ch. 3:24
Ananiah	f. of Maaseiah, priest.	Neh. 3:22f.
Ananias	A. 1. s. of Emmer.	1 Es. 9:21
	is Hanani.	Ezr. 10:20
	A. 2. s. of Bebai	1 Es. 9:29
	is Hananiah.	Ezr. 10:28
	A. 3. He stood with Ezra.	1 Es. 9:43
	is Anaiah.	Neh. 8:4
	A. 4. Levite.	1 Es. 9:48
	is Hanan.	Neh. 8:7
	A. 5. Anc. of Judith.	Jth. 8:1
	6. h. of Sapphira.	Ac. 5:1ff.
	7. Disciple living in Damascus.	Ac. 9:10-18
	8. High Priest.	Ac. 23:1f.
A. Ananiel	Anc. of Tobit.	To. 1:1
A. Anasib	f. of priests.	1 Es. 5:24
	is Sanasib (AV.)	
Anath	f. of Shamgar.	Jg. 3:31
Anathoth	1. s. of Becher, Benjamite.	1 Ch. 7:8
	2. Chief who sealed the covenant	Neh. 10:19
Andrew	First Apostle; b. of Peter.	Mk. 1:16-20
Andronicus	A. 1. An official at Antioch.	2 Mac. 4:31-38
	2. Christian relative of Paul.	Ro. 16:7
	A. 3. Officer at Gerizim.	2 Mac. 5:23
Aner	Amorite Chieftain, covenanted with Abraham.	Gn. 14:13.
Aniam	Man of Manasseh.	1 Ch. 7:19

Anna	A. 1. w. of Tobit.	To. 1:9
	2. Prophetess.	Lk. 2:36-38
A. Annan	is Annas 2.	
Annas	1. High Priest during lifetime of Jesus Christ.	Jn. 18:13
	A. 2. Jew.	1 Es. 9:32
	is Harim.	Ezr. 10:31
A. Annis	Head of post-exilic family.	1 Es. 5:16
A. Annus AV. Anus	Levite.	1 Es. 9:48
A. Annuus	Jew, returned from exile with Ezra.	1 Es. 8:48
A. Anos	desc. of Baani.	1 Es. 9:34
	is Vaniah.	Ezr. 10:36
Anthothijah AV Anto-thijah	Benjamite.	1 Ch. 8:24
A. Antiochis	Concubine of Antiochus Epiphanes.	2 Mac. 4:30
A. Antiochus	1. f. of Numenius.	1 Mac. 12:16
	2. Antiochus III (The Great).	1 Mac. 1:10
	3. Antiochus IV (Epiphanes). second s. of Antiochus III.	1 Mac. 1:20ff.
	4. Antiochus V, s. of Antiochus IV.	1 Mac. 6:17
	5. Antiochus VI, s. of Alexander Balas and Cleopatra.	1 Mac. 13:31
	6. Antiochus VII, second s. of Demetrius.	1 Mac. 15:1-10
Antipas (Antipater)	1. S. Herod.	
	2. Martyr.	Rev. 2:13
A. Antipater	Ambassador.	1 Mac. 12:16
Anub	Judahite.	1 Ch. 4:8
A. Apame	d. of Bartacus.	1 Es. 4:29
Apelles	Christian at Rome.	Ro. 16:10
A. Apherra	Descendants returned with Zerubbabel.	1 Es. 5:34

Aphiah	Anc. of Saul.	1 S. 9:1
A. Apollonius	1. s. of Thraseus.	2 Mac. 3:5
	2. s. of Menestheus.	2 Mac. 4:21
	3. sent with army to Judea.	2 Mac. 5:24-26
	4. s. of Genneus, who vexed the Jews.	2 Mac. 12:2
	5. Governor in Syria.	1 Mac. 10:67-86
A. Apollophanes	Syrian.	2 Mac. 10:37
Apollos	Alexandrian Jew at Ephesus.	Ac. 18:24
Appaim	Judahite s. of Nadab.	1 Ch. 2:30, 31
Apphia	Christian lady of Colossae.	Philem. v. 2
A. Apphus	Surname of Jonathan the Maccabee.	1 Mac. 2:5
Aquila	Jewish Christian, h. of Priscilla, and friend of Paul.	Ac. 18:2, 24-28
Ara	Asherite.	1 Ch. 7:38
Arad	Benjamite.	1 Ch. 8:15
Arah	1. Asherite.	1 Ch. 7:39
	2. Descendants returned with Zerubbabel.	Ezr. 2:5
Aram R.V. Ram	1. s. of Shem.	Gn. 10:22
	2. s. of Kemuel, desc. of Nahor.	Gn. 22:21
	3. Asherite.	1 Ch. 7:34
	4. S. genealogy of Jesus.	Mt. 1:3
Aran	Hurrian (Horite) desc. of Esau.	Gn. 36:28
A. Arathes AV. Ariarathes	K. of Cappadocia.	1 Mac. 15:22
Araunah	Jebusite. is Ornan.	2 S. 24:18ff. 1 Ch. 21:15
Arba	f. of Anak.	Jos. 14:15
Archelaus	S. Herod.	
Archippus	Christian at Colossae.	Philem. v. 2; Col. 4:17

Ard	1. s. of Benjamin.	Gn. 46:21
	2. grands. of Benjamin.	Nu. 26:40
	is Addar.	1 Ch. 8:3
Ardon	s. of Caleb.	1 Ch. 2:18
Areli	s. of Gad.	Gn. 46:16
A. Ares	descendants returned with Zerubbabel.	1 Es. 5:10
	is Arah.	Neh. 7:10
A. Aretas	1. k. of Arabians (Aretus 1).	2 Mac. 5:8
	2. k. of the Nabataeans (Aretus IV).	2 Cor. 11:32
Argob	Officer of Pekahiah, k. of Israel.	2 K. 15:25
A. Ariarathes	S. Arathes.	
Aridai	Ninth s. of Haman.	Est. 9:9
Aridatha	Sixth s. of Haman.	Est. 9:8
Arieh	killed with Argob.	2 K. 15:25
Ariel	1. one of Ezra's chief men.	Ezr. 8:16
	2. Moabite.	2 S. 23:20
Arioch	1. Vassal King.	Gn. 14:1
	2. Captain of the guard.	Dn. 2:14
	A. 3. King of Elymaeans.	Jth. 1:6
Arisai	Eighth s. of Haman.	Est. 9:9
Aristarchus	Thessalonian Christian.	Ac. 20:4, 27:2
Aristobulus	1. Head of a household.	Ro. 16:10
	A. 2. Ptolemy's tutor.	2 Mac. 1:10
A. Arius	K. of Sparta.	1 Mac. 12:7
Armoni	s. of Saul.	2 S. 21:8
A. Arna	Anc. of Ezra.	2 Es. 1:2
	is Zerahiah.	Ezr. 7:4
Arnan	desc. of David.	1 Ch. 3:21
Arni	Anc. of Jesus.	Lk. 3:33
AV. Aram	is Ram.	Mt. 1:3, 4
Arod	s. of Gad.	Nu. 26:17
	is Arodi.	Gn. 46:16
A. Arom	desc. returned with Zerubbabel.	1 Es. 5:16

Arpachshad AV. Arphaxad	Third s. of Shem. is Arphaxad.	Gn. 10:22, 24 Lk. 3:36
A. Arphaxad	1. K. of the Medes. S. Arpachshad.	Jth. 1:1
A. Arsaces	K. of the Parthians.	1 Mac. 15:22
A. Arsiphurith AV. Azephurith	sons returned from exile. is Jorah. is Hariph.	1 Es. 5:16 Ezr. 2:18 Neh. 7:24
Arta xerxes I	S. Xerxes. Persian King.	Ezr. 4:7-23
Artemas	Companion of Paul.	Tit. 3:12
Arza	Steward of the palace at Tirzah.	1 K. 16:9
Asa	1. K. of Judah. 2. Levite.	1 K. 15:9f. 1 Ch. 9:16
A. Asadias	Anc. of Baruch. is Hasadiah.	Bar. 1:1
Asahel	1. s. of Zeruiah, swift of foot. 2. Levite. 3. in charge of Tithes. 4. f. of Jonathan.	2 S. 23:24 2 Ch. 17:8 2 Ch. 31:13 Ezr. 10:15
Asahiah	S. Asaiah 1.	
Asaiah AV. Asahiah	1. sent by Josiah to the prophetess. 2. Simeonite prince. 3. Levite. 4. Judahite living in Jerusalem. is Maaseiah.	2 K. 22:12 1 Ch. 4:36 1 Ch. 6:30 1 Ch. 9:5 Neh. 11:5
A. Asaias	5. Aseas	1 Es. 9:32
A. Asana	His descendants returned with Zerubbabel. is Asnah.	1 Es. 5:31 Ezr. 2:50
Asaph	1. f. of Joah the chronicler. 2. keeper of the King's forest. 3. Korahite. is Ebiasaph. 4. Head of family of Temple musicians.	2 K. 18:18 Neh. 2:8 1 Ch. 26:1 1 Ch. 6:23 1 Ch. 15:17

A. Asara AV. Azara	His sons were Temple servants.	1 Es. 5:31
Asarel AV. Azareel	s. of Jehallelel.	1 Ch. 4:16
A. Asbasareth AV. Azba- zareth	k. of Assyria. is Esarhaddon	1 Es. 5:69 Ezr. 4:2
A. Aseas	s. of Annas. is Isshijah.	1 Es. 9:32 Ezr. 10:31
A. Asebebias	Levite.	1 Es. 8:47
A. Asebias AV. Asebia	Levite.	1 Es. 8:48
Asenath	w. of Joseph.	Gn. 41:45, 50
Asharelah AV. Asarelah	s. of Asaph. is Jesharelah.	1 Ch. 25:2 1 Ch. 25:14
Ashbea	uncertain.	1 Ch. 4:21
Ashbel	Second s. of Benjamin.	1 Ch. 8:1
Asher	Eighth s. of Jacob.	Gn. 35:26
Ashhur AV. Ashur	f. of Tekoa.	1 Ch. 2:24
Ashkenaz	Eldest s. of Gomer.	Gn. 10:3
Ashpenaz	Chief of Nebuchadnezzar's eunuchs.	Dn. 1:3
Ashvath	Asherite.	1 Ch. 7:33
A. Asibias	s. of Phoros. is Malchijah (2).	1 Es. 9:26 Ezr. 10:25
Asiel AV. Asael	1. grandf. of Jehu. A. 2. one of Ezra's writers. A. 3. Anc. of Tobit.	1 Ch. 4:35 2 Es. 14:24 To. 1:1
A. Asipha	His sons were Temple servants. is Hasupha.	1 Es. 5:29 Ezr. 2:43
Asnah	Head of post-exilic family. is Asana.	Ezr. 2:50 1 Es. 5:31
Asnapper	S. Osnapper.	
A. Asom	Head of post-exilic family. is Hashum.	1 Es. 9:33 Ezr. 10:33

21

Aspatha	Third s. of Haman.	Est. 9:7
A. Aspharasus	leader under Zerubbabel.	1 Es. 5:8
	is Mispar.	Ezr. 2:2
	is Mispereth.	Neh. 7:7
Asriel AV Ashriel	Manassite.	Jos. 17:2
A. Assamias AV. Assanias	Priest.	1 Es. 8:54
A. Assaphioth AV. Azaphion	His descendants returned from exile.	1 Es.5:33
	is Hassophereth.	Ezr. 2:55
	is Sophereth.	Neh. 7:57
Asshur	Founder of Nineveh.	Gn. 10:22
Assir	1. s. of Korah.	Ex. 6:24
	2. s. of Ebiasaph.	1 Ch. 6:23
	3. s. of Jeconiah.	1 Ch. 3:17
Assurbanipal	is Asnapper, k. of Assyria.	Ezr. 4:10
A. Astad AV. Sadas	His descendants returned from exile.	1 Es. 5:13
	is Astath.	1 Es. 8:38
	is Azgad.	Ezr. 2:12
A. Astath	S. Astad.	
A. Astyages	k. of the Medes.	Bel. 1
A. Asur AV. Assur	his sons returned from exile. is Harhur.	1 Es. 5:31 Ezr. 2:51
Asyncritus	Christian.	Ro. 16:14
A. Atar AV. Jatal	sons returned from exile. is Ater.	1 Es. 5:28 Ezr. 2:42
Atarah	w. of Jerahmeel.	1 Ch. 2:26
Ater AV. Aterezias	1. S. Atar A. 2. s. of Hezekiah.	Ezr. 2:16 1 Es. 5:15
A. Ateta AV. Teta	his children returned from exile. is Hatita.	1 Es. 5:28 Ezr. 2:42
Athaiah	Judahite.	Neh. 11:4
Athaliah	1. d. of Ahab and Jezebel.	2 K. 8:18 2 Ch. 21:6

	2. Benjamite.	1 Ch. 8:26
	3. f. of Jeshaiah.	Ezr. 8:7
A. Athenobius	friend of Antochus VII.	1 Mac. 15:28
Athlai	Jew.	Ezr. 10:28
Atipha	S. Hatipha.	
Attai	1. Jerahmeelite slave.	1 Ch. 2:35
	2. Gadite.	1 Ch. 12:11
	3. s. of Rehoboam.	2 Ch. 11:20
A. Attalus	k. of Pergamum.	1 Mac. 15:22
A. Attharias AV. Atharias	Post exilic official.	1 Es. 5:40
Attus AV. Lettus	grands. of Shecaniah. is Hattush.	1 Ch. 3:22 Ezr. 8:2
A. Augia	d. of Barzillai.	1 Es. 5:38
Augustus	1. First Roman emperor.	Lk. 2:1
	2. Nero.	Ac. 25:21
A. Auranus	Foolish rebel.	2 Mac. 4:40
A. Auteas	Levite. is Hodiah.	1 Es. 9:48 Neh. 8:7
Avaran	S. Eleazar 7.	
A. Azael	f. of Jonathan. is Asahel.	1 Es. 9:14 Ezr. 10:15
A. Azaelus	Follower of Ezra.	I Es. 9:34
Azaliah	f. of Shaphan the scribe.	2 K. 22:3
Azaniah	Levite.	Neh. 10:9
A. Azaraias AV. Saraias	Anc. of Ezra.	1 Es. 8:1
Azarel AV. Azareel	1. Follower of David.	1 Ch. 12:6
	2. s. of Heman. is Uzziel.	1 Ch. 25:18 1 Ch. 25:4
	3. s. of Jeroham, Danite.	1 Ch. 27:22
	4. s. of Bani.	Ezr. 10:41
	5. Priest.	Neh. 11:13
AV. Azarael	6. Levite musician.	Neh. 12:36
Azariah	1. S. Uzziah.	

	2. is Ahaziah 2.	2 Ch. 22:6
	3. Prophet.	2 Ch. 15:1f.
	4. High Priest of Solomon.	1 K. 4:2
	5. s. of Ahimaaz.	1 Ch. 6:9
	6. f. of Amariah.	1 Ch. 6:11
	7. High priest in reign of Uzziah.	2 Ch. 26:16f.
	8. High priest of Hezekiah.	2 Ch. 31:10
	9. s. of Hilkiah.	1 Ch. 6:13
A.	is Ezerias.	1 Es. 8:1
A.	is Azarias.	2 Es. 1:1
	10. s. of Nathan.	1 K. 4:5
	11. s. of Ethan the wise man.	1 Ch. 2:8
	12. Judahite.	1 Ch. 2:38
	13. Levite, anc. of Samuel.	1 Ch. 6:36
	is Uzziah.	1 Ch. 6:24
	14. s. of Hilkiah.	1 Ch. 9:11
	15. } sons of Jehoshaphat. 16. }	2 Ch. 21:2
	17. Military captain.	2 Ch. 23:1
	18. Military captain.	2 Ch. 23:1
	19. Tribal leader, Ephraimite.	2 Ch. 28:12
	20. } Levites. 21. }	2 Ch. 29:12
	22. Worker with Nehemiah.	Neh. 3:23
	23. Leader under Zerubbabel.	Neh. 7:7
	is Seraiah.	Ezr. 2:2
A.	is Zacharias.	1 Es. 5:8
	24. Interpreter.	Neh. 8:7
A.	is Azarias.	1 Es. 9:48
	25. Priest.	Neh. 10:2
	26. Priest.	Neh. 12:33
	27. Military captain.	Jer. 43:2
	is Jaazaniah.	2 K. 25:23
	is Jezaniah.	Jer. 40:8
	28. S. Abednego.	

A. Azarias	1. Priest.	1 Es. 9:21
	is Uzziah	Ezr. 10:21
	2. Companion of Ezra.	1 Es. 9:43
	3. Interpreter.	1 Es. 9:48
	is Azariah 24.	Neh. 8:7

	4. Angel Raphael's human name.	To. 5:12
	5. Military captain.	1 Mac. 5:18
	6. is Azariah 9.	
A. Azaru AV. Azuran	Head of family.	1 Es. 5:15
Azaz	Reubenite.	1 Ch. 5:8
Azaziah	1. Levite musician.	1 Ch. 15:21
	2. f. of Hoshea.	1 Ch. 27:20
	3. Temple overseer.	2 Ch. 31:13
Azbuk	f. of Nehemiah who helped to repair the walls of Jerusalem.	Neh. 3:16
Azel	desc. of Jonathan, s. of Saul.	1 Ch. 8:37
A. Azetas	Head of family.	1 Es. 5:15
Azgad	S. Astad.	Neh. 10:15
A. Aziei	Anc. of Ezra.	2 Es. 1:2
	is Azariah.	Ezr. 7:3
	is Ozias (AV. Ezias).	1 Es. 8:2
Aziel	Levite.	1 Ch. 15:20
	is Jaaziel.	1 Ch. 15:18
Aziza	Jew.	Ezr. 10:27
	A. is Zardeus.	1 Es. 9:28
Azmaveth	1. desc. of Saul.	1 Ch. 8:36
	2. One of David's mighty men.	2 S. 23:31
	3. f. of archers.	1 Ch. 12:3
	4. s. of Adiel.	1 Ch. 27:25
Azor	Anc. of Jesus.	Matt. 1:13
Azriel	1. Manassite.	1 Ch. 5:24
	2. Naphtalite.	1 Ch. 27:19
	3. f. of Seraiah.	Jer. 36:26
Azrikam	1. s. of Neariah.	1 Ch. 3:23
	2. desc. of Saul.	1 Ch. 8:38
	3. Levite.	1 Ch. 9:14
	4. Officer under Ahaz.	2 Ch. 28:7
Azubah	1. w. of Caleb.	1 Ch. 2:18
	2. m. of Jehoshaphet.	1 K. 22:42
Azzan	f. of Paltiel.	Nu. 34:26

Azzur	1. Levite who sealed the covenant.	Neh. 10:17
AV. Azur	2. f. of Hananiah.	Jer. 28:1
AV. Azur	3. f. of Jaazaniah.	Ezk. 11:1

B

Baal	1. Reubenite chieftain.	1 Ch. 5:5
	2. Gibeonite.	1 Ch. 8:30
Baal-Hanan	1. k. of Edom.	Gn. 36:38
	2. Gederite, official under David.	1 Ch. 27:28
Baalis	k. of Ammonites.	Jer. 40:14
A. Baalsamus AV. Bala-samus	Helped Ezra to interpret the law to the people. is Maaseiah.	1 Es. 9:43 Neh. 8:7
Baana	1. One of Solomon's twelve commissariat officers.	1 K. 4:12
	2. One of Solomon's twelve commissariat officers.	1 K. 4:16
	3. f. of Zadok, of the builders of Jerusalem under Nehemiah.	Neh. 3:4
A.	4. Leader of the people who returned with Zerubbabel. is Baanah.	1 Es. 5:8 Ezr. 2:2
Baanah	1. Benjamite who murdered Ishbosheth.	2 S. 4:5-12
	2. f. of Heled.	2 S. 23:29
	3. One who returned from exile with Zerubbabel.	Ezr. 2:2
	4. One who sealed the covenant.	Neh. 10:27
A. Baani AV. Maani	His sons had taken foreign wives. is Bani.	1 Es. 9:34 Ezr. 10:34
Baara	w. of Shaharaim, Benjamite.	1 Ch. 8:8
Baaseiah	Kohathite.	1 Ch. 6:40
Baasha	s. of Ahijah, of the tribe of Issachar (1 K. 15:16-21). Of lowly origin, he reigned over Israel for 24 years.	

26

A. Babi	Head of family which returned with Ezra.	1 Es. 8:37
	is Bebai.	Ezr. 8:11
A. Bacchides	Friend of Antiochus Epiphanes.	1 Mac. 7:8-20
A. Bacchurus	One who put away his foreign wife.	1 Es. 9:24
A. Bacenor	Jewish officer in army of Judas Maccabaeus.	1 Mac. 5:58
A. Bago	Head of family who returned with Ezra.	1 Es. 8:40
	is Bagoi.	1 Es. 5:14
	is Bigvai.	Ezr. 2:14
A. Bagoas	Eunuch in service of Holofernes.	Jth. 12:11
A. Bagoi	His descendants returned with Zerubbabel.	1 Es. 5:14
	is Bigvai.	Ezr. 2:14
	is Bago.	1 Es. 8:40
A. Baiterus AV. Meterus	Sons returned with Zerubbabel.	1 Es. 5:17
Bakbakkar	Levite.	1 Ch. 9:15
Bakbuk	His descendants returned with Zerub.	Ezr. 2:15
A. is Acub.		1 Es. 5:31
Bakbukiah	1. Levite singer.	Neh. 11:17
	2. Porter and storekeeper.	Neh. 12:25
Balaam	s. of Beor (Nu. 22-24). He was a soothsayer resident at Pethor on the Euphrates, hired by Balak, king of Moab, to lay a curse on the Israelites. In this he was thwarted by supernatural means, and instead uttered blessings. Later he went to live with Midianites, joining with them in an attempt to lure the Israelites into false worship, (Nu. 31:16). He and the Midianite king were subsequently slain by the Israelites, (31:8). In the N.T. he was a symbol of avarice (2 P. 2:15; Jude 11) and idolatry (Rev. 2:14).	

Baladan	f. of Merodach Baladan, k. of Babylon.	2 K. 20:12
Balak	k. of Moab hired Balaam to lay a curse on the Israelites as they were about to enter Canaan.	Nu. 22
A. Balnuus	Had married foreign wife.	1 Es. 9:31
	is Binnui.	Ezr. 10:30
Baltasar	Greek form of Belshazzar.	Dan. 5
A. Ban	Head of family at return under Zerubbabel.	1 Es. 5:37
	is Tobiah.	Ezr. 2:60 / Neh. 7:62
A. Banaias	One who took a foreign wife.	1 Es. 9:35
	is Benaiah.	Ezr. 10:43
Bani	1. Gadite, one of David's heroes.	2 S. 23:36
	2. Levite, Merarite.	1 Ch. 6:46
	3. Levite, f. of Rehum.	Neh. 3:17
	4. Levite and instructor in the law.	Neh. 8:7
	is Binnui	Ezr. 8:33; Neh. 10:9
	5. Judahite.	1 Ch. 9:4
	6. Head of family of returning exiles.	Ezr. 2:10
	is Binnui.	Neh. 7:15
	7. One who married a foreign wife.	Ezr. 10:38
	8. f. of Uzzi.	Neh. 11:22
	9. One who sealed the covenant.	Neh. 10:13
	10. Two Levites.	Neh. 9:4
A. Banias AV. Banid	Anc. of Salimoth.	1 Es. 8:36
A. Bannas AV. Banuas	Levite who returned with Zerub. is Shebaniah.	1 Es. 5:26 / Neh. 10:9
A. Banneas AV Baanias	One who took a foreign wife. is Benaiah.	1 Es. 9:26 / Ezr. 10:25
A. Bannus	One who took a foreign wife. is either Bani or Binnui.	1 Es. 9:34 / Ezr. 10-38

Barabbas	Criminal who was released in preference to Jesus Christ.	Mt. 27:16 Lk. 23:19
Barachel	f. of Elihu, Job's friend.	Job. 32:2
Barachiah AV. Barachias	f. of Zachariah.	Mt. 23:35

Barak — s. of Abinoam (Jg. 4, 5), summoned by Deborah to be her ally in the struggle against the Canaanites, under the command of Sisera. In return Barak insisted on Deborah's presence with him. They gained a great victory (Jg. 5:19-22). Barak was listed in the roll call of Heb. 11 (v. 32).

A. Barchus AV. Charchus is Barkos.	Returned with Zerubbabel.	1 Es. 5:32 Ezr. 2:53
Bariah	s. of Shemaiah.	1 Ch. 3:22
Barjesus	Jew. 'Prophet of lies' in the train of the Proconsul Sergius Paulus.	Ac. 13:6-11
Barkos	S. Barchus.	

Barnabas — s. of Consolation, encouragement (Ac. 4:36, 11:25ff., 13:2, 3, 14, 15). A Cypriot Jew of the Diaspora and a Levite (Ac. 4:36), who sold land in Cyprus and gave the proceeds to the Church. An early convert and a prominent Christian, he persuaded the Jerusalem Christians to accept Paul, their erstwhile opponent, after his conversion (Ac. 9:27). Later he represented the Jerusalem church at Antioch, and helped in the spread of Christianity there. He sought Paul at Tarsus and together they returned to exercise a joint ministry for a whole year. He went with Paul and Mark on the first missionary journey, returning to Antioch (Ac. 13-14). Then Barnabas and Paul gave an account of the work among the Gentiles, to the Jerusalem church in the controversy concerning circumcision (Ac. 15). For the second missionary journey the two friends parted, Barnabas taking his cousin John Mark, and

Paul taking Silas, as their companions respectively (Ac. 15:36). Barnabas was no more mentioned in Acts, but Paul referred to him several times in his letters, always with great respect. The change from Barnabas and Paul to Paul and Barnabas in 13:43 was significant, and thereafter with exceptions (*e.g.* Ac. 15), Barnabas was mentioned second. Luke described him as 'a good man, full of the Holy Spirit and of faith' (Ac. 11:24).

A. Barodis	Returned with Zerubbabel.	1 Es. 5:34
Barsabbas	1. S. Joseph.	Ac. 1:23
	2. S. Judas.	Ac. 15:22
A. Bartacus	f. of Apame, concubine of Darius.	1 Es. 4:29

Bartholomew One of the Apostles (Ac. 1:13; Jn. 1:45f.) according to the four lists in the N.T. (Mt. 10:3; Mk. 3:18; Lk. 6:14; Ac. 1:13). In the Gospel lists he appears after Philip. He may have been Nathanael.

Bartimaeus One of two blind beggars healed by our Lord at the gate of Jericho (Mk. 10:46-52). His name means 'son of Timaeus', and he doubtless had another name.

Baruch 1. s. of Neriah (Jer. 36:45), of illustrious family and devoted friend and secretary of the prophet Jeremiah. Also quartermaster to k. Zedekiah. He prepared an edition of Jeremiah's prophecies (Jer. 36:4, 32). He went with the prophet to Anathoth (32), and to Egypt (43:6).

	2. Repairer of wall.	Neh. 3:20
	3. Sealed the covenant.	Neh. 10:6
	4. f. of Maaseiah.	Neh. 11:5

Barzillai 1. Gileadite of Rogelim (2 S. 17:27, 19:31-40). He was a faithful and aged friend of David.

	2. Meholathite f.-in-law of Michal.	2 S. 21:8
	3. Priest, h. of Barzillai I's d.	Ezr. 2:61
A. Basaloth	Returned with Zerubbabel.	1 Es. 5:31

	is Bazluth.	Ezr. 2:52
	is Bazlith.	Neh. 7:54
Basemath, AV.	1. d. of Elon and w. of Esau.	Gn. 26:34
	is Adah.	Gen. 36:2
Bashemath	2. d. of Ishmael and w. of Esau.	Gn. 36:3-4
	is Mahalath.	Gen. 28:9
AV. Basmath	3. d. of Solomon and w. of Ahimaaz.	1 K. 4:15
A. Bassai AV. Bassa	His family returned with Zerubbabel.	1 Es. 5:16
	is Bezai.	Ezr. 2:17
A. Basthai AV. Bastai	His family returned with Zerubbabel.	1 Es. 5:31
	is Besai.	Ezr. 2:49
Bathsheba	d. of Eliam (2 S. 11:3), w. of Uriah the Hittite, and then of David. m. of Solomon (2 S. 12). Intrigued with Nathan the prophet to procure Solomon's accession to the throne.	
	is Bathshua	1 Ch. 3:5
Bathshua	1. S. Shua. 2. S. Bathsheba.	
Bavvai, AV. Bavai	s. of Henadad, rebuilt a portion of the wall of Jerusalem.	Neh. 3:18
	is Binnui.	Neh. 3:24
Bazlith	Founder of a family of Nethinim who returned with Zerubbabel.	Neh. 7:54
	is Bazluth.	Ezr. 2:52
	A. is Basaloth.	1 Es. 5:31
Bealiah	Benjamite archer.	1 Ch. 12:5
Bebai	1. Head of a family of returning exiles.	Ezr. 2:11
	2. One who sealed the covenant.	Neh. 10:15
Becher	1. s. of Ephraim, anc. of Becherites.	Nu. 26:35
	is Bered.	1 Ch. 7:20
	2. s. of Benjamin.	Gn. 46:21

Bechorath	One of Saul's ancestors.	1 S. 9:1
Bedad	f. of Hadad, k. of Edom.	Gn. 36:35
Bedan	1. One of the deliverers of Israel. Perhaps is Barak.	1 S. 12:11
	2. Manassite.	1 Ch. 7:17
Bedeiah	One of those who had taken foreign wives.	Ezr. 10:35
A. is Pedias.		1 Es. 9:34
Beeliada	s. of David.	1 Ch. 14:7
	is Eliada.	2 S. 5:16
A. Beelsarus	One of the leaders of Jews who returned to Jerusalem with Zerubbabel.	1 Es. 5:8
	is Bilshan.	Ezr. 2:2
A. Beeltethmus	Officer of Artaxerxes.	1 Es. 2:16
Beera	Asherite, eleventh s. of Zophah.	1 Ch. 7:37
Beerah	Reubenite.	1 Ch. 5:6
Beeri	1. f. of Judith, one of Esau's wives.	Gn. 26:34
	2. f. of the prophet Hosea.	Hos. 1:1
Bela	1. s. of Beor, first k. of Edom.	Gn. 36:32f.
	2. eldest s. of Benjamin.	Gn. 46:21
	3. s. of Azaz, Reubenite.	1 Ch. 5:8
A. Belemus	Officer of Artaxerzes.	1 Es. 2:16
	is Bishlam.	Ezr. 4:7
Belshazzar	s. of Nabonidus and prob. grands. of Nebuchadnezzar II and last reigning k. of Babylon who died when the city fell in 539 B.C. (Dan. 5:1).	
Belteshazzar	Chaldaean name given to Daniel.	Dan. 1:7
Ben	Levite.	1 Ch. 15:18
Ben-Abinadab AV. 'son of Abinadab'	One of Solomon's commissariat officers.	1 K. 4:11
Benaiah	1. s. of Jehoiada the priest (2 S. 23:20). Famed for three exploits, he was one of David's 'Thirty', and commanded the army in the third month. He was also captain of the foreign mercenaries	

who formed David's bodyguard (2 S. 8:18, 20:23). Benaiah supported Solomon and slew Adonijah, Joab and Shimei (1 K. 2).

2. One of David's Thirty mighty men (2 S. 23:30), and commander in the eleventh month.

		1 Ch. 27:14
	3. Prince of Simeon.	1 Ch. 4:36
	4. Levite singer.	1 Ch. 15:18
	5. Priest in David's time.	1 Ch. 15:24
	6. Asaphite Levite.	2 Ch. 20:14
	7. Levite in Hezekiah's time.	2 Ch. 31:13
	8. One of those who had taken foreign wives.	Ezr. 10:25
A.	is Banneas.	1 Es. 9:26
	9. One of those who had taken foreign wives.	Ezr. 10:30
A.	is Naidus.	1 Es. 9:31
	10. One of those who had taken foreign wives.	Ezr. 10:35
A.	is Mamdai.	1 Es. 9:34
	11. One of those who had taken foreign wives.	Ezr. 10:43
A.	is Banaias.	1 Es. 9:35
	12. f. of Pelatiah.	Ezk. 11:1, 13

Ben-Ammi	s. of Lot's younger daughter.	Gn. 19:38
Ben-Deker	One of Solomon's twelve commissariat officers.	1 K. 4:9
Ben-Geber, AV. 'son of Geber'	One of Solomon's twelve commissariat officers. S. Geber.	1 K. 4:13
Ben-Hadad	1. Benhadad I, s. of Tabrimmon, k. of Damascus.	1 K. 15:18

2. Benhadad II, k. of Damascus (1 K. 20; 2 K. 8:7-15), enemy of Ahab, slain by Hazael about 843 B.C.

3. Benhadad III (2 K. 13:3, 24), s. of Hazael, k. of Damascus (796-770). (It may be that Benhadad I and II were the same person.)

Ben-Hail	Prince sent by Jehoshaphat to teach in the cities of Judah.	2 Ch. 17:7

Ben-Hanan	Man of Judah.	1 Ch. 4:20
Ben-Hesed AV. 'son of Hesed'	One of Solomon's twelve commissariat officers.	1 K. 4:10
Hinnom	See Jer. 19:2, 6.	
Ben Hur	One of Solomon's twelve commissariat officers. S. Hur.	1 K. 4:8
Beninu	One who sealed the covenant.	Neh. 10:13
Benjamin	1. Youngest s. of Jacob ('Son of the right hand') (Gn. 35:18). He and Joseph were sons of Rachel, who died giving birth to Benjamin (35: 18, 24). After Joseph, he was his father's favourite son, and figured prominently in the stories of Joseph in Egypt (Gn. 42-45). He was the anc. of the tribe of Benjamin. is Benoni.	
	2. Gt-grands. of Benjamin	1 Ch. 7:10
	3. One of those who had married a foreign wife.	Ezr. 10:32
	4. Priest in time of Nehemiah.	Neh. 12:34
	5. A builder of the wall.	Neh. 3:23
Beno	s. of Jaaziah.	1 Ch. 24:26f.
Ben-Zoheth	Man of Judah.	1 Ch. 4:20
Beor	1. f. of Balaam.	Nu. 22:5
	2. f. of Bela, k. of Edom.	Gn. 36:32
Bera	K. of Sodom.	Gn. 14:2
Beracah, AV. Berachah	One of Saul's relations.	1 Ch. 12:3
Beraiah	Benjamite.	1 Ch. 8:21
Berechiah, AV. Berachiah	1. f. of Asaph.	1 Ch. 6:39
	2. s. of Zerubbabel.	1 Ch. 3:20
	3. f. of Meshullam.	Neh. 3:4
	4. Levite guard of the ark.	1 Ch. 9:16
	5. f. of the prophet Zechariah.	Zec. 1:1
	6. Ephraimite.	2 Ch. 28:12
	7. Levite, Gatekeeper for the Ark.	1 Ch. 15:23

Bered	S. Becher 1.	
Beri	s. of Zophah	1 Ch. 7:36
Beriah	1. Fourth s. of Asher.	Gn. 46:17
	2. s. of Ephraim.	1 Ch. 7:23
	3. Levite, fourth s. of Shimei.	1 Ch. 23:10
	4. Fourth s. of Elpaal.	1 Ch. 8:13
Bernice, or Berenice	S. Herod. A d. of Agrippa 1.	Ac. 25:13, 23
Berzelus	S. Zorzelleus.	
Besai	His descendants returned with Zerubbabel.	Ezr. 2:49
	A. is Basthai.	1 Es. 5:31
A. Bescaspasmys is Mattaniah.		1 Es. 9:31
Besodeiah	His son helped in repairing the old gate.	Neh. 3:6
Bethuel	s. of Nahor.	
	n. of Abraham.	Gn. 22:23, 24:15
	f. of Laban and Rebecca.	
Bezai	1. One who sealed the covenant.	Neh. 10:18
	2. His family returned with Zerubbabel.	Ezr. 2:17
	A. is Bassai.	
Bezalel	1. Judahite, s. of Huri, grands. of Hur (Ex. 31:1-11, 35:30-35), craftsman in wood, metal and stone, became gifted with the spirit. Foreman for the construction of the Tabernacle.	
	2. One of the eight sons of Pahath-moab (Ezr. 10:30) that had married foreign wives.	
Bezer	desc. of Asher.	1 Ch. 7:37
Bichri	A Benjamite, f. of rebel Sheba.	2 S. 20:1
Bidkar	Chief officer of Ahab.	2 K. 9:25
Bigtha	One of the chamberlains of k. Ahasuerus.	Est. 1:10
Bigthan	One of the two chamberlains of Ahasuerus who conspired against the king's life (Est. 2:21).	
Bigvai	1. companion of Zerubbabel.	Ezr. 2:2

	2. One who sealed the covenant.	Neh. 10:16
Bildad	One of Job's three friends.	Job 2:11
Bilgah	1. Priest in time of David.	1 Ch. 24:14
	2. Priest who returned with Zerubbabel.	Neh. 12:5
	is Bilgai.	Neh. 10:8
Bilgai	S. of Bilgah 2.	
Bilhah	Slave girl given to Rachel.	Gn. 29:29
Bilhan	1. Horite chief.	Gn. 36:27
	2. desc. of Benjamin.	1 Ch. 7:10
Bilshan	Companion of Zerubbabel.	Ezr. 2:2
	A. is Beelsarus.	1 Es. 5:8
Bimhal	desc. of Asher.	1 Ch. 7:33
Binea	desc. of Jonathan.	1 Ch. 8:37
Binnui	1. Head of family that returned with Zerubb.	Neh. 7:15
	is Bani.	Ezr. 2:10
	2. Levite (post-exilic).	Ezr. 8:33
	3. s. of Pahath-Moab.	Ezr. 10:30
	A. is Balnuus.	1 Es. 9:31
	4. s. of Bani who had married a foreign wife.	Ezr. 10:38
	5. s. of Henadad.	Neh. 3:24
	6. Levite	Neh. 12:8
Birsha	K. of Gomorrah.	Gn. 14:2
Birzaith	Asherite	1 Ch. 7:31
Bishlam	Officer of Artaxerxes.	Ezr. 4:7
	A. is Belemus.	1 Es. 2:16
Bithiah	d. of a Pharaoh.	
	w. of Mered the Judahite.	1 Ch. 4:18
Biztha	One of the seven eunuchs of k. Ahasuerus.	Est. 1:10
Blastus	Chamberlain of Herod Agrippa 1.	Ac. 12:20
Boanerges	Surname given by our Lord to His disciples James and John.	Mk. 3:17
Boaz	Head of family who lived in Beth-lehem-judah.	

	Gt. grandf. of David (Ru. 2:1). A good-natured and wealthy farmer (Ru. 2) who redeemed Ruth and married her under the law of the Levirate marriage.	Ru. 3-4
Bocheru	desc. of Jonathan.	1 Ch. 8:38
Bohan	s. of Reuben.	Jos. 15:6
A. Borith	Anc. of Ezra.	2 Es. 1:2
	is Boccas.	1 Es. 8:2
	is Bukki.	1 Ch. 6:5
Bukki	1. s. of Jogli, a prince of the tribe of Dan.	Nu. 34:22
	2. s. of Abishua High Priest.	1 Ch. 6:5
	A. is Boccas.	1 Es. 8:2
	A. is Borith.	2 Es. 1:2
Bukkiah	Levite, s. of Heman.	1 Ch. 25:4
Bunah	Man of Judah, Jerahmeelite.	1 Ch. 2:25
Bunni	1. Levite (post-exilic).	Neh. 9:4
	2. Levite, f. of Hashabiah.	Neh. 11:15
	3. A Chief of the people.	Neh. 10:15
Buz	1. second s. of Nahor, n. of Abraham.	Gn. 22:21
	2. of the tribe of Gad.	1 Ch. 5:14
Buzi	f. of the prophet Ezekiel, member of the priestly house of Zadok.	Ezk. 1:3

C

Caesar	The family name of a Roman family who ruled the Republic of Rome 31 B.C. to 68 A.D. This family name then became a title found nearly thirty times in the N.T. It refers to:
	1. Augustus (27 B.C.-A.D. 14) (Lk. 2:1). Name and title of Julius Caesar's adopted son.
	2. Tiberius (A.D. 14-37) (Lk. 3:1; Mk. 12:14-17). He was reigning at the beginning of Jesus' ministry.
	3. Claudius (A.D. 41-54) (Ac. 11:28). Mentioned incidentally in Ac. 11:28 and 18:2.
	4. Nero (A.D. 54-68) (Ac. 25:10f.). A gt.-gt.-grands. of Claudius, and adopted by him as

Caiaphas

	his heir. Weak, cruel, despotic, artistic, he had his mother executed and eventually killed himself. Paul appealed to him from his deputy Festus (Ac. 25:10f.). Peter and Paul were probably martyred during his reign.
Caiaphas	High priest of the Jews (c. A.D. 18-13) who resolved to take Jesus by subtlety (Mt. 26:3, 27:1). The procedure under his presidency was a travesty of justice. He continued to harass the Church (Ac. 5:17). He was Annas' s.-in-law (Jn. 18:13).
Cain	First-born of Adam and Eve (Gn. 4:1). He was an agriculturalist and slew his only b. Abel (Gn. 4:8). He bore a distinguishing mark, and built the first city. He was the f. of Enoch.
Cainan	1. s. of Enos. Lk. 3:37 2. s. of Arphaxad. Lk. 3:36
Calcol AV. Chalcol	Judahite famous for wisdom 1 K. 4:31 but surpassed by Solomon.
Caleb	means 'dog'. This name may refer to one, or two or even three persons in the O.T. 1. Caleb, third s. of Hezron, and grands. of Pharez. (1 Ch. 2:9). He was gt.-grandf. of Bezaleel. F. of Achsah. Jos. 15:16 2. Hezron's eldest s. was Jerahmeel, and Caleb was his b. and f. of Ahsah (1 Ch. 2:9, 42, 49). Almost certainly is Caleb 1. 3. The s. of Jephunneh (1 Ch. 4:15). He was one of the spies sent by Moses from Kadesh to reconnoitre the land of Canaan (Nu. 13, 14). He subsequently conquered the district of Hebron and controlled it. cp. 'Negeb of Caleb' (1 S. 30:14).
A. Calitas	Levite. 1 Es. 9:23
A. Callisthenes	Syrian captured by the Jews. 2 Mac. 8:33
Canaan	s. of Ham, grands. of Noah (Gn. 9:22f.), one of the three men from whom the world was re-peopled after the flood.

Candace	Q. of the Aethiopians.	Ac. 8:27
A. Carabasion	Corrupt name of one who put away foreign wives.	1 Es. 9:34
	is Meremoth.	Ezr. 10:36
Carcas	One of the seven chamberlains of k. Ahasuerus.	Est. 1:10
Carmi	1. Judahite f. of Achan.	Jos. 7:1
	2. is Chelubai.	1 Ch. 2:9
	3. Reubenite.	Gn. 46:9
Carpus	Inhabitant of Troas with whom St. Paul stayed. One of the seventy disciples.	2 Ti. 4:13
Carshena	One of the seven counsellors of k. Ahasuerus.	Est. 1:14
A. Cathua	Head of family who returned with Zerubbabel.	1 Es. 5:30
	is Giddel.	Ezr. 2:47
A. Cendebaeus	General of Antiochus VII overcome by the Jews under Judas Maccabaeus. 1 Mac. 15:38	
Cephas	S. Peter.	
A. Chabris	One of the three rulers of Bethulia.	Jth. 6:15
A. Chaereas AV. Chereas	In command of Ammonites.	2 Mac 10:32
A. Chalphi AV. Calphi	f. of Judas, captain of Jonathan Maccabaeus against the Syrians at Hazor. 1 Mac. 11:70	
A. Chanuneus AV. Channuneus	Levite.	1 Es. 8:48
A. Charaathalan AV. Charaathalar	Leader of certain families who returned from Babylon.	1 Es. 5:36
A. Charea	Head of family that returned with Zerubbabel.	1 Es. 5:32
	is Harsha.	Ezr. 2:52
A. Charme AV. Carme	Returned from captivity. is Harim.	1 Es. 5:25 Ezr. 2:39

A. Charmis	s. of Melchiel.	Jth. 6:15
A. Chaseba	Returned with Zerubbabel.	1 Es. 5:31
Chedor-Laomer	k. of Elam, in command in the war against the Canaanite princes.	Gn. 14:1-16
Chelal	One who had married a foreign wife.	Ezr. 10:30
Chelod	k. of Assyrians.	Jth. 1:6b
Chelub	1. desc. of Judah.	1 Ch. 4:11
	2. f. of Ezri.	1 Ch. 27:26
Chelubai	Another form of Caleb.	1 Ch. 2:9
Cheluhi AV. Chelluh	One who had married a foreign wife.	Ezr. 10:35
Chenaanah	1. Benjamite.	1 Ch. 7:10
	2. f. of Zedekiah the false prophet.	1 K. 22:11
Chenani	Levite.	Neh. 9:4
Chenaniah	1. Chief of the Levites at the removal of the ark from the house of Obededom.	1 Ch. 15:22
	2. An Izharite.	1 Ch. 26:29
Cheran	desc. of Seir, the Horite.	Gn. 36:26
Cherub	Leading exile.	Ez. 2:59
Chesed	s. of Nahor.	Gn. 22:22
Chezib	is Chaseba.	1 Ez. 5:31
Chidon	is Nachon.	
Chileab	s. of David and Abigail.	2 S. 3:3
	is Daniel.	1 Ch. 3:1
Chilion	s. of Elimelech and Naomi.	Ru. 1:1
Chimham	s. of Barzillai the Gileadite.	2 S. 19:37f.
Chislon	f. of Elidad. Benjamite.	Nu. 34:21
Chloe	Members of her household had told Paul of dissensions in the Corinthian Church.	1 Cor. 1:11
A. Chorbe	Returned from exile.	1 Es. 5:12

AV. Corbe	is Zaccai.	Ezr. 2:9
A. Chosamaeus	One who had taken a foreign wife.	1 Es. 9:32
	is Shimeon.	Ezr. 10:31
Chuza RV. Chuzas	Steward of Herod Antipas.	His wife Joanna ministered to our Lord. Lk 8:3
Claudia	Christian lady of Rome on intimate terms of friendship with St. Paul.	2 Ti. 4:21
Claudius	Fourth emperor of Rome. In his time was a famine over the whole world.	Ac. 11:28
	He commanded all the Jews to depart from Rome. S. Caesar.	Ac. 18:2
Claudius Lysias	Military tribune in Jerusalem.	Ac. 21:23
Clement	Fellow labourer with St. Paul at Philippi.	Ph. 4:3
Cleopas	One of the two to whom Jesus appeared on the road to Emmaus.	Lk. 24:18
	is Clopas?	Jn. 19:25
	is Alphaeus?	Mt. 10:3
Cleopatra	A. 1. w. of Philometor.	Add. Est. 11:1
	A. 2. d. of Cleopatra and Ptolemy Philometor.	1 Mac. 10:57
	3. w. of Herod the Great, Tetrarch of Ituraea.	m. of Philip, Lk. 3:1
Clopas AV. Cleophas	h. of the sister of Jesus' mother.	Jn. 19:25
Col-Hozeh	Judahite.	Neh. 3:15
A. Colius	Levite. is Calitas.	1 Es. 9:23
Conaniah AV. Cononiah	1. Levite in time of Hezekiah.	2 Ch. 31:12
	2. Chief of Levites in Josiah's reign.	2 Ch. 35:9
Coniah	S. Jehoiachin.	
Cornelius	Centurion in the garrison of Caesarea, a devout man and ideal gentile.	Ac. 10:1

Cosam	Ancestor of Jesus.	Lk. 3:28
Cozbi	Midianitess slain by Phinehas.	Nu. 25:15
Crescens	Companion of St. Paul in his final imprisonment.	2 Ti. 4:10
Crispus	Ruler of the Jewish synagogue at Corinth who believed that Jesus was the Messiah (Ac. 18:8).	
Cush	1. f. of Nimrod.	Gn. 10:8
	2. Benjamite.	Ps. 7 title
Cushan-Rishathaim AV. Chushan-rishathaim	k. of Mesopotamia, first oppressor into whose hands God delivered Israel.	Jg. 3:8-10
Cushi	1. gt. grandf. of Jehudi.	Jer. 36:14
	2. f. of the prophet Zephaniah.	Zeph. 1:1
A. Cutha AV. Coutha	His sons returned from Babylon with Zerubbabel.	1 Es. 5:32
Cyrus	k. of Media as well as Persia (Ezr. 1:1ff., 5:13f.). He captured Babylon in 539 B.C., and gave liberty to the Jews to return from Babylon to Jerusalem (Is. 44:28, 45:1), sanctioned the rebuilding of the Temple (2 Ch. 36:22f.), returned the Temple vessels (Ez. 1:7), and provided funds (3:7).	

D

A. Dabria	One of the five scribes of Ezra.	2 Es. 14:24
A. Dacubi AV. Dacobi	His family returned with Zerubbabel.	1 Es. 5:28
	is Akkub.	Ezr. 2:42
A. Daisan	His sons returned from exile.	1 Es. 5:31
	is Rezin.	Ezr. 2:48
A. Dalan AV. Ladan	Returned from exile but could not prove Jewish descent.	1 Es. 5:37
	is Delaiah.	Ezr. 2:60
Dalphon	s. of Haman.	Est. 9:7

Damaris	A woman converted by St. Paul Ac. 17:34 at Athens.
Dan	One of Jacob's twelve sons and elder of the two sons borne to Jacob by Bilhah (Gn. 30:6), Rachel's maidservant. He was the Anc. of the tribe of Dan.
Daniel	1. David's second s. by Abigail. 1 Ch. 3:1 is Chileab. 2 S. 3:3
	2. A priest of the family of Ithamar (Ezr. 8:2), companion of Ezra, who also sealed the covenant (Neh. 10:6).
	3. Hero and traditional author of the Bk. of Daniel, the fourth Book of the Prophets. He was carried captive to Babylon, given another name, Belteshazzar (1:7). A wise and prudent man gifted with the interpretation of dreams. He also became himself the recipient of a series of visions (7-12).
	4. In Ezk. 14:14, 28:3, a Daniel is mentioned and linked with Noah and Job. He was an ancient king, known in Phoenician-Canaanite lore, and mentioned in the texts from Ugaint. His name may be read as Danel, or Daniel.
Dara	S. Darda.
Darda	Mentioned as a son of Mahol, a 1 K. 4:31 proverbial type of wisdom.
Darius	1. Darius I. Darius the Great (522-486 B.C.) (Ezr. 4:5, 24, 6:1). Son of Hystaspes and founder of the Persian empire. In his reign the second temple of Jerusalem was finished.
	2. probably Darius II (Neh. 12:22), Nothus called Darius the Persian. (May be Darius III Codomanus).
	3. The Mede, k. of the Chaldeans (Dan. 9:1), and k. or governor of Babylon (Dan. 11:1). He was the son of Ahasuerus (Xerxes. Dan. 6:1, 11:1), and succeeded Balshazzar. Identity otherwise unknown.

Darkon	His family returned with Zerubbabel.	Ezr. 2:56
	A. is Lozon.	1 Es. 5:33
Dathan	Reubenite rebel against Moses.	Nu. 16:1
David	Name given to no one except the great king of Israel (1 S. 16, 1. K. 2, 1 Ch. 2-29). 'Beloved'. He was the eighth s. of Jesse, his mother's name being unknown, and gt. grands. of Boaz and Ruth. He had eight principal wives besides others. At least six sons were born to him during his days at Hebron (2 S. 3:2-5), and at least 13 more in his Jerusalem days (5:14). Brought up as a shepherd, he was chosen by Samuel to succeed Saul, Israel's first king (1 S. 16). He became Israel's greatest king, ruling for forty years, and was an ancestor of Jesus Christ. He was the 'man after God's own heart'. David was introduced to Saul's court, and through various exploits, the killing of Goliath and many other Philistines, he became the great friend of Saul's son, Jonathan, and husband of Saul's daugher, Michal. Owing to Saul's increasing jealousy and insanity, David fled to the south, becoming leader of a large group of outlaws. He even allied himself with the Philistines, but was not allowed to fight for them in the battle of Gilboa in which both Saul and Jonathan were slain and Israel defeated, (2 S. 1). Then David became a puppet king of the Philistines at Hebron, ruling for two years over Judah only, and then for five-and-a-half years over Israel and Judah (2 S. 5:1-5). David captured Jerusalem (2 S. 5:7), and removed Israel's chief religious emblem, the ark, there. His dance on that occasion was long remembered as an extraordinary feat of strength and piety (2 S. 6). Thereafter he reigned for thirty-three years in Jerusalem, the story of the reign	

being given in 2 S. 7-20, 1 K. 1-2, the so-called succession document.

David was obviously a handsome man who had handsome and beautiful children. He was brave, tender hearted and magnanimous, zealous and pious. His faults were many for he was lustful and wilful, though quick to recognise his faults. He was ever loyal to Saul and his own friends, very tactful in difficult situations, a great warrior and a statesman, an outstanding poet and musician, but above all he was a deeply religious man, devoted to God. He was a great experimentalist in prayer, and an individualist in personal piety. He was the acknowledged and beloved head of the nation in religion and politics.

Debir	k. of Eglon.	Jos. 10:3
Deborah	'Bee'.	
	1. Nurse of Rebekah.	Gn. 35:8
	2. w. of Lappidoth.	Jg. 4:4

Prophetess and Judge in the hill country of Ephrain (Jg. 4 and 5). Her work was centred under 'the palm tree of Deborah' between Ramah and Bethel. She joined Barak, and together they defeated Sisera and his army in the great battle of the Kishon (Jg. 4:15, 5:19ff.). She is described in Jg. 5:7 as 'a mother in Israel'.

AV. Debora	A. 3. grandm. of Tobit.	To. 1:8
Dedan	desc. of Abraham and Keturah.	Gn. 10:7, 25:3
Delaiah AV. Dalaiah	1. desc. of David.	1 Ch. 3:24
	2. Priest and leader in the time of David.	1 Ch. 24:18
	3. s. of Shemaiah.	Jer. 36:12
	4. s. of Mehetabel.	Neh. 6:10
	5. Head of family who returned with Zerubbabel.	Ezr. 2:60
	A. is Dalan.	1 Es 5:37.

Delilah	A Philistine woman of Sorek who betrayed Samson into the hands of the Philistines.	
		Jg. 16:4-22
Demas	Fellow labourer with St. Paul but 'he loved this present world'. is Dysmas.	Col. 4:14, 2 Ti. 4:10

A. Demetrius 1. Demetrius I, Soter, k. of Syria (162-151 B.C.) (1 Mac. 7:1-4, 10, 11:20). At first a Syrian hostage at Rome, he escaped and proclaimed himself king of Syria. After much fighting with the Jews, he was worsted and died after his horse had fallen into a swamp.

2. s. of Demetrius I, Nicator (146-139 B.C.) (1 Mac. 11). Ally of Ptolemy VI of Egypt, and h. of Cleopatra. He became k. of Syria in 146 B.C. and remained on good terms with the Jews and their leader, Jonathan. Later he was defied by Jonathan, and still later was captured by the Persians. His reign ended in confusion.

3. A silversmith at Ephesus and a ringleader in a riot at Ephesus directed against Paul.

Ac. 19:24

4. Disciple commended by St. John. 3 Jn. 12

A. Demophon	Syrian commandant in Palestine, hostile towards the Jews.	2 Mac. 12:2
Deuel	f. of Eliasaph, prince of Gad. is Reuel.	Nu. 1:14 Nu. 2:14
Diblaim	f. of Gomer, Hosea's wife.	Hos. 1:3
Dibri	Danite.	Lv. 24:11
Didymus	S. Thomas.	
Diklah	s. of Joktan.	Gn. 10:27
Dinah	d. of Jacob by Leah (Gn. 30:21). Shechem the prince of Shechem raped her, and the tribes of Simeon and Levi attacked that city (Gn. 34).	

Dionysius	One of the few converts made by St. Paul at Athens.	Ac. 17:34
Diotrephes	An ambitious person standing in the way of the hospitable reception of brethren who visited the Church.	3 Jn. vv. 9, 10
Diphath	is Riphath	
Dishan	Seventh s. of Seir.	Gn. 36:21
	is Dishon.	Gn. 36:26
Dishon	1. Fifth s. of Seir.	Gn. 36:21
	2. s. of Anah, grands. of Seir.	Gn. 36:25
Dives	In the parable of the rich man, Jesus did not mention the name of the rich man. He was an imaginary person traditionally called Dives.	Lk. 16:19-31.
Dodai	S. Dodo.	
Dodanim	Fourth s. of Javan.	Gn. 10:4
Dodavahu, AV. Dodavah	f. of Eliezer.	2 Ch. 20:37
Dodo	1. f. of Eliezer, the second of the three captains over the Thirty.	2 S. 23:9
	2. Bethlehemite, f. of Elhanan.	2 S. 23:24
	3. Man of Issachar.	Jg. 10:1
Doeg	Edomite, chief of Saul's runners.	1 S. 21:7
Dorcas	Name given to Tabitha, a disciple at Joppa (Ac. 9:36). She was renowned for her charity and was raised from the dead by Peter.	
A. Dorymenes	f. of Ptolemy Macron.	2 Mac. 4:45
A Dositheus	1. Priest.	Ad.Est. 11:1
	2. Soldier of Judas Maccabaeus.	2 Mac. 12:35
	3. Renegade Jew favoured by Ptolemy Philopator.	3 Mac. 1:3
	4. Officer of Judas Maccabaeus.	2 Mac. 12:19
Drusilla	w. of Felix.	Ac. 24:24
Dumah	s. of Ishmael.	Gn. 25:14
Dysmas	S. Demas.	
	Apocryphal name of penitent thief.	

47

E

Ebal	1. s. of Shobal.	Gn. 36:23
	2. s. Abal.	
Ebed	1. f. of Gaal who headed the rebellion against Abimelech.	Jg. 9:26
	2. One who returned from Babylon with Ezra.	Ezr. 8:26
A.	is Obeth.	1 Es. 8:32
Ebed-Melech	Ethiopian eunuch at whose intercession Jeremiah was released from the pit-prison.	Jer. 38:7ff.
Eber	1. Anc. of the Hebrews, gt. grands. of Shem.	Gn. 10:24f.
	2. Post-exilic Priest.	Neh. 12:20
	3. Gadite.	1 Ch. 5:13
	4. Benjamite.	1 Ch. 8:12
	5. Benjamite.	1 Ch. 8:22
Ebiasaph	S. Abiasaph.	
A. Eddinus AV. Jeduthun	One of the holy singers at Josiah's passover.	1 Es. 1:15
	is Jeduthun.	2 Ch. 35:15
Eden	1. Levite in the time of Hezekiah.	2 Ch. 29:12
	2. Another Levite (? Eden 1).	2 Ch. 31:15
Eder	1. Levite in time of David.	1 Ch. 23:23
	2. Benjamite.	1 Ch. 8:15
A. Edna	w. of Raguel of Ecbatana.	To. 7:2
Edom	s. Esau.	
A. Edos AV. Edes	One who had taken a foreign wife.	1 Es. 9:35
	is Iddo.	Ezr. 10:43
Eglah	w. of David.	2 S. 3:5
Eglon	k. of Moab during the period of the Judges. Slain by Ehud, a judge.	Jg. 3:12ff.
Ehi	Benjamite.	Gn. 46:21
Ehud	1. s. of Gera, Benjamite, who slew Eglon, k. of Moab.	Jg. 3:12-30

	2. s. of Bilhan, gt. grands. of Benjamin.	1 Ch. 7:10
Eker	Jerahmeelite.	1 Ch. 2:27
Ela AV. Elah	1. f. of Shimei.	1 K. 4:18
A.	2. One who had taken a foreign wife.	1 Es. 9:27
	is Elam.	Ezr. 10:26
Elah	1. Duke of Edom.	Gn. 36:41
	2. K. of Israel, s. of Baasha.	1 K. 16:6
	3. f. of Hoshea, last k. of Israel.	2 K. 15:30
	4. second s. of Caleb.	1 Ch. 4:15
	5. Benjamite.	1 Ch. 9:8
Elam	1. s. of Shem.	Gn. 10:22
	2. Korahite in David's time.	1 Ch. 26:3
	3. Benjamite.	1 Ch. 8:24
	4. His family returned with Zerubbabel and Ezra.	Ezr. 2:7, 10:26
	5. His family returned with Zerubbabel (may be 4 above).	Ezr. 2:31
	6. One who sealed the covenant.	Neh. 10:14
	7. Priest in Nehemiah's time.	Neh. 12:42
Elasah	1. One who had married a foreign wife.	Ezr. 10:22
	2. s. of Shaphan.	Jer. 29:3
Eldaah	s. of Midian.	Gn. 25:4

Eldad   One of the seventy elders appointed to assist Moses (Nu. 11:26-29). Once he and Medah remained in the camp when the others had gone out to worship. They began to prophesy, and Moses refused to reprimand them.

Elead	Ephraimite.	1 Ch. 7:21
Eleadah AV. Eladah	Ephraimite.	1 Ch. 7:20
Eleasah	1. Judahite, Jerahmeelite.	1 Ch. 2:39
	2. Descendant of Saul. Benjamite.	1 Ch. 8:37

Eleazar			
		1. Third s. of Aaron (Ex. 6:23). When Aaron died he succeeded him in his functions.	Nu. 20:25
		2. s. of Abinadab.	1 S. 7:1
		3. s. of Dodo, one of David's three principal mighty men.	2 S. 23:9
		4. Levite, Merarite.	1 Ch. 23:21
		5. Priest of the time of Ezra.	Ezr. 8:33
		6. One who married a foreign woman.	Ezr. 10:25
		7. Levite musician post-exilic.	Neh. 12:42
	A.	8. s. of Mattathias and b. of Judas Maccabaeus.	1 Mac. 2:5
	A.	9. One of the principal scribes martyred.	2 Mac. 6:18-31
	A.	10. f. of Jason.	1 Mac. 8:17
	A.	11. f. of Sirach	Sir. 50:27
		12. Anc. of our Lord.	Mt. 1:15
Elhanan		1. s. of Jaare-oregim the Bethlehemite (2 S. 21:19). Slew Goliath the Gittite. Elhanan either slew Goliath's brother (1 Ch. 20:5) or Elhanan was David's original pre-court name.	
		2. s. of Dodo the Bethlehemite.	2 S. 23:24
Eli		desc. of Aaron, through Ithamar (1 S. 1-4). Eli was the leader of the priests in God's house at Shiloh. He was the guardian and mentor of young Samuel. He 'judged Israel' forty years, but great judgment fell on his family.	
Eliab		1. s. of Helon, prince of Zebulun.	Nu. 1:9
		2. Reubenite.	Nu. 16:1b
		3. Eldest s. of Jesse, b. of David.	1 S. 16:6
		4. Anc. of Samuel. Ephraimite.	1 Ch. 6:27
		5. Gadite warrior.	1 Ch. 12:9
		6. Levite musician.	1 Ch. 15:20ff.
	A.	7. Anc. of Judith, Simeonite.	Jth. 8:1
Eliada		1. s. of David. is Beeliada.	2 S. 5:16 / 1 Ch. 14:7
		2. f. of Rezon, a Syrian.	1 K. 11:23
		3. Warrior of Benjamin.	2 Ch. 17:17

A. Eliadas	Jew who had married a foreign wife.	1 Es. 9:28
	is Elioenai.	Ezr. 10:27
Eliahba	One of David's 'Thirty'.	2 S. 23:32
Eliakim	1. s. of Hilkiah and prefect of the palace.	2 K. 18:18ff.
	2. Orig. name of Jehoiakim, k. of Judah.	2 K. 23:34
	3. Priest in time of Nehemiah.	Neh. 12:41
	4. Anc. of our Lord.	Mt. 1:13
	5. Anc. of our Lord.	Lk. 3:30
A. Eliali(s)	He had married a foreign wife.	1 Es. 9:34
Eliam	1. f. of Bathsheba.	2 S. 11:3
	is Ammiel.	1 Ch. 3:5
	2. s. of Ahithophel.	2 S. 23:34
A. Eliaonias	Desc. of Paath-moab who returned from Babylon.	1 Es. 8:31
	is Eliehoenai.	Ezr. 8:4
Elias	S. Elijah.	
Eliasaph	1. s. of Deuel prince of Gad.	Nu. 1:14
	2. s. of Lael, Gershonite.	Nu. 3:24
Eliashib	1. s. of Joiakim. High priest contemporary with Nehemiah.	Neh. 12:10
	2. Singer of the time of Ezra.	Ezr. 10:24
A.	is Eliasibus.	1 Es. 9:24
	3. Of the family of Zattu.	Ezr. 10:27
A.	is Eliasimus.	1 Es. 9:28
	4. Of the family of Bani.	Ezr. 10:36
A.	is Eliasis.	1 Es. 9:34
	5. desc. of David.	1 Ch. 3:24
	6. Priest of time of David.	1 Ch. 24:12
	7. f. of Jehohanan, and High Priest in time of Nehemiah (Ezr. 10:6). may be 1 above.	
A. Eliasib	High Priest in time of Neh.	1 Es. 9:1
	is Eliashib 7.	Ezr. 10:6
A. Eliasibus AV. Eleazurus	Singer who put away his foreign wife.	1 Es. 9:24
	is Eliashib 2.	Ezr. 10:24
A. Eliasimus	S. Eliashib 3.	1 Es. 9:28

A. Eliasis	S. Eliashib 4.	1 Es. 9:34 Ezr. 10:36
Eliathah	Hemanite musician.	1 Ch. 25:4
Elidad	s. of Chislon, Benjamite.	Nu. 34:21
Eliehoenai AV. Elioenai	1. Korahite gatekeeper.	1 Ch. 26:3
AV. Elihoenai	2. Head of family that returned.	Ezr. 8:4
A.	is Eliaonias.	1 Es. 8:31
Eliel	1. Korahite, Levitical singer.	1 Ch. 6:34
	is Eliab.	1 Ch. 6:27
	is Elihu.	1 S. 1:1
	2. Mighty man of David.	1 Ch. 11:46
	3. Mighty man of David.	1 Ch. 11:47
	4. Mighty man of David.	1 Ch. 12:11
	5. Chief of Manasseh.	1 Ch. 5:24
	6. Benjamite.	1 Ch. 8:20
	7. Benjamite.	1 Ch. 8:22
	8. Levite of family of Hebron.	1 Ch. 15:9, 11
	9. Levite in time of Hezekiah.	2 Ch. 31:13
Elienai	Benjamite.	1 Ch. 8:20
A. Eliezar	S. Eliezer 6 and 7.	
Eliezer	1. Abraham's chief servant, a Damascene.	Gn. 15:2
	2. Second s. of Moses.	Ex. 18:4
	3. s. of Becher, a Benjamite.	1 Ch. 7:8
	4. s. of Zichri, captain of the tribe of Reuben.	1 Ch. 27:16
	5. A prophet, s. of Dodavahu.	2 Ch. 20:37
	6. Among the 'chief men' whom Ezra sent to find Levites.	Ezr. 8:16f.
	7. Priest who married a foreign woman.	Ezr. 10:18
	8. Levite who married a foreign woman.	Ezr. 10:23
	9. s. of Harim who married a foreign woman.	Ezr. 10:31
	10. One of the priests appointed to blow with the trumpets.	1 Ch. 15:24

	11. Levite.	1 Ch. 26:25
	12. Anc. of our Lord.	Lk. 3:29
Elihoreph	One of Solomon's scribes.	1 K. 4:3
Elihu	1. Anc. of Samuel.	1 S. 1:1
	is Eliel.	1 Ch. 6:34
	is Eliab.	1 Ch. 6:27
	2. David's eldest b.	1 Ch. 27:18
	is Eliab.	1 S. 16:6
	3. Manassite chief.	1 Ch. 12:20
	4. Korahite porter.	1 Ch. 26:7
	5. s. of Barachel the Buzite, descended from Nahor (Job. 32:2). Fourth to speak to Job.	
A.	6. Anc. of Judith.	Jth. 8:1
Elijah	1. Elijah the Tishbite (uncertain location) was a prophet, whose story is told in 1 K. 17-19, 21; 2 K. 1:2. Six incidents were related about him; his prediction of drought and hiding (1 K. 17); the contact with false prophets on Mount Carmel (1 K. 18); the pilgrimage to Horeb (1 K. 19); his denunciation of Ahab in the affair of Naboth's vineyard (1 K. 21); the oracle to king Ahaziah (2 K. 1); his ascension (2 K. 2). He was a great prophet link between Samuel and Amos. It was believed he would re-appear shortly before the advent of the Messiah (Mal. 4:5f.; Mk. 8:28). He appeared with Moses in the transfiguration (9:4).	
AV. Eliah	2. Benjamite chief.	1 Ch. 8:27
	3. Priest who married a foreign wife.	Ezr. 10:21
	4. Layman who married a foreign wife.	Ezr. 10:26
Elika	One of David's 'Thirty'.	2 S. 23:25
Elimelech	A man of Bethlehem, married to Naomi (Ru. 2:1). They and their two sons migrated to Moab, where he died.	
Elioenai	1. Simeonite chief.	1 Ch. 4:36
	2. Benjamite.	1 Ch. 7:8

		3. desc. of David.	1 Ch. 3:23
		4. s. of Pashur.	Ezr. 10:22
	A.	is Elionas.	1 Es. 9:22
		5. s. of Zattu.	Ezr. 10:27
	A.	is Eliadas.	1 Es. 9:28
		6. Priest post-exilic.	Neh. 12:41
Elionas	A. 1.	S. Elioenai 4.	
	A. 2.	Jew who had taken a foreign wife.	1 Es. 9:32
		is Eliezer.	Ezr. 10:31
Eliphal		One of David's mighty men.	1 Ch. 11:35
		is Eliphelet.	2 S. 23:34
A. Eliphalat AV. Eliphalet	1.	Jew who returned from exile. is Eliphelet 4.	1 Es. 8:39
	2.	Jew who married a foreign wife. is Eliphelet 5.	1 Es. 9:33
Eliphaz		1. s. of Esau.	Gn. 36:4
		2. Oldest and most important friend of Job.	Job 4, 5, 15 and 22.
Eliphelehu, AV. Elipheleh		Musical Levite of David's day.	1 Ch. 15:18
Eliphelet, AV. Eliphalet		1. One of David's sons. is Elpelet.	2 S. 5:16 / 1 Ch. 14:5
		2. s. of David	1 Ch. 3:6
		3. One of David's mighty men. is Eliphal.	2 S. 23:34 / 1 Ch. 11:35
		4. desc. of Jonathan.	1 Ch. 8:39
		5. Returned from exile.	Ezr. 8:13
	A.	is Eliphalat.	1 Es. 8:39
		6. s. of Hashum who married a foreign wife.	Ezr. 10:33
	A.	is Eliphalat.	1 Es. 9:33
Elisabeth		w. of Zacharias, m. of John the Baptist, belonged to the priestly family of Aaron and was a kinswoman of the Virgin Mary. Lk. 1:5ff.	
Eliseus		S. Elisha.	
Elisha		God is salvation (1 K. 19:16-21; 2 K. 2:12;	

AV. Eliseus	2 K. 6:14, 32). s. of Shaphat of the tribe of Issachar, disciple and successor of the prophet Elijah. He came from the Jordan valley. His ministry extended over fifty years during six reigns in C. 9 B.C. He was head of a school of prophets. Some 18 stories, including several miracles, were told about him in 1 K. 19; 2 K. 2:9, 13. Chief influence was in the contemporary history of Israel and Syria.	
Elishah	s. of Javan.	Gn. 10:4
Elishama	1. Prince of the tribe of Ephraim. grandf. of Joshua.	Nu. 1:10
	2. One of David's sons.	2 S. 5:16
	3. s. of David. is Elishua.	1 Ch. 3:6 2 S. 5:15
	4. desc. of Judah.	1 Ch. 2:41
	5. f. of Nethaniah.	2 K. 25:25
	6. Secretary to Jehoiakim.	Jer. 36:12
	7. Priest of time of k. Jehoshaphat.	2 Ch. 17:8
Elishaphat	Captain under Jehoiada.	2 Ch. 23:1
Elisheba	d. of Amminadab, w. of Aaron.	Ex. 6:23
Elishua	s. of David. is Elishama.	2 S. 5:15 1 Ch. 3:6
Eliud	Anc. of Jesus.	Mt. 1:15
Elizaphan	1. s. of Uzziel, Levite. is Elzaphan.	Nu. 3:30 Ex. 6:22.
	2. Zebulun's representative for dividing the land.	Nu. 34:25
Elizur	Prince of Reuben.	Nu. 1:5
Elkanah	1. s. of Korah.	Ex. 6:24
	2. s. of Jeroham, Ephraimite. and f. of Samuel.	h. of Hannah 1 S. 1:1
	3. s. of Assir, the s. of Korah.	1 Ch. 6:23
	4. f. of Zuph.	1 Ch. 6:26
	5. Anc. of Berechiah.	1 Ch. 9:16
	6. One of David's mighty men.	1 Ch. 12:6
	7. One of the ark doorkeepers.	1 Ch. 15:23

	8. 'He was next to the king' (Ahaz) slain by Zichri.	2 Ch. 28:7
A. Elkiah	Anc. of Judith.	Jth. 8:1
Elmadam AV. Elmodam	Anc. of Jesus.	Lk. 3:28
Elnaam	f. of two of David's mighty men.	1 Ch. 11:46
Elnathan	1. f. of Nehushta, the m. of Jehoiachin.	2 K. 24:8
	2. s. of Achbor.	Jer. 26:22
	3. ⎱ Three men of this name 4. ⎰ in the list of those sent for 5. ⎰ by Ezra.	Ezr. 8:16
Elon	1. Of the tribe of Zebulun, one of the minor Judges.	Jg. 12:11-12
	2. s. of Zebulun.	Gn. 46:14
	3. Hittite, f.-in-law of Esau.	Gn. 26:34
Elpaal	Benjamite.	1 Ch. 8:11
Elpelet AV. Elpalet	One of David's sons. is Eliphelet 1.	1 Ch. 14:5
Eluzai	Warrior who joined David at Ziklag.	1 Ch. 12:5
Elymas	S. Bar-jesus.	
Elzabad	1. Gadite chief.	1 Ch. 12:12
	2. Korahite doorkeeper.	1 Ch. 26:7
Elzaphan	S. Elizaphan.	
A. Emadabun AV. Madia- bun	Mentioned amongst he Levites who superintended the restoration of the temple. 1 Es. 5:58	
A. Ematheis AV. Amatheis	One who took a foreign wife. is Athlai.	1 Es. 9:29 Ezr. 10:28
A. Emmer	Jew who had married a foreign wife. is Immer.	1 Es. 9:21 Ezr. 10:20
A. Emmeruth AV. Meruth	His family returned from exile.	1 Es. 5:24
Enan	Prince of Naphtali at first census.	Nu. 1:15

A. Enasibus	Jew who had married a foreign wife.	1 Es. 9:34
	is Eliashib 4.	Ezr. 10:36
A. Enemessar	K. of Assyria.	To. 1:2
A. Eneneus AV. Enenius	One of the leaders of the return from Babylon	1 Es. 5:8
	is Nahamani.	Neh. 7:7
Enoch	1. Eldest s. of Cain and f. of Irad.	Gn. 4:17, 18
	2. s. of Jared, f. of Methuselah (Gn. 5:24; Heb. 11:5). The words 'He was not; for God took him' describe his close fellowship with God and his death.	
Enos RV. Enosh	s. of Seth.	Gn. 4:26
Epaenetus	One of the Christians greeted by St. Paul.	Ro. 16:5
Epaphras	Native of Colossae, founder of the Colossae Church and fellow prisoner of Paul.	
		Col. 1:4-8, 4:12
Epaphroditus	From one or two allusions in the Ep. to the Philippians (Ph. 2:25-30) we learn that he visited St. Paul during his first Roman imprisonment. Fellow worker and fellow soldier with St. Paul.	
Ephah	1. s. of Midian.	Gn. 25:4
	2. concubine of Caleb.	1 Ch. 2:46
	3. Judahite.	1 Ch. 2:47
Ephai	The Netophathite whose sons were among the captains of the forces who joined Gedaliah at Mizpah.	Jer. 40:8
Epher	1. s. of Midian.	Gn. 25:4
	2. s. of Ezrah, Judahite.	1 Ch. 4:17
	3. Head of Manassite family.	1 Ch. 5:24
Ephlal	desc. of Judah.	1 Ch. 2:37
Ephod	f. of Hanniel.	Nu. 34:23
Ephraim	Joseph, s. of Jacob, had two sons, Manasseh and Ephraim, by Asenath, d. of Potipherah	

	(Gn. 41:50ff.). The dying Jacob crossed his arms and so blessed Ephraim the younger boy with the right hand, thus predicting the ascendancy of Ephraim over his elder brother.	
Ephrath	w. of Caleb.	1 Ch. 2:19
Ephron	s. of Zohar the Hittite from whom Abraham purchased the field in which was the cave of Machpelah.	Gn. 23:8-17
Epiphanes	S. Antiochus IV.	
Er	1. Firstborn s. of Judah. He was married to Tamar but died childless.	Gn. 38:3-7
	2. s. of Shelah the s. of Judah.	1 Ch. 4:21
	3. Anc. of our Lord.	Lk. 3:28
Eran	grands. of Ephraim.	Nu. 26:36
Erastus	1. Companion of St. Paul (Ac. 19:22), sharing a mission with Timothy to Macedonia. He is probably the Erastus of 2 Ti. 4:20.	
	2. Companion of St. Paul, Treasurer of the city of Corinth.	Ro. 16:23
Eri	s. of Gad.	Gn. 46:16
Esaias	AV. spelling of Isaiah in Apoc. and N.T.	
Esar-Haddon	The favourite s. of Sennacherib, k. of Assyria.	2 K. 19:37
Esau	1. Elder of Isaac's twin sons (Gn. 25:25). He was Isaac's favourite son, but was tricked by Jacob his younger brother in many ways. Esau was the ancestor of Edom, and the rivalry between the brothers was continued between the two peoples, Israel and Edom.	Num. 20, 1 K. 11
A.	2. Returned from exile with Zerubbabel.	1 Es. 5:29
	is Ziha.	Ezr. 2:43
A. Esdris	is Gorgias AV.	2 Mac. 12:36
A. Eserebias AV. Esebrias	Priest. S. Sherebiah.	1 Es. 8:54
Eshbaal	S. Ishbosheth.	

Eshban	Edomite chief.	Gn. 36:26
Eshcol	Amorite confederate of Abraham in his pursuit and defeat of Chedorlaomer's forces.	
		Gn. 14:13
Eshek	desc. of Saul.	1 Ch. 8:39
Eshtemoa	1. s. of Ishba, Calebite.	1 Ch. 4:17
	2. A Maacathite, s. of Hodiah.	1 Ch. 4:19
Eshton	Judahite.	1 Ch. 4:11
Esli	Anc. of Jesus.	Lk. 3:25
Esther	is Hadassah (Myrtle) (Est. 2:7). Jewess of the tribe of Benjamin who spent her life in the Captivity in Persia as the orphan ward of her cousin Mordecai (Est. 2:5ff.). She was the fairest of many beautiful maidens brought before the king. She married Ahasuerus (Xerxes), and risked her life to save her people.	
Esyelus AV. Syelus	One of the rulers of the temple in Josiah's time. is Jehiel.	2 Ch. 35:8
Ethan	1. He was surpassed in wisdom by Solomon.	1 K. 4:31
	2. s. of Zerah, grands. of Judah.	1 Ch. 2:6
	3. Anc. of Asaph.	1 Ch. 6:42
	4. Anc. of a guild of temple singers.	1 Ch. 6:44
A. Ethanus	'Swift scribe' who wrote to the dictation of Ezra.	2 Es. 14:24
Ethbaal	k. of the Sidonians, and f. of Jezebel who married Ahab.	1 K. 16:31
Ethnan	Judahite, s. of Helah.	1 Ch. 4:7
Ethni	Anc. of Asaph.	1 Ch. 6:41
	is Jeatherai.	1 Ch. 6:21
Eubulus	Leading member of the Christian community at Rome.	2 Ti. 4:21
A. Eumenes	Eumenes II, k. of Pergamus.	1 Mac. 8:8

Eunice	m. of Timothy. She was a Jewess and famed for her goodness and faith (2 Ti. 1:5; Ac. 16:1).
Euodia AV. Euodias	Christian woman of Philippi. Ph. 4:2
A. Eupator	surname of Antiochus V. 1 Mac. 6:17
A. Eupolemus	grands. of one of the Ambassadors sent to Rome by Judas Maccabaeus. 1 Mac. 8:17
Eutychus	At Troas, a young man restored Ac. 20:7-12 to life by St. Paul.
Eve	First woman (Gn. 3:20). w. of Adam and m. of Cain, Abel and Seth. She was created out of a rib of Adam to provide a suitable mate for him. She succumbed to the blandishments of a speaking serpent in the garden of Eden, and in turn persuaded her husband to defy God and eat forbidden fruit. She, with her husband, was expelled from Eden, and the pain of childbirth became her punishment.
Evi	One of the five kings of Midian. Nu. 31:8
Evil-merodach	s. and successor of the great Nebuchadnezzar on the throne of Babylon (2 K. 25:27-30). He released Jehoiakin of Judah from prison.
Ezbai	f. of Naarai. 1 Ch. 11:37
Ezbon	1. Gadite. Gn. 46:16 is Ozni. Nu. 26:15 2. grands. of Benjamin 1 Ch. 7:7
A. Ezekias AV. Ezechias AV. Ezecias	1. One who had a foreign wife. 1 Es. 9:14 is Jahzeiah. Ezr. 10:15 2. Stood on Ezra's right hand. 1 Es. 9:43 is Hilkiah. Neh. 8:4
Ezekiel	God strengthens (Ezk. 1f.). s. of Buzi, a Zadokite priest deported to Babylon in 597, and resided in Tel Abib by the river Chebar. Five years later he was called to be a prophet when thirty years old (1:1). He lived for not less than another twenty-two years (29:17). On the day of his call (592) when he received a most majestic vision, he was presumably

struck dumb (3:26) and only recovered his speech the night before the fugitive from captured Jerusalem arrived to tell the news in Babylon (33:21f.). His wife had died the very day that Nebuchadnezzar had besieged Jerusalem (24:1-2, 15-18). He possessed an exact knowledge of Jerusalem and its Temple. He was a visionary, a prophet, a priest and a great poet.

Ezer		
	1. Horite Duke.	Gn. 36:21
	2. s. of Ephraim.	1 Ch. 7:21
	3. Judahite, f. of Hushah.	1 Ch. 4:4
	4. Gadite chief.	1 Ch. 12:9
	5. s. of Jeshua who helped to repair the wall.	Neh. 3:19
	6. Priest.	Neh. 12:42
A. Ezora	His sons had married non-Jewish wives.	1 Es. 9:34
	is Machnadebai.	Ezr. 10:40

Ezra

1. Either in 458 or 398 B.C. (Ezr. 7-10; Neh. 8-10) and by a royal decree proclaimed in Aramaic (7:11-26), Ezra, priest and scribe, returned from Babylon to Jerusalem at the head of a company of returning exiles (Ezr. 8). He first brought about the dissolution of mixed marriages which the Jewish men had contracted with non-Jewish women (9). A census of such marriages was made. Then a public reading of the Law, and the Feast of Tabernacles was held and a day of penance and confession observed (Neh. 7 and 8). The alternatives of date, 458 or 598, depends on whether Artaxerxes I or II is intended (Ezr. 7:8), and if the former, then Ezra was a contemporary of Nehemiah.

2. Head of a priestly family which returned with Zerubbabel.   Neh. 12:1
   is Azariah.   Neh. 10:2

3. A priest, contemporary of Nehemiah.   Neh. 12:33

	4. A priest.	Neh. 12:13
Ezrah AV. Ezra	Judahite.	1 Ch. 4:17
Ezri	s. of Chelub, David's superinten- dent of agriculture.	1 Ch. 27:26
A. Ezril AV. Esril	Married a foreign wife. is Azarel.	1 Es. 9:34 Ezr. 10:41

F

Felix	Marcus Antonius Felix was the Roman pro- curator in Judea from 52-60 A.D. and he lived in Caesarea, the Roman capital of the province (Ac. 23-24, 24:27). After Claudius Lysias had arrested Paul, he sent him for trial before Felix at Caesarea. The case was heard and Felix, having exact knowledge of the Christian way, postponed his decision, and with his Jewish wife Drusilla, heard Paul often. Felix probably hoped to receive bribes from Paul. At the end of two years, when Felix was relieved of his post, he left Paul in gaol.
Festus	Porcius Festus (Ac. 25-26) succeeded Felix as the Roman procurator of Judea, (60-62 A.D.). (Ac. 24:27). He tried Paul very soon (25-6), but Paul appealed to Caesar. After hearing Paul's defence before king Agrippa, Festus thought Paul mad, but the king was impressed and would have been prepared to release Paul, had he not appealed to Caesar (26:32).
Fortunatus	An important member of the Church at Corinth, mentioned as being present with Paul in Ephesus. 1 Cor. 16:17

G

| Gaal | s. of Ebed. Canaanite rebel at   Jg. 9:26-41
Shechem. |

A. Gabael	1. Anc. of Tobit.	To. 1:1
	2. Kinsman of Tobit.	To. 1:14
Gabatha	A. Persian Eunuch.	Ad. Est. 12:1
	is Bigthan.	Est. 2:21
	is Bigthana.	Est. 6:2
Gabbai	Benjamite.	Neh. 11:8
A. Gabrias	b. of Gabael.	To. 1:14
	f. of Gabael.	To. 4:20
Gabriel	Interpreter of Daniel's vision.	Dan. 8:15f. Lk. 1:11f. Lk. 1:26

Gad	1. 'Good fortune' (Gn. 30:11). Jacob's seventh son, and his first son by Leah's handmaid, Zilpah. He was himself the father of seven sons, and the anc. of the tribe of Gad.	
	2. Seer at David's court (2 S. 24:11), and his adviser (1 Ch. 29:29) concerning the consequences of David's census, David's Altar (2 S. 25:10ff.), and the planning of David's music (2 Ch. 29:25). He was a historian of David's reign (29:29).	

Gaddi	Manassite spy.	Nu. 13:11
Gaddiel	Zebulunite spy.	Nu. 13:10
A. Gaddis	Surname of John (Maccabaeus) b. of Judas Maccabaeus.	1 Mac. 2:2
Gadi	f. of Mehahem king of Israel.	2 K. 15:14, 17
Gaham	s. of Nahor.	Gn. 22:24
Gahar	Family of Nethinim.	Ezr. 2:47
	A. is Geddur.	1 Es. 5:30

Gaius	A Latin name.	
	1. A Christian from Macedon (Ac. 19:29) arrested at Ephesus with Paul and another in the riots caused by Demetrius the silversmith.	
	2. A Christian from either Derbe or Doubenis, both in Macedonia (Ac. 20:4). He accom-	

panied Paul from Ephesus to Macedon, when Paul was on his way to Jerusalem.

(Gaius 1 and 2 may be the same person.)

3. A Christian at Corinth, one of two baptised by Paul himself (1 Cor. 1:14). Gaius housed the Church in his home, and Paul lodged with him during his third visit to Corinth (Ro. 16:23).

4. A Gaius was the recipient to whom John 3 is written.   3 Jn. 1

| Galal | 1. Levite, s. of Jeduthun. | 1 Ch. 9:16 |
| | 2. Levite. | 1 Ch. 9:15 |

| Gallio | s. of M. Annaeus Seneca, Proconsul of Achaia under Claudius. | Ac. 18:12-17 |

| A. Gamael | s. of Ithamar. | 1 Es. 8:29 |
| | is Daniel. | Ezr. 8:2 |

| Gamaliel | 1. s. of Pedahzur and prince of Manasseh. | Nu. 1:10 |

2. The s. of Simon and grands. of Hillel. He was the first to be styled 'Rabban', a higher title than Rabbi. He was a famous Pharisee, learned in the law and a member of the Sanhedrin (Ac. 5:34-39, 22:3). He was Paul's teacher (Ac. 22:3), and pleaded for moderation in the trial of Peter and the other apostles (Ac. 5:34-39).

| Gamul | Chief of Levites. | 1 Ch. 24:17 |

| Gareb | From the hill country of Judah, one of David's 'Thirty'. | 2 S. 23:38 |

| A. Gas AV. Gar | His sons were Temple Servants. | 1 Es. 5:34 |

| Gashmu | is Geshem. | Neh. 6:6 |

| Gatam | s. of Eliphaz. | Gn. 36:11 |

| A. Gazera | His sons were Temple Servants. | 1 Es. 5:31 |
| | is Gazzam. | Ezr. 2:48 |

| Gazez | 1. s. of Ephah. | 1 Ch. 2:46 |
| | 2. s. of Haran. | 1 Ch. 2:46 |

Geshan

Gazzam	Head of family who returned with Zerubbabel.	Ezr. 2:48
	is Gazera.	1 Es. 5:31
Geber	One of Solomon's twelve commissariat officers.	1 K. 4:19
Gedaliah	1. s. of Ahikam. Nebuchadnezzar made him governor over the poor of the people that were left in the land (Jer. 40, 41; 2 K. 25:22-25).	
	2. s. of Jeduthun, leader of the second course of temple musicians (1 Ch. 25:3, 9).	
	3. A Priest of the sons of Jeshua.	Ezr. 10:18
A.	is Joadanus.	1 Es. 9:19
	4. s. of Pashhur.	Jer. 38:1
	5. grandf. of Zephaniah.	Zeph. 1:1
Gedor	1. Anc. of King Saul.	1 Ch. 8:31
	2. s. of Penuel, Judahite.	1 Ch. 4:4
	3. s. of Jered, Judahite.	1 Ch. 4:18
Gehazi	Servant of Elisha.	2 K. 4:8-37
Gemalli	f. of the Danite spy.	Nu. 13:12
Gemariah	1. s. of Shaphan the scribe.	Jer. 36:10
	2. s. of Hilkiah, messenger from k. Zedekiah to Nebuchadrezzar.	Jer. 29:3
A. Gennaeus AV. Genneus	f. of Apollonius, Syrian Commander.	2 Mac. 12:2
Genubath	s. of Hadad, Edomite prince.	1 K. 11:19-20
Gera	1. s. of Benjamin.	Gn. 46:21
	2. s. of Bela, 2nd grands. of Benjamin.	1 Ch. 8:3
	3. and 4. f. and s. of Ehud.	Jg. 3:15; Ch. 8:7
	5. f. of Shimei.	2 S. 16:5
A. Geron	an Athenian.	2 Mac. 6:1
Gershom	1. s. of Moses.	Ex. 2:22
	2. s. of Levi.	
	is Gershon.	1 Ch. 6:1
A.	3. a desc. of Phinehas.	Ezr. 8:2
	is Gershon.	1 Es. 8:29
Geshan AV. Gesham	desc. of Caleb.	1 Ch. 2:47

Geshem	an Arabian opponent of Neh.	Neh. 2:19, 6:1-2
	is Gashmu.	Neh. 6:6
Gether	s. of Aram.	Gn. 10:23
	s. of Shem.	1 Ch. 1:17
Geuel	a Gadite. One of the twelve spies.	Nu. 13:15
Gibbar	Returned with Zerub.	Ezr. 2:20
	is Gibeon.	Neh. 7:25
Gibea	grandf. of Caleb.	1 Ch. 2:49
Gibeon	S. Gibbar.	
Giddalti	s. of Heman.	1 Ch. 25:4, 29
Giddel	1. Head of family of Nethinim.	Ezr. 2:47; Neh. 7:49
A.	is Cathua.	1 Es. 5:30
	2. Head of family of Solomon's servants.	Ezr. 2:56; Neh. 7:58
A.	is Isdael.	1 Es. 5:33
Gideon	s. of Joash, member of the clan of Abiezer, part of the tribe of Manasseh (Jg. 6:11, 15). One of Israel's most famous judges. Favoured with several signs and delivered Israel from the annual raids of the Midianites (Jg. 6:11-8:35). Also destroyed Canaanite cult symbols (Jg. 6:25-32); was signally favoured in that 'the Spirit of the LORD clothed itself with Gideon'(Jg. 6:34), and later presumably refused a hereditary kingship (Jg. 8:22-27).	
Gideoni	f. of Abidan, Benjamite prince.	Nu. 1:11
Gilalai	Levitical Musician.	Neh. 12:36
Gilead	1. s. of Machir.	Nu. 27:1
	2. s. of Michael, Gadite.	1 Ch. 5:14
	3. f. of Jephthah.	Jg. 11:1-2
Ginath	f. of Tibni.	1 K. 16:21, 22
Ginnethoi AV. Ginnetho	1. A Priest who returned from exile.	Neh. 12:4
	is Ginnethon.	Neh. 10:6
	2. Head of family of priests.	Neh. 12:16

Ginnethon	S. Ginnethoi.	Neh. 12:16
Gishpa	Overseer of the Nethinim.	Neh. 11:21
Gog	1. Head of a Reubenite family.	1 Ch. 5:4
	2. Prince from the north, representative of invading hordes.	Ezk. 38
Goliath	1. Philistine Giant from Gath slain by David (1 S. 17). He is said to have been 10½ ft. high, if the cubit is reckoned as 21 inches. His sword was kept at the Nob sanctuary, and later given to David himself (1 S. 21:9).	
	2. Philistine giant slain by Elhanan (2 S. 21:19). If Elhanan was David's original name, then there was only one Goliath. But 1 Ch. 20:5 gives the name of this second Goliath as Lahmi.	
Gomer	1. s. of Japheth.	Gn. 10:2, 3
	2. d. of Diblaim, w. of Hosea, the prophet and mother of three children.	Hos. 1:3
A. Gorgias	General of Antiochus Epiphanes, a mighty man.	1 Mac. 4:1; 2 Mac. 8:9
A. Gotholias	f. of Jesias, returned with Ezra.	1 Es. 8:33
	is Athaliah.	Ezr. 8:7
A. Gothoniel	f. of Chabris, one of the rulers of Bethulia.	Jth. 6:15
Guni	1. Head of a Naphtalite family.	Gn. 46:24
	2. A Gadite chief.	1 Ch. 5:15

H

Haahashtari	desc. of Judah.	1 Ch. 4:6
Habaiah	Head of priestly family which returned with Zerubbabel.	Ezr. 2:61
	is Hobaiah.	Neh. 7:63
A.	is Obdia.	1 Es. 5:38
Habakkuk	Habakkuk is the author of the Book of Prophecies bearing his name, the eighth of the Minor Prophets. He was a prophet attached	

	to the Jerusalem temple in the days of k. Josiah (640-609) and later.	
Habazziniah	grandf. of Jaazaniah, a Rechabite.	Jer. 35:3
Hacaliah, AV. Hachaliah	f. of Nehemiah.	Neh. 1:1, 10:1
Hachmoni	f. of Jehiel. S. Jashobeom.	1 Ch. 27:32
Hadad AV. Hadar	1. Eighth s. of Ishmael.	Gn. 25:15
	2. k. of Edom, s. of Bedad.	Gn. 36:35
	3. k. of Edom.	1 Ch. 1:50
	is Hadar.	Gn. 36:39
	4. Member of Royal House of Edom. f. of Genubath.	1 K. 11:14ff.
Hadadezer	K. of Zobah, s. of Rehob.	2 S. 8:3, 12
	is Hadarezer.	2 S. 10:16, 19
Hadar	S. Hadad 3.	
Hadarezer	S. Hadadezer.	
Hadassah	Jewish name of Esther.	Est. 2:7
Hadlai	Ephraimite.	2 Ch. 28:12
Hadoram	1. s. of Joktan (fifth).	Gn. 10:27
	2. s. of Tou, k. of Hamath.	1 Ch. 18:10
	is Joram.	2 S. 8:10
	3. Superintendent of levies in the reign of Rehoboam.	2 Ch. 10:18
	is Adoram.	1 K. 12:18
Hagab	His descendants returned from Babylon with Zerubbabel.	Ezr. 2:46
	A. is Accaba.	1 Es. 5:30
Hagaba	Head of family of Nethinim who returned with Zerrubbabel.	Neh. 7:48
	is Hagabah.	Ezr. 2:45
	A. is Aggaba.	1 Es. 5:29
Hagabah	S. Hagaba.	
Hagar	The name of an Egyptian woman who was maid to Sarah, Abraham's wife (Gn. 16:1-16, 21:8-21). Because of her own barrenness	

	Sarah gave Hagar to her husband for child bearing. In her pregnancy Hagar became arrogant, and later Abraham expelled her and her son Ismael from his household.	
Haggai	'Festival'. Haggai is the author of the tenth of the books of the Minor Prophets. He and Zechariah are named as prophets in Jerusalem after the return from exile. They were active in the re-building of the Second Temple 520-516 B.C.	
Haggedolim	f. of Zabdiel. (?. Text).	Neh. 11:14
Haggi	Second s. of Gad.	Gn. 46:16
Haggiah	Levite (Merarite).	1 Ch. 6:30
Haggith	w. of David. m. of Adonijah.	}2 S. 3:4
Hagri, AV. Haggeri	f. of Mibhar.	1 Ch. 11:38
Hajehudijah AV. Jehu-dijah	Jewess, m. of Jered and Heber.	1 Ch. 4:18
Hakkatan	Head of family of returning exiles.	Ezr. 8:12
A. is Akatan.		1 Es. 8:38
Hakkoz AV. Coz or Koz	1. Judahite. 2. Head of a priestly family. 3. Head of family.	1 Ch. 4:8 1 Ch. 24:10; Ezr. 2:61
A. is Akkos.		1 Es. 5:38
Hakupha	Anc. of family of Nethinim.	Ezr. 2:51; Neh. 7:53
A. is Achipha.		1 Es. 5:31
Hallohesh AV. Halohesh	Assisted at the repairing of the wall.	Neh. 3:12
Ham	second s. of Noah, resident in a survivor of the flood.	Noah's ark and Gn. 10:1
Haman	s. of Hammedatha, enemy of the Jews, chief minister of Ahasuerus.	Est. 3:1, 10 etc.

Hammath	f. of the house of Rechab.	1 Ch. 2:55
Hammedatha	f. of Haman.	Est. 3:1, 10
Hammelech	Proper name in AV. and RVm. 'the King' in AVm. and RV.	Jer. 36:26
Hammolecheth	d. of Machir. sister of Gilead.	1 Ch. 7:17
Hammuel	Simeonite.	1 Ch. 4:26
Hamor	Hivite f. of Shechem.	Gn. 33:19, 34
Hamran	An Edomite.	1 Ch. 1:41
AV. Amram	is Hemdan.	Gn. 36:26
Hamul	s. of Perez. grands. of Judah.	Gn. 46:12
Hamutal	w. of Josiah. m. of kings Jehoahaz and Zedekiah.	2 K. 23:31
Hana	S. Hanan 7.	
Hanamel	cousin of Jeremiah. s. of Shallum.	Jer. 32:7
Hanan	1. Levite—signed the Covenant.	Neh. 8:7; 10:10
	2. s. of Zaccur. One of Nehemiah's four treasurers.	Neh. 13:13
	3. Benjamite chief.	1 Ch. 8:23
	4. Youngest s. of Azel.	1 Ch. 8:38
	5. One of David's mighty men.	1 Ch. 11:43
	6. s. Igdaliah and head of prophetic guild.	Jer. 35:4
	7. Head of family of Nethinim who returned with Zerubbabel.	Ezr. 2:46; Neh. 7:49
A.	is Anan.	1 Es. 5:30
	8. Chief of the people, sealed the covenant.	Neh. 10:22
	9. Chief of the people, sealed the covenant.	Neh. 10:26
Hanani	1. Near kinsman of Nehemiah. One of the governors of Jerus.	Neh. 1:2 Neh. 7:2
	2. s. of Heman.	1 Ch. 25:4
	3. f. of Jehu the seer.	1 K. 16:1
	4. Priest who married a foreign wife.	Ezr. 10:20
A.	is Ananias.	1 Es. 9:21

		5. Chief musician.	Neh. 12:36
Hananiah		1. The first of Daniel's three companions.	Dan. 1:19
		named Shadrach.	Dan. 2:49

2. Governor of the fortress; a faithful man, one of two officers in command of Jerusalem.
Neh. 7:2

		3. s. of Zerubbabel.	1 Ch. 3:19
		4. Benjamite.	1 Ch. 8:24
		5. One of the temple musicians.	1 Ch. 25:4
		6. One of Uzziah's captains.	2 Ch. 26:11
		7. One who married a foreign woman.	Ezr. 10:28
	A.	is Ananias.	1 Es. 9:29

8. One of the guild of perfumers (or apothecaries) who repaired a portion of the wall of Jerusalem. Neh. 3:8
9. s. of Shelemiah.
One who repaired the wall. Neh. 3:30, 41
10. A priest under Joiakim. Neh. 12:12
11. f. of Zedekiah. Jer. 36:12
12. grandf. of Irijah, a captain of the ward. Jer. 37:13
13. A prophet, who was an opponent of Jeremiah. He died two months after Jeremiah had predicted his death within one year (Jer. 28).
14. One who sealed the covenant. Neh. 10:23
15. s. Chanuneus.

Hannah	w. of Elkanah. m. of Samuel who fulfilled a vow made whilst she was still barren, of dedicating her child to God.	1 S. 1:2ff.
Hanniel	1. Manassite leader and s. of Ephod.	Nu. 34:23
	2. Hero of tribe of Asher.	1 Ch. 7:39
Hanoch	1. grands. of Abraham.	Gn. 25:4
	2. eldest s. of Reuben.	Gn. 46:9
Hanun	1. s. of Nahash, k. of Ammonites.	2 S. 10:1ff.
	2. One who repaired the wall.	Neh. 3:13
	3. One who repaired the wall. sixth s. of Zalaph.	Neh. 3:30

Happizzez AV. Aphses	Head of an order of priests.	1 Ch. 24:15
Haran	1. s. of Terah. f. of Lot. 2. Levite, s. of Shimli. 3. Judahite, s. of Caleb.	Gn. 11:26 1 Ch. 23:9 1 Ch. 2:46
Harbona	is Harbonah, third of seven eunuchs who waited on king Ahasuerus.	Est. 1:10
Hareph	Judahite Chief.	1 Ch. 2:51
Harhaiah	f. of Uzziel, repairer of wall.	Neh. 3:8
Harhas	Anc. of Shallum. is Hasrah.	2 K. 22:14 2 Ch. 34:22
Harhur	Head of a family of Nethinim who returned from exile. A. is Asur.	Ezr. 2:51 1 Es. 5:31
Harim	1. lay family, who returned from exile and signed the covenant. 2. Priestly family, that went up with Zerubbabel. 3. A priest who sealed Ezra's covenant. 4. A chief who sealed the covenant. 5. Head of an order of priests.	Ezr. 2:32 Ezr. 2:39 Neh. 10:5 Neh. 10:27 1 Ch. 24:8
Hariph	1. Family that returned with Zerubbabel, and signed the covenant. is Jorah. 2. One who sealed the covenant.	Neh. 7:24 Ezr. 2:18 Neh. 10:19
Harnepher	Asherite.	1 Ch. 7:36
Haroeh	s. of Shobal, Judahite. is Reaiah.	1 Ch. 2:52 1 Ch. 4:2
Harsha	Head of family who returned from exile. A. is Charea.	Ezr. 2:52 1 Es. 5:32
Harum	Judahite.	1 Ch. 4:8
Harumaph	f. of Jedaiah.	Neh. 3:10
Haruz	grandf. of Amon, k. of Judah.	2 K. 21:19
Hasadiah	1. s. of Zerubbabel.	1 Ch. 3:20

	A. 2. s. of Hilkiah.	Bar. 1:1
Hashabiah	1. Levite, Anc. of a musician.	1 Ch. 6:45
	2. Levite, Anc. of Shemaiah.	1 Ch. 9:14
	3. s. of Jeduthun.	1 Ch. 25:3
	4. Hebronite, and royal deputy.	1 Ch. 26:30
	5. Ruler of the Levites (David).	1 Ch. 27:17
	6. Levite in time of Josiah.	2 Ch. 35:9
A.	is Sabias.	1 Es. 1:9
	7. Levite, returned under Ezra.	Ezr. 8:19
A.	is Asebias.	
	8. Priest, caretaker of the vessels.	Ezr. 8:24
A.	is Assamias.	1 Es. 8:54
	9. Ruler who helped to repair the wall and sealed the covenant.	Neh. 10:11
	10. Levite, desc. of Asaph.	Neh. 11:22
	11. Priest of house of Hilkiah.	Neh. 12:21
	12. Layman who had married a foreign wife.	Ezr. 10:25
	13. A builder of Nehemiah's wall wall (is perhaps 9).	Neh. 3:17
	14. Shared in dedication of wall.	Neh. 12:24
Hashabnah	One who sealed the covenant.	Neh. 10:25
Hashabneiah	1. f. of a builder of the wall.	Neh. 3:10
	2. Levite in time of Ezra.	Neh. 9:5
	is Hashabiah.	Ezr. 8:19
Hashbaddanah	One who stood on the left hand of Ezra at the reading of the law.	Neh. 8:4
A. is Nabarias.		1 Es. 9:44
Hashem	Gizonite, Davidic hero. is Jashen.	1 Ch. 11:34
Hashubah	s. of Zerubbabel.	1 Ch. 3:20
Hashum	1. Head of family of returning exiles.	Ezr. 2:19
A. is Asom.		1 Es. 9:33
	2. One who stood on Ezra's left hand at the reading of the law.	Neh. 8:4
A. is Lothasubus.		1 Es. 9:44
	3. One who sealed the covenant.	Neh 10:18
Hasrah	1. is Harhas.	

73

	A. 2. Head of family of temple servants.	1 Ezr. 5:31
Hassenaah	His sons built the fish gates. is Senoah.	Neh. 3:3
Hassenuah	1. Benjamite inhabitants of Jerusalem.	1 Ch. 9:7
	2. Benjamite inhabitants of Jerusalem.	Neh. 11:9
Hasshub	1. Builder of the wall.	Neh. 3:11
	2. Builder of the wall.	Neh. 3:23
	3. One who signed the covenant.	Neh. 10:23
	4. Levite, Merarite.	1 Ch. 9:14
Hassophereth	s. Sophereth.	
Hasupha, AV. Hashupha	Head of family of Nethinim who returned with Zerubbabel.	Neh. 7:46
	A. is Asipha.	1 Es. 5:29
Hathach AV. Hatach	Eunuch who attended Q. Esther.	Es. 4:5
Hathath	s. of Othniel.	1 Ch. 4:13
Hatipha	Head of family of Nethinim who returned from exile with Zerubbabel.	Ezr. 2:54
	A. is Atipha.	1 Es. 5:32
Hatita	Head of family of porters.	Ezr. 2:42
	A. is Ateta.	1 Es. 5:28
Hattil	Head of family of servants in Solomon's household.	Ezr. 2:57
	A. is Agia.	1 Es. 5:34
Hattush	1. Post-exilic priest.	Neh. 12:2
	2. desc. of David, contemporary of Ezra.	Ezr. 8:2
	3. Builder at the wall of Jerusalem.	Neh. 3:10
	4. One who sealed the covenant.	Neh. 10:4
A. Hauran	Leader of armed men in Jerusalem.	2 Mac. 4:40
Havilah	1. s. of Cush.	Gn. 10:7
	2. s. of Joktan.	Gn. 10:29
Hazael	Powerful king of Syria (842-796) (2 K. 9:15).	

	He was anointed king by Elijah the prophet, and soon murdered Benhadad the reigning king (2 K. 8:7-15). He fought against Jehoram, Jehu and Jehoahaz and widely extended his domains. He was probably Syria's greatest king.	
Hazaiah	desc. of Judah.	Neh. 11:5
Hazarmaveth	s. of Joktan.	Gn. 10:26
Haziel	Levite in time of Solomon.	1 Ch. 23:9
Hazo	s. of Nahor and Milcah.	Gn. 22:22
Hazzelponi, AV. Hazelelponi	d. of Etam, Judahite.	1 Ch. 4:3
Heber	1. Man of Asher, s. of Beriah.	Gn. 46:17
	2. Kenite, h. of Jael.	Jg. 4:17
	3. Man of Judah, s. of Mered.	1 Ch. 4:18
	4. Benjamite.	1 Ch. 8:17
Hebron	1. Third s. of Kohath.	Ex. 6:18
	2. s. of Mareshah, Calebite.	1 Ch. 2:42, 3
Hegai or Hege	Eunuch of Ahasuerus.	Est. 2:8, 15
Hegemonides	Officer left in command by Lysias.	2 Mac. 13:24
Heglam	s. of Ehud and f. of Uzza and Ahihud.	1 Ch. 8:7
Helah	w. of Ashhur.	1 Ch. 4:5, 7
Heldai	1. Captain of temple guard.	1 Ch. 27:15
	is Heleb, s. of Baanah.	2 S. 23:29
	is Heled.	1 Ch. 11:30
	2. One of small band who brought gifts of gold and silver from Babylon to make a crown for Joshua the High Priest.	Zec. 6:10
	is Helem.	Zec. 6:14
Helek	s. of Gilead, Manassite.	Nu. 26:30
Helem	1. Man of Asher.	1 Ch. 7:35
	2. An exile who brought gifts of gold and silver to Jerusalem.	Zec. 6:14
	is Heldai 2.	Zec. 6:10
Helez	1. One of David's 'Thirty.'	2 S. 23:26; 1 Ch. 27:10

	2. Judahite.	1 Ch. 2:39
Heli	1. f. of Joseph, f. of Jesus.	Lk. 3:23
A.	2. Anc. of Ezra.	2 Es. 1:2
A. Heliodorus	Chancellor of Seleucus IV.	2 Mac. 3:7f.
Helkai	Priest.	Neh. 12:15
A. Helkias	is Hilkiah, Chelcias.	
	1. High Priest in Josiah's reign.	1 Es. 1:8
	gt.-grandf. of Ezra.	1 Es. 8:1
	f. of Joakim.	Bar. 1:7
	S. Hilkiah 2.	
	2. Anc. of Baruch.	Bar. 1:1
	3. f. of Susanna.	Sus. vv. 2-29
Helon	Zebulunite f. of Eliab.	Nu. 1:9
Hemam	s. of Lotan the Horite.	Gn. 36:22
	is Homam.	1 Ch. 1:39
Heman	1. One of four sages whom Solomon excelled in wisdom.	1 K. 4:31
	2. s. of Zerah, Judahite.	1 Ch. 2:6
	3. A Kohathite Levite, s. of Joel.	1 Ch. 6:33
Hemdan	Edomite.	Gn. 36:26
	is Hamran.	1 Ch. 1:41
Hen	s. of Zephaniah.	Zec. 6:14
	May be the same as Josiah 2.	Zec. 6:10
Henadad	Levite chief.	Ezr. 3:9
Hepher	1. s. of Gilead the Manassite. f. of Zelophehad.	Nu. 26:32
	2. Judahite.	1 Ch. 4:6
	3. One of David's 'Thirty'.	1 Ch. 11:36
Hephzibah	m. of Manasseh, K. of Judah.	2 K. 21:1
Heresh	Levite.	1 Ch. 9:15
Hermas	One saluted by St. Paul.	Ro. 16:14
Hermes	A Christian saluted by St. Paul.	Ro. 16:14
Hermogenes	One in Asia who turned away from St. Paul.	2 Ti. 1:15
Herod	Herod is the name of the dynasty which ruled Palestine A.D. 37-70. The family began to	

rise through Antipater, or Antipas, appointed Procurator of Judaea by Julius Caesar in 47 B.C. He made his second son, Herod, Governor of Galilee.

1. Herod the Great.

Herod, the governor of Galilee, soon became governor of Coele-Syria, and was later given the title 'King of the Jews' by the Roman Senate. After three years of fighting he became the real king and reigned for thirty-three years. He ruled in the interests of Rome and was a very great builder. He built in cities such as Athens, rebuilt Samaria, built Caesarea and built many fortresses, such as Masada on the Dead Sea and Antonia in Jerusalem. He also reconstructed the Temple in Jerusalem. He was Edomite by birth, and this, together with his idolatry and cruel murders, especially of the old Hasmonean rulers, made him hated by his subjects. The greatest of his dynasty, he figured in the Gospel story in the massacre of the babies of Bethlehem (Mt. 2), and in reference to his last Will and Testament (Mt. 2:22; Lk. 3:1).

2. Herod Archaelaus, elder s. of Herod the Great and Malthace (Mt. 2:22). He succeeded Herod the Great and ruled as Elhnarch 4-6 B.C. He was later deposed and banished to France in A.D. 6, dying in A.D. 18.

3. Herod Antipas (Lk. 3:19). Herod the Tetrarch, younger son of Herod the Great and Malthace. He was responsible for the arrest and execution of John the Baptist who had condemned Antipas' second wedding as unlawful (Mk. 6:14-28). Jesus described him as 'that fox' (Lk. 13:31f.). Pilate sent Jesus to appear before this Herod (Lk. 23:7f.).

4. Herod Philip Tetrarch of Galilee (Lk. 3:1).

5. Another Philip (Mt. 14:3; Lk. 3:19).

6. Herod Agrippa was grands. of Herod the Great, and s. of Aristobulus. The Roman

emperor Gaius (Caligula) made him a king, and eventually this Herod ruled over a kingdom as extensive as Herod the Great. He persecuted the church and the apostles (Ac. 12:2f.), and his sudden death is recorded in Ac. 12:20. His s. was Agrippa, and his ds. Bernice (Ac. 25:13f.), and Drusilla, third w. of Felix (24:24).

7. Herod Agrippa II.

Son of Herod Agrippa I, he was a minor when his f. died (A.D. 44). Later he became k. and was famous for his encounter with Paul (Ac. 25:13, 26:32), and for his words, 'Almost thou persuadest me to be a Christian' (26:28). The dynasty ended with him.

Herodias	grandd. of Herod, and d. of Aristobulus (Mt. 14:3). Second w. of Herod Antipas, her second h. By her first h. was Herod, half-b. of Antipas, by whom she had Salome.
Herodion	Christian, apparently a Jew. Ro. 16:11
Heth	s. of Canaan, Anc. of Hittites. Gn. 10:15
Hezekiah	1. K. of Judah, s. of Ahaz, f. of Manasseh (2 K. 18; Is. 36-39; 2 Ch. 29-32). His reign is of uncertain length and dates (?716-701). He was one of Judah's greatest kings, and was commended for good behaviour because he reformed Jewish worship (2 K. 18:3). He also fortified the city and constructed the Siloam water tunnel, thereby protecting the city's water supply (2 K. 20:21).
	2. Anc. of the prophet Zephaniah. Zeph. 1:1
	3. Head of family of exiles who returned. Ezr. 2:16
	4. s. of Neariah of royal family of Judah. 1 Ch. 3:23
	5. One who sealed the covenant. Neh. 10:17
Hezion	grandf. of Benhadad, the Syrian king. 1 K. 15:18

Hezir	1. Priest. Seventeenth of the Priestly courses.	1 Ch. 24:15
	2. Head of a lay family who signed the covenant.	Neh. 10:20
Hezro AV. Hezrai	One of David's 'Thirty'.	2 S. 23:35
Hezron	1. s. of Reuben.	Gn. 46:9
	2. s. of Perez. grands. of Judah.	Gn. 46:12
Hiddai	One of David's 'Thirty'. is Hurai.	2 S. 23:30 1 Ch 11:32
Hiel	A Bethelite famed as the rebuilder of Jericho in the reign of Ahab.	1 K. 16:34
A. Hiereel	s. of Harim. is Jehiel.	1 Es. 9:21 Ezr. 10:21
A. Hieremoth	1. s. of Elam. is Jeremoth.	1 Es. 9:27 Ezr. 10:26
	2. s. of Bani. is Jeremoth. RV.= and Ramoth.	1 Es. 9:30 Ezr. 10:29
A. Hiermas	s. of Parosh. is Ramiah.	1 Es. 9:26 Ezr. 10:25
Hieronymus	Syrian officer under Antiochus V.	2 Mac. 12:2
Hilkiah	1. f. of Eliakim.	2 K. 18:18
	2. High Priest in reign of Josiah.	2 K. 22f.
A.	is Helkias.	1 Es. 1:8
	3. f. of Jeremiah.	Jer. 1:1
	4. f. of Gemariah.	Jer. 29:3
	5. Levite, Merarite, pre-Davidic.	1 Ch. 6:45
	6. Levite, Merarite, of David's day.	1 Ch. 26:11
	7. Contemporary of Ezra.	Neh. 8:4
	8. Chief of priests in days of Nehemiah.	Neh. 12:7
A.	9. Anc. of Baruch.	Bar. 1:1
A.	10. f. of Susanna.	Sus. 2:29
Hillel	f. of Judge Abdon in Ephraim.	Jg. 12:13
Hirah	Adullamite 'friend' of Judah.	Gn. 38:1, 12

79

Hiram	1. K. of Tyre and contemporary with David and Solomon.	2 S. 5:11
	2. Artificer procured by k. Solomon from Tyre.	1 K. 7:13f.
Hizki, AV. Hezeki	Benjamite.	1 Ch. 8:17
Hizkiah, AV. Hezekiah	s. of Neariah, a desc. of David.	1 Ch. 3:23
Hobab	s. of Reuel the Midianite. relation of Moses' w. Zipporah. S. Heber 2.	Nu. 10:29
Hobaiah	Head of priestly family which returned from exile.	Neh. 7:63
	is Habaiah.	Ezr. 2:61
A.	is Obdia.	1 Es. 5:38
Hod	Asherite.	1 Ch. 7:37
Hodaviah	1. Head of Manassite clan.	1 Ch. 5:24
	2. Head of Benjamite clan.	1 Ch. 9:7
	3. Levite.	Ezr. 2:40
	is Hodevah.	Neh. 7:43
AV. Hodaiah	4. desc. of David.	1 Ch. 3:24
Hodesh	w. of Shaharaim, a Benjamite.	1 Ch. 8:9
Hodevah	Levite.	Neh. 7:43
	is Hodaviah.	Ezr. 2:40
Hodiah	1. Man of Judah.	1 Ch. 4:19
	2. Levite, interpreter of the law.	Neh. 8:7; 10:10
	3. Levite, signatory of covenant.	Neh. 10:13
	4. One of those who sealed the covenant.	Neh. 10:18
Hoglah	d. of Zelophehad.	Nu. 26:33
Hoham	K. of Hebron.	Jos. 10:3ff.
A. Holofernes	Arch enemy of Jews, captain of the army of Nebuchadnezzar.	Jth. 2:4
Homam	s. of Lotan.	1 Ch. 1:39
	is Hemam.	Gn. 36:22
Hophni	s. of Eli, priest at Shiloh.	1 S. 1:3
Hophra	K. of Egypt.	Jer. 44:30

Horam	K. of Gezer.	Jos. 10:33
Hori	1. s. of Lotan.	Gn. 36:22
	2. f. of Shaphat the Simeonite spy.	Nu. 13:5
Hosah	Levitical doorkeeper of the temple.	1 Ch. 16:38

Hosea	was the first or second of the canonical prophets of the O.T., who lived during the last twenty years of Israel. He was a northerner, possibly a baker or priest who presumably shared the fate of the kingdom. His ministry was his marriage. He married either a harlot or a woman who became a harlot. The story is told in cc. 1 and 3. The two chapters may be parallel accounts of the same event, or of marriage with two men, but most probably 3 is the sequel of 1, and the renewal of Hosea's marriage with the wife whom he found he could not give up. Likewise there was a future for God's people. Hosea's great word was 'mercy'. i.e. 'loving kindness', his message was love, and his principles included claiming of the agricultural order for God (Hos. 2:8)

Hoshaiah	1. Leader of the Princes of Judah.	Neh. 12:32
	2. f. of Jezaniah.	Jer. 42:1
Hoshama	s. of Jehoiachin. desc. of David.	1 Ch. 3:18
Hoshea	1. K. of Israel (2 K. 17:1). s. of Elah. He is the nineteenth and last k. of Israel. Though a vassal of Assyria, he intrigued with Egypt, and thereby brought about his own end.	
	2. is Oshea.	Nu. 13:8
	is Joshua.	Deut. 32:44
	3. Davidic officer.	1 Ch. 27:20
	4. is Hosea the prophet.	
	5. Signatory of the covenant.	Neh. 10:2
Hotham AV. Hothan.	1. Asherite.	1 Ch. 7:32
	2. f. of two of David's 'Thirty'.	1 Ch 11:44
Hothir	s. of Heman.	1 Ch. 25:4
Hozai	Historian.	2 Ch. 33:19

Hul	s. of Aram, grands. of Shem.	Gn. 10:23
Huldah	A prophetess during the reign of Josiah.	2 K. 22:14-20
Hupham	S. Huppim.	Nu. 26:39
Huppah	Priest in days of David.	1 Ch. 24:13
Huppim	Head of Benjamite family. is Hupham.	Gn. 46:21 Nu. 26:39
Hur	1. Companion of Moses.	Ex. 17:10
	2. Judahite, grandf. of Bezalel.	Ex. 31:2
	3. One of the five kings of Midian.	Nu. 31:8
	4. Ephraimite.	1 K. 4:8
	5. f. of Rephaiah.	Neh. 3:9
Hurai	S. Hiddai.	
Huram	1. Benjamite.	1 Ch. 8:5
	2. S. Hiram 1 and 2.	2 Ch. 2:13f.
Huri	Gadite.	1 Ch. 5:14
Hushah	s. of Ezer. grands. of Hur. of the tribe of Judah.	1 Ch. 4:4
Hushai	The Archite, friend of David.	2 S. 16:16
Husham	K. of Edom.	Gn. 36:34
Hushim	1. Danite. is Shuham.	Gn. 46:23 Nu. 26:42
	2. s. of Aher, Benjamite man of valour.	1 Ch. 7:12
	3. w. of Shararaim the Benjamite.	1 Ch. 8:8
Hymenaeus	False teacher of time of St. Paul.	1 Ti. 1:19, 20 2 Ti. 2:17, 18
A. Hyrcanus AV. Hircanus	s. of Tobias.	2 Mac. 3:11

I

A. Iadinus	Levite teacher under Ezra. is Jamin 3.	1 Es. 9:48 Neh. 8:7

Ibhar	s. of David.	1 Ch. 3:6
Ibneiah	Benjamite.	1 Ch. 9:8
Ibnijah	Benjamite.	1 Ch. 9:8
Ibri	Levite (David's days).	1 Ch. 24:27
Ibsam AV. Jibsam	desc. of Issachar.	1 Ch. 7:2
Ibzan	One of the Minor Judges.	Jg. 12:8-10
Ichabod	s. of Phinehas. grands. of Eli	1 S. 4:21
Idbash	s. of Etam, Judahite.	1 Ch. 4:3
Iddo	1. Chief of temple servants from Casiphia.	Ezr. 8:17
	2. s. of Zechariah, Manassite.	1 Ch. 27:21
AV. Jadau	3. One of those who had taken foreign wives.	Ezr. 10:43
A.	is Edos.	1 Es. 9:35
	4. f. of Ahinadab.	1 K. 4:14
	5. Levite of clan of Gershom.	1 Ch. 6:21
	is Adaiah.	1 Ch. 6:41
	6. Seer and prophet.	2 Ch. 9:29
	7. grandf. of Zechariah.	Zec. 1:1
A.	is Addo.	1 Es. 6:1
	8. Head of one of the priestly clans that went up with Zerubbabel.	Neh. 12:4, 16
A. Iduel	One of the 'chief men' sent by Ezra to fetch Levites.	1 Es. 8:43
	is Ariel.	Ezr. 8:16
A. Ieddias	One of those who agreed to put away their foreign wives.	1 Es. 9:26
	is Izziah.	Ezr. 10:25
Iezer	Manassite.	Nu. 26:30
	is Abiezer.	Jos. 17:2
Igal	1. Of the tribe of Issachar, one of the twelve spies sent by Moses.	Nu. 13:7
	2. One of David's 'Thirty'.	2 S. 23:36
AV. Igeal	3. s. of Shemaiah of the royal house of David.	1 Ch. 3:22

Igdaliah	'Man of God.' f. of Hanan.	Jer. 35:4
Ikkesh	f. of Ira, one of David's 'Thirty'.	2 S. 23:26
Ilai	One of David's 'Thirty'. is Zalmon.	1 Ch. 11:29 2 S. 23:28
A. Iliadun AV. Eliadun	A Levite. is Henadad.	1 Es. 5:58 Ezr. 3:9
A. Imalcue	Arab Prince.	1 Mac. 11:39
Imla	f. of Micaiah, a prophet. is Imlah.	2 Ch. 18:7, 8 1 K. 22:8, 9
Immanuel	Symbolic name of child predicted by Isaiah.	Is. 7:14
Immer	1. Head of a priestly family. Ezr. 2:37; Neh. 2. Priest contemp. with Jeremiah.	1 Ch. 9:12; 7:40, 11:13 etc. Jer. 20:1
Imna	Asherite chief.	1 Ch. 7:35
Imnah AV. Jimna	1. Eldest s. of Asher. 2. Levite in the time of Hezekiah.	Nu. 26:44 2 Ch. 31:14
Imrah	Asherite chief.	1 Ch. 7:36
Imri	1. Judahite. 2. f. of Zaccur.	1 Ch. 9:4 Neh. 3:2
Iob AV. Job	Third s. of Issachar. is Jashub.	Gn. 46:13 Nu. 26:24
Iphdeiah	Benjamite chief.	1 Ch. 8:25
Ir	Benjamite. is Iri.	1 Ch. 7:12 1 Ch. 7:7
Ira	1. A Jairite, priest to David. 2. An Ithrite, one of David's 'Thirty'. 3. Another of David's 'Thirty'. s. of Ikkesh the Tekoite.	2 S. 20:26 2 S. 23:38 1 Ch. 27:9
Irad	s. of Enoch. grands. of Cain. antediluvian patriarch.	Gn. 4:18

Iram	Duke of Edom.	Gn. 36:43
Iri	S. Ir.	
Irijah	Captain who arrested Jeremiah.	Jer. 37:13f.
Iru	Eldest s. of Caleb.	1 Ch. 4:15
Isaac	lit. he laughs.	

Isaac was the s. of Abraham and Sarah, born to them in their old age, when his mother was past the age for conception. He was the son of promise, because his birth was promised to his aged parents (Gn. 17 and 18). When Isaac was a youth Abraham came to believe he was required to offer his son to God as a sacrifice, but was prevented. From this Abraham and Israel learnt that human sacrifice was wicked (Gn. 22). Isaac's marriage with Rebekah is one of the greatest stories in Genesis (24), and after twenty years of marriage they became the parents of Esau and Jacob, and so the promise to Abraham (Gn. 12:1-3) went on. Isaac was a gentle man.

Isaiah   Jehovah is salvation.

Isaiah was the author of most of chapters 1-39 of the book that bears his name. To distinguish him from the authors of 40-55, and 55-66, he is commonly called Isaiah of Jerusalem. He must have been born about 760 B.C., and continued as a prophet through four reigns and at least until 701 B.C. Tradition has it that he was martyred. A contemporary of Micah, and son of Amoz, he was married and had two sons at least. He ministered mainly to Jerusalem and Judah and faced severe crises in 734 B.C. Syrian invasion, 722 B.C. fall of Samaria, 711 B.C. when he went naked and barefoot for three years, and 701 B.C. Assyrian invasions. His main themes were the Holiness of God, Israel's political neutrality, the importance of Jerusalem and the Davidic House with its Messianic associations, the inviolability of

Zion, the remnant, which he not only attempted to create (8:16-18) but also proclaimed.

(See Is. 1:12, 36:39 and 2 K. 18:13, 20:21.)

Iscah	d. of Haran. Sister of Milcah.	Gn. 11:29
A. Isdael	His family returned with Zerubbabel. is Giddel 2.	1 Es. 5:33 Ezr. 2:56
Ishbah	Judahite.	1 Ch. 4:17
Ishbak	s. of Abraham and Keturah.	Gn. 25:2
Ishbi-Benob	One of the Philistines slain by the mighty men of David.	2 S. 21:15-17
Ishbosheth	lit: Man of shame. fourth s. of Saul. is Ishbaal. is Ishvi.	2 S. 2:8 1 Ch. 8:34 1 S. 14:49

Saul's general, Abner, made Ishbosheth king at Mahanaim, a place beyond Jordan. He became king at 40 and reigned for two years only. He had a very small entourage, and was assassinated by two of his own officers. His rival David then became king of all Israel.   2 S. 2:4

Ishhod AV. Ishod	Manassite.	1 Ch. 7:18
Ishi	1. Jerahmeelite. 2. Judahite chief. 3. Chief of East Manasseh. 4. Simeonite captain.	1 Ch. 2:31 1 Ch. 4:20 1 Ch. 5:24 1 Ch. 4:42
Ishma	One of the sons of Etam.	1 Ch. 4:3
Ishmael	God hears.	

1. Son of Abraham by Hagar, the Egyptian handmaiden to Sarah, his wife. He was circumcised when he was thirteen, and later became a rival to Isaac, Sarah's son (Gn. 17:25f.). Ishmael begat twelve sons (25:12-16), and so was ancestor of twelve clans. He was

		called 'a wild ass of a man' (16:12), and lived for 137 years.	
	2.	s. of Azel, a desc. of Saul.	1 Ch. 8:38
	3.	Anc. of Zebadiah, Judahite.	2 Ch. 19:11
	4.	s. of Jehohanan.	2 Ch. 23:1
	5.	Priest who put away his foreign wife.	Ezr. 10:22
A.		is Ismael.	1 Es. 9:22
	6.	s. of Nethaniah, member of the royal house of David.	2 K. 25:23f. Jer. 40-42
Ishmaiah	1.	Disaffected warrior of Benjamin.	1 Ch. 12:4
	2.	Of the tribe of Zebulum.	1 Ch. 27:19
Ishmerai		Benjamite chief.	1 Ch. 8:18
Ishpah		Benjamite.	1 Ch. 8:16
Ishpan		Benjamite chief.	1 Ch. 8:22
Ishvah		Second s. of Asher.	Gn. 46:17
Ishvi	1.	Third s. of Asher.	Gn. 46:17
	2.	Second s. of Saul.	1 S. 14:49
Ismachiah		Levite. Temple officer.	2 Ch. 31:13
A. Ismael		S. Ishmael no. 5.	
A. Ismaerus		One who had taken a foreign wife.	1 Es. 9:34
		is Amram.	Ezr. 10:22
Israel		is Jacob.	Gn. 43:6
Issachar	1.	Ninth s. of Jacob.	Gn. 30:18
	2.	Korahite doorkeeper.	1 Ch. 26:5
Isshiah	1.	Head of tribe of Issachar.	1 Ch. 7:3
AV. Jesiah	2.	Korahite Davidic warrior.	1 Ch. 12:6
AV. Jesiah	3.	s. of Uzziel, Levite.	1 Ch. 23:20
	4.	Levite.	1 Ch. 24:21
Isshijah AV. Ishijah		One who married a foreign wife.	Ezr. 10:31
A.		is Aseas.	1 Es. 9:32
A. Istalcurus		Returned from exile.	1 Es. 8:40
		S. Zabbud.	Ezr. 8:14

Ithai

Ithai	Benjamite, one of David's 'Thirty'.	1 Ch. 11:31
	is Ittai.	2 S. 23:29
Ithamar	Youngest s. of Aaron.	Ex. 6:23, 28:1
Ithiel	1. Benjamite.	Neh. 11:7
	2. To whom Agur addressed his oracular sayings.	Pr. 30:1
Ithmah	Moabite, one of David's 'Thirty'.	1 Ch. 11:46
Ithra	h. of Abigail, David's sister.	
	an Israelite.	2 S. 17:25
	S. Jether, the Ishmaelite.	1 Ch. 2:17
Ithran	1. desc. of Seir the Horite.	Gn. 36:26
	2. Asherite chief.	1 Ch. 7:37
Ithream	s. of David and Eglah.	1 Ch. 3:3
Ittai	1. Native of Gath.	2 S. 15:19
	2. One of David's 'Thirty'.	2 S. 23:29
	is Ithai.	1 Ch. 11:31
Ishar	1. s. of Kohath the s. of Levi.	Ex. 6:18, 21
	2. Judahite.	1 Ch. 4:7
Izliah	Benjamite.	1 Ch. 8:18
Izrahiah	Chief of tribe of Issachar.	1 Ch. 7:3
Izri	chief of Levitical choir.	1 Ch. 25:11
	is Zeri.	1 Ch. 25:3
Izziah,	One who married a foreign wife.	Ezr. 10:25
AV. Jesiah	A. is Ieddias.	1 Es. 9:26

J

Jaakan	Third s. of Ezer (Edomite).	1 Ch. 1:42
Jaakobah	Simeonite Prince.	1 Ch. 4:36
Jaala	Returned to Palestine with Zerubbabel.	Neh. 7:58
	A. is Jeeli.	1 Es. 5:33
Jaare-Oregim	Bethlehemite. f. of Elhanan.	2 S. 21:19
	S. Jair 4.	

Jaareshiah, AV. Jaresiah	Benjamite chief.	1 Ch. 8:27
Jaasiel	1. 'Ruler' of Benjamin, s. of Abner.	1 Ch. 27:21
	2. Mezobaite, or Zobite, one of David's warriors.	1 Ch. 11:47
Jaasu AV. Jaasau	One who married a foreign wife.	Ezr. 10:37
Jaazaniah	1. Judaean military commander who came to Mizpah to give allegiance to Gedaliah, the Governor of Judah.	2 K. 25:23
	is Jezaniah.	Jer. 40:8
	2. Chieftain of the Rechabites.	Jer. 35:3
	3. s. of Shaphan, ringleader of secret idolatry in Jerusalem.	Ezk. 8:11
	4. s. of Azzur, against whose counsels Ezekiel was commanded to prophesy.	Ezk. 11:1ff.
Jaaziah	s. of Merari.	1 Ch. 24:26
Jaaziel	Levite skilled in use of the psaltery.	1 Ch. 15:18
	is Aziel.	1 Ch. 15:20
Jabal	s. of Lamech—originator of the nomadic form of life.	Gn. 4:20
Jabesh	f. of Shallum who assassinated K. Zechariah.	2 K. 15:10
Jabez	desc. of Judah.	1 Ch. 4:9
Jabin	1. K. of Hazor, defeated by Joshua.	Jos. 11:1
	2. K. of Canaan, reigning from Hazor.	Jg. 4
Jacan AV. Jachan	Gadite chief.	1 Ch. 5:13
Jachin	1. Fourth s. of Simeon.	Gn. 46:10
	is Jarib.	1 Ch. 4:24
	2. Head of priestly family.	1 Ch. 9:10
Jacob	'He overreaches.'	Gn. 35:23-26
	1. s. of Isaac and Rebekah, younger twin-b. of	

D

89

Esau, h. of Leah and Rachel, and two concubine wives Zilpah and Bilhah, maids of his wives respectively, and f. of twelve sons, six by Leah, and two each by the three women, and one d., Dinah, by Leah (30:21). Because Jacob is renamed Israel (35:10), the children of Jacob became the children of Israel, from whom the people of Israel sprang. The story of Jacob is told in Gn. 25:50. He robbed his brother of his birthright and fled from his home at Beersheba to his mother's people in Harran (27). En route he experienced in a dream the vision of Jacob's ladder and the promises of divine blessing and protection (28:10-22). At Harran he married his elder cousin, Leah, and then the more beautiful Rachel, her sister, who was his favourite wife. After twenty years, and after building up a considerable wealth in flocks, he fled from Harran (29:31). After various adventures at Jabbok (32), Shechem and Bethel, he settled near Hebron. During a great famine at the end of his life, he moved down to Egypt where he died 130 years old. He was buried in the cave of Machpelah with his parents. (50:13). He is mentioned often in the O.T. and N.T.

2. f. of Joseph h. of Mary.   Mt. 1:15f.

Jacubus	A. Interpreted the law to the people.	1 Es. 9:48
	is Akkub.	Neh. 8:7
Jada	Jerahmeelite, s. of Onam.	1 Ch. 2:28
Jaddua	1. One who sealed the covenant.	Neh. 10:21
	2. High Priest.	Neh. 12:11
Jaddus AV. Addus	A. Priest whose descendants were unable to trace their genealogy at the time of the return. 	 1 Es. 5:38
	is Barzillai.	Ezr. 2:61
Jadon	Meronothite who took part in rebuilding the wall of Jerusalem.	Neh. 3:7
Jael	w. of Heber the Kenite.	Jg. 4:17
	She treacherously killed Sisera.	5:24ff.

Jahath	1. grands. of Judah.	1 Ch. 4:2
	2. Gt.-grands. of Levi.	1 Ch. 6:20
	3. s. of Shimei.	1 Ch. 23:10
	4. s. of Shelomoth, Izharite Levite.	1 Ch. 24:22
	5. Merarite Levite, in time of Josiah.	2 Ch. 34:12
Jahaziel	1. Benjamite who joined David.	1 Ch. 12:4
	2. Priest who blew trumpet before the ark.	1 Ch. 16:6
	3. Kohathite Levite.	1 Ch. 23:19
	4. Asaphite Levite.	2 Ch. 20:14
	5. Anc. of family of exiles who returned.	Ezr. 8:5
	A. is Jezalus.	1 Es. 8:32
Jahdai	f. of six sons.	1 Ch. 2:47
Jahdiel	Manassite chief.	1 Ch. 5:24
Jahdo	Gadite.	1 Ch. 5:14
Jahleel	Third s. of Zebulun. Anc. of Jahleelites.	Gn. 46:14
Jahmai	Man of Issachar, s. of Tola.	1 Ch. 7:2
Jahzeel	Naphtali's firstborn.	Gn. 46:24
	is Jahziel.	1 Ch. 7:13
Jahzeiah, AV. Jahaziah	s. of Tikvah, opposed Ezra in the matter of the foreign wives.	Ezr. 10:15
Jahzerah	Priest.	1 Ch. 9:12
	is Ahzai.	Neh. 11:13
Jahziel	S. Jahzeel.	
Jair	1. s. of Manasseh.	Nu. 32:41
	2. One of the Judges who judged Israel for twenty-two years.	Jg. 10:3ff.
	3. f. of Mordecai.	Est. 2:5
	A. is Jairus.	Est. 11:2
	4. f. of Elhanan.	1 Ch. 20:5
	is Jaare-oregim.	2 S. 21:19
Jairus	A. 1. f. of Mordecai.	Est. 11:2
	is Jair 3.	Est. 2:5

A. 2.	Temple servant. AV. is Airus.	1 Es. 5:31
3.	Ruler of the synagogue. Jesus raised his daughter from the dead.	Mk. 5:22
Jakeh	f. of Agur, author of proverbs.	Pr. 30:1
Jakim	1. Benjamite.	1 Ch. 8:19
	2. Priest.	1 Ch. 24:12
Jalam	s. of Esau, and an Edomite chief.	Gn. 36:5
Jalon	s. of Ezrah. desc. of Caleb.	1 Ch. 4:17

James is the same word as Jacob=supplanter.

1. s. of Zebedee, b. of John (Mt. 4:21), and one of the twelve apostles (Mt. 4:21), nicknamed by Jesus 'Boanerges' 'sons of thunder' (Mk. 3:17). He was one of the inner group of three disciples with Jesus at the raising of Jairus' daughter (5:37), the transfiguration (9:2), and Gethsemane, (14:33). James and John figure by themselves twice in the records (Lk. 9:51-56 and Mk. 10:35-45). He was a witness of the Resurrection (Jn. 21:1-8). He was eventually martyred by the sword, by Herod Agrippa I, about 44 A.D.
(Cp. Mk. 10:39 and Ac. 12:2.)

2. s. of Alphaeus, one of the twelve disciples (Mk. 2:14, 3:18), and is always the first name of the third group of four disciples in the list of the twelve disciples. He is not mentioned by name in the Gospels, unless he is the same person as James, *i.e.* James the less (Mk. 15:40), son of the Mary present at the Cross and empty tomb, and b. of Joses (or Joseph).

3. b. of the lord, and b. of Joses. Simon and Judas (Mt. 13:55). After the resurrection he became a leader in the church at Jerusalem, and perhaps its first minister or bishop. He presided at the first council of Jerusalem (Ac. 15). He was surnamed the 'Just' and was martyred about 61, and probably author of the Epistle of James.

	4. An otherwise unknown James, f. (and not b. as AV.) of Judas, not Iscariot, one of the twelve disciples.	Lk. 6:16
Jamin	1. s. of Simeon.	Gn. 46:10
	2. Judahite, Jerahmeelite.	1 Ch. 2:27
	3. Priest. S. Iadinus.	Neh. 8:7
Jamlech	Simeonite chief.	1 Ch. 4:34
Janai AV. Jaanai	Gadite chief.	1 Ch. 5:12
Jannai	Anc. of Jesus.	Lk. 3:24
Jannes and Jambres	Traditional names of two Egyptian magicians who opposed Moses.	2 Ti. 3:8
Japheth	s. of Noah, Anc. of peoples in region of Anatolia and Aegean.	Gn. 10:2-4
Japhia	1. K. of Lachish belonging to the Amorite coalition.	Jos. 10:3ff.
	2. s. of David.	2 S. 5:14b-16
Japhlet	Asherite, s. of Heber.	1 Ch. 7:32f.
Jarah	desc. of Saul.	1 Ch. 9:42
	is Jehoaddah.	1 Ch. 8:36
Jareb	K. of Assyria.	Hos. 5:13, 10:6
Jared	s. of Seth.	
	f. of Enoch	Gn. 5:15
	is Jered.	1 Ch. 4:18
Jarha	Egyptian slave.	1 Ch. 2:34f.
Jarib	1. Simeonite.	1 Ch. 4:24
	is Jachin.	Gn. 46:10
	2. Chief sent by Ezra to Casiphia.	Ezr. 8:16
A.	is Joribus.	1 Es. 8:44
	3. Priest who married foreign wife.	Ezr. 10:18
A.	is Joribus.	1 Es. 9:19
A. Jarimoth	One who sealed the Covenant.	1 Es. 9:28
	is Jeremoth.	Ezr. 10:27
Jaroah	Gadite chief.	1 Ch. 5:14

93

A. Jasaelus AV. Jasael	One who sealed the Covenant. is Sheal.	1 Es. 9:30 Ezr. 10:29
Jashen	f. of David's 'Thirty' mighty men. is Hashem.	2 S. 23:32 1 Ch. 11:34
Jashobeam	One of David's mighty men and commander for the first month.	1 Ch. 11:11
Jashub	1. Fourth s. of Issachar. is Iob. 2. Returned exile, married to foreign wife.	Nu. 26:24 Gn. 46:13 Ezr. 10:29
Jashubi-Lehem	Judahite.	1 Ch. 4:22
Jason	A. 1. Jason II, s. of Eleazer, envoy sent by Judas Maccabaeus.	1 Mac. 8:17
	A. 2. f. of Antipater.	1 Mac. 12:16, 14:22
	A. 3. High Priest, leader of the Hellenizing party among Jews. b. of Onias III.	2 Mac. 4:7-17
	A. 4. Jason of Cyrene, Historian of Maccabees in five volumes.	2 Mac. 2:23
	5. Befriended St. Paul during his visit to Thessalonica.	Ac. 17:5ff.
Jasubus	A. Priest who married a foreign wife. is Jashub 2.	1 Es. 9:30 Esr. 10:29
A. Jathan, AV. Jonathas	s. of Shemaiah 'the great'.	To. 5:13
Jathniel	Levite, Korahite gatekeeper.	1 Ch. 26:2
Javan	s. of Japheth.	Gn. 10:2, 4
Jaziz	Superintendent over the flocks of K. David.	1 Ch. 27:31
Jeatherai	Anc. of Asaph. is Ethni.	1 Ch. 6:21 1 Ch. 6:41
Jeberechiah	f. of Zechariah, friend of Isaiah.	Is. 8:2
Jechiliah, AV. Jecoliah	m. of K. Uzziah. is Jecholiah.	2 Ch. 26:3 2 K. 15:2

Jechonias	1. Gk. form of Jeconiah, s. of Josiah.	Ad. Est. 11:4
	is Jechoniah.	Mt. 1:11f.
	A. 2. Spokesman for Israelites who returned from exile.	1 Es. 8:92
	is Shecaniah.	Ezr. 10:2
	A. 3. S. Jeconias, 1.	1 Es. 1:9
Jecoliah, AV. Jecholiah	S. Jechiliah.	
Jechoniah	S. Jehoiachin.	
Jeconias S. Joachaz	A. 1. Captain in the time of Josiah.	1 Es. 1:9
	A. 2. S. Joachaz.	1 Es. 1:34
Jedaiah	1. Priest among returned exiles.	1 Ch. 9:10
	2. Exile sent from Babylon with gifts for the sanctuary at Jerusalem.	Zec. 6:10
	3. Simeonite.	1 Ch. 4:37
	4. One who repaired the wall of Jerusalem.	Neh. 3:10
	5. Post-exilic priest.	Neh. 11:10
	6. A priest among the returned exiles.	Neh. 12:6
	7. Another priest.	Neh. 12:7
	8. Head of priestly course.	1 Ch. 24:7
A. Jeddu	Priest.	1 Es. 5:24
	is Jedaiah 1.	Ezr. 2:36
A. Jedeus	One who put away his foreign wife.	1 Es. 9:30
	is Adaiah.	Ezr. 10:29
Jediael	1. Benjamite.	1 Ch. 7:6
	2. One of David's 'Thirty'.	1 Ch. 11:45
	3. Manassite deserter to David.	1 Ch. 12:20
	4. Korahite porter.	1 Ch. 26:2
Jedidah	m. of Josiah, k. of Judah.	2 K. 22:1
Jedidiah	Name given to Solomon by the prophet Nathan.	2 S. 12:25
Jeduthun	Anc. of family of temple singers.	Neh. 11:17

A. Jeeli		f. of family who returned from exile.	1 Es. 5:33
		is Jaala.	Neh. 7:58
		is Jaalah.	Ezr. 2:56
A. Jeelus		f. of Shecaniah.	1 Es. 8:92
		is Jehiel.	Ezr. 10:2
Jehallelel		1. Judahite.	1 Ch. 4:16
		2. Levite, Merarite.	2 Ch. 29:12
Jehdeiah		1. Levite of David's day.	1 Ch. 24:20
		2. officer of David in charge of royal she-asses.	1 Ch. 27:30
Jehezkel		Priest.	1 Ch. 24:16
Jehiah		Levite gatekeeper for the ark.	1 Ch. 15:24
Jehiel		1. One of David's chief Levite musicians.	1 Ch. 15:18
		2. Chief of Ladan Levites, Gershonite.	1 Ch. 23:8
		3. s. of Hachmoni, companion to the king's sons.	1 Ch. 27:32
		4. s. of Jehoshaphat.	2 Ch. 21:2
		5. One of Hezekiah's overseers.	2 Ch. 31:13
		6. Ruler of the house of God in Josiah's reign.	2 Ch. 35:8
		7. f. of Obadiah, returning exiles.	Ezr. 8:9
	A.	is Jezelus.	1 Es. 8:35
		8. f. of Shecaniah.	Ezr. 10:2
	A.	is Jeelus.	1 Es. 8:92
		9. One who married a foreign wife.	Ezr. 10:26
	A.	is Jezrielus.	1 Es. 9:27
		10. Priest who married a foreign wife.	Ezr. 10:21
	A.	is Hiereel.	1 Es. 9:21
Jehieli		Levite.	1 Ch. 26:21
		is Jehiel.	1 Ch. 23:8
Jehizkiah		Ephraimite, s. of Shallum.	2 Ch. 28:12ff.

Jehoaddah	desc. of Saul.	1 Ch. 8:36
	is Jarah.	1 Ch. 9:42
Jehoaddan, RV. Jehoaddin	m. of Amaziah, k. of Judah.	2 Ch. 25:1
		2 K. 14:2
Jehoahaz, RV. Joahaz	1. K. of Israel.	2 K. 13:1
	s. of Jehu.	2 K. 14:1
	2. K. of Judah.	
	s. of Josiah.	2 K. 23:30
A.	is Joachaz.	1 Es. 1:34
A.	is Zarakes.	1 Es. 1:38
	is Shallum.	
	3. s. of Jehoram.	2 Ch. 21:17
	is Ahaziah.	2 Ch. 22:1
Jehoash or Joash	1. k. of Judah.	2 K. 11
	2. K. of Israel, s. of Jehoahaz.	2 K. 13:10f.
Jehohanan	1. Korahite doorkeeper.	1 Ch. 26:3
	2. One of Jehoshaphat's five captains.	2 Ch. 17:15
	3. High Priest, friend of Ezra.	Ezr. 10:6
A.	is Jonas.	1 Es. 9:1
	is Johanan.	Neh. 12:22
	is Jonathan.	Neh. 12:11
	4. Israelite, who had a foreign wife.	Ezr. 10:28
A.	is Joannes.	1 Es. 9:29
	5. s. of Tobiah the Ammonite.	Neh. 6:18
	6. A priest.	Neh. 12:13
	7. Priest at dedication of the walls.	Neh. 12:42
	8. f. of Ishmael, concerned in Jehoiada's revolt.	2 Ch. 23:1
Jehoiachin	K. of Judah, s. of Jehoiakim.	2 K. 24:6ff.
	is Jeconiah.	Jer. 27:20
	is Coniah.	Jer. 22:24
A.	is Joakim.	1 Es. 1:43
A.	is Jechonias.	Bar. 1:3
	is Jechoniah.	Mt. 1:11
Jehoiada	1. f. of Benaiah, David's commander.	1 Ch. 11:22

97

	2. grands. of Jehoiada 1, and s. of Benaiah, counsellor to David after Ahithophel.	1 Ch. 27:34.
	3. High Priest in reigns of Ahaziah, Athaliah and Jehoash. He organised revolt against Queen Athaliah.	2 K. 11:4-21.
Jehoiakim	1. k. of Judah, s. of Josiah.	1 Ch. 3:15
A. is Joakim.		1 Es. 1:37
A. 2. High priest.		Bar. 1:7
Jehoiarib	1. Priest in Jerusalem.	1 Ch. 9:10
	2. Head of priestly course.	1 Ch. 24:7
A. is Joarib.		1 Mac. 2:1
Jehonadab or Jonadab	1. s. of Shimeah, David's b.	2 S. 13:3ff.
	2. s. of Rechab and very conservative Rechabite.	Jer. 35:6
Jehonathan or Jonathan	1. Levite sent out by Jehoshaphat to teach the people.	2 Ch. 17:8
	2. Head of priestly family of Shemaiah, s. of Uzziah.	Neh. 12:18; 1 Ch. 27:25
Jehoram RV. Joram	1. k. of Israel, second eldest s. of Ahab. b. and successor of Ahaziah.	2 K. 3:1
	2. k. of Judah (c. 849-842), s. of Jehoshaphat and b.-in-law of Jehoram, k. of Israel, h. of Athaliah.	2 K. 8:16ff.
	3. Priest appointed by Jehoshaphat to teach the Law.	2 Ch. 17:8
Jehoshabeath	S. Jehosheba.	
Jehoshaphat	Yahweh had judged.	2 Ch. 17
	1. s. of Asa and fourth k. of Judah. He reorganised defences, foreign policy and judicial system of his kingdom.	1 K. 22:41-50
	2. s. of Ahilud. Recorder in the reign of David, and Solomon, and a chief official.	2 S. 8:16; 1 K. 4:3
	3. One of Solomon's twelve commissariat officers.	1 K. 4:17
	4. f. of Jehu, k. of Israel.	2 K. 9:2

	5. is Joshaphat 2.	
Jehosheba	d. of k. Jehoram of Judah, w. of Jehoiada the High Priest.	2 K. 11:2
	is Jehoshabeath.	2 Ch. 22:11
Jehoshua Jehoshuah	} RV. is Joshua.	Nu. 13:16 1 Ch. 7:27
Jehozabad	1. s. of Shomer. Servant of k. Joash, and one of his murderers (2 K. 12:21).	
	2. Benjamite chief.	2 Ch. 17:18
	3. Levite, temple gatekeeper.	1 Ch. 26:4
Jehozadak	f. of Joshua the High Priest.	1 Ch. 6:14
	AV. Josedech.	Zec. 6:11
A.	is Josedek, AV. Josedec.	1 Es. 5:5 etc.
	is Jozadak.	Ezr. 3:2
Jehu	1. Prophet of Northern Kingdom. s. of Hanani, who predicted the end of the dynasty of Jeroboam 1 of Israel.	1 K. 16:1-7
	2. King of Israel, 842-815 (2 K. 9). s. of Jehoshaphat, grands. of Nimshi. Anointed k. by the authority of Elisha, proclaimed k. by his fellow officers, he slew his predecessor, Jehoram and his family. Founded the fourth and what proved to be the longest lived dynasty of Israel. But he had to submit and pay tribute to Shalmanezer III of Assyria.	
	3. Judahite, s. of Obed, and a Jerahmeelite.	1 Ch. 2:38
	4. Simeonite, s. of Joshibiah.	1 Ch. 4:35
	5. One of David's 'Thirty', a Benjamite from Anathoth.	1 Ch. 12:3
Jehubbah	Asherite.	1 Ch. 7:34
Jehucal	Courtier under k. Zedekiah.	Jer. 37:3f.
	is Jucal.	Jer. 38:1
Jehudi	s. of Nethaniah, gt.-grands of Cushi. Officer of Jehoiakim.	Jer. 36:14ff.
Jehudijah	S. Hajehudijah.	
Jehuel	Levite, s. of Heman.	2 Ch. 29:14
	is Jehiel 5.	

Jeiel	1. Reubenite and tribal chief.	1 Ch. 5:7
	2. f. of Gibeon and Anc. of Saul.	1 Ch. 9:35; 1 Ch. 8:29
	3. One of David's 'Thirty'.	1 Ch. 11:44
	4. Levite gatekeeper.	1 Ch. 15:18
	5. Levite musician.	1 Ch. 15:21
	6. Levite chief in time of Josiah.	2 Ch. 35:9
	7. Scribe in reign of Uzziah.	2 Ch. 26:11
	8. One who had married a foreign wife.	Ezr. 10:43
	9. Levite, Asaphite.	2 Ch. 20:14
	10. Worshipping Levite.	1 Ch. 16:5
	is Jaaziel.	1 Ch. 15:18
Jekameam	Levite, s. of Hebron.	1 Ch. 23:19
Jekamiah	1. Judahite.	1 Ch. 2:41
	2. s. of k. Jehoiachin.	1 Ch. 3:18
Jekuthiel	Man of Judah.	1 Ch. 4:18
Jemimah	Eldest of Job's daughters after his restoration to prosperity.	Job 42:14
Jemuel	s. of Simeon.	Gn. 46:10
	is Nemuel.	Nu. 26:12
Jephthah	Judge. Conq. of Ammonites, who sacrificed his d. in fulfilment of a vow.	Jg. 11:1, 12:7
Jephunneh	1. f. of Caleb.	Nu. 13:6
	2. s. of Jether. Asherite.	1 Ch. 7:38
Jerah	s. of Joktan.	Gn. 10:26
Jerahmeel	1. desc. of Judah, and head of a Hebrew clan listed among Judah.	1 Ch. 2:9
	2. Merarite Levite, s. of Kish.	1 Ch. 23:21, 24:29
	3. s. of k. Jehoiakim.	Jer. 36:26
Jered RV. Jared	Judahite desc. of David.	1 Ch. 4:18
Jeremai	Jew who married a foreign wife.	Ezr. 10:33
Jeremiah	1. The Prophet. s. of Hilkiah, and native of Anathoth. As a youth he became a prophet	

in 626 B.C., and remained a prophet at least until 586 B.C., forty years later. He lived through the reigns of the last five kings of Judah, predicting from the beginning the end of the kingdom of Judah, (1:13-19). He seems at first to have supported the Deuteronomic Reform of 621(11), but then withdrew from public ministry until about 609, the year of Josiah's death. Soon after Jehoiakim had begun to reign, Jeremiah made an appeal for national repentance in the course of a sermon preached in the temple (7:1-15; 26:1ff.). A period of plots against his life followed. In 605 B.C. he prepared an edition of his prophecies to date, only to have it destroyed by the king's command. He prepared a new edition of his oracles (36). About this time he was in the stocks. In these years too he composed what are called his 'Confessions', the record of his debate with God—found dispersed through chapters 11-20. When at last Jerusalem fell, he uttered a lament (13:15-17). Jeremiah continued to prophesy and to maintain that a still greater captivity was to be expected (27-28). He advised the exiles in Babylon to prepare for a long captivity. The city was finally captured in 587 B.C., though Jeremiah gave various proofs of a new life for the community beyond the destruction (32:1-15). Later he was taken down to Egypt where presumably he died. In his prophecy of the new covenant he is the link between Moses and Jesus. He was one of the greatest prophets of the O.T. and more is known about him than almost any other character in the Bible.

2. A warrior of the tribe of Gad, 1 Ch. 12:10 who joined David.

3. a Gadite warrior, who also 1 Ch. 12:13 joined David.

4. Slinger of the tribe of 1 Ch. 12:4 Benjamin.

	5. Head of Manassite family.	1 Ch. 5:24
	6. Jew of Libnah, f. of Hamutal w. of k. Josiah.	2 K. 23:31
	7. f. of Jaazaniah, head of the Rechabites.	Jer. 35:3
	8. Priest who came back to Jerusalem.	Neh. 12:1
	9. Priest who sealed Nehemiah's great covenant.	Neh. 10:2
	10. Prince of Judah at the dedication of the walls.	Neh. 12:34
Jeremias	A. s. of Maani.	1 Es. 9:34
	is Jeremai.	Ezr. 10:33
Jeremoth	1. Benjamite.	1 Ch. 7:8
	2. Benjamite.	1 Ch. 8:14
	3. Levite, Merarite, s. of Mushi.	1 Ch. 23:23
	4. Levite, s. of Heman. is Jerimoth.	1 Ch. 25:4, 22
	5. Naphtalite, tribal chief.	1 Ch. 27:19
	6. One who had married a foreign wife.	Ezr. 10:26
	7. One who had married a foreign wife.	Ezr. 10:27
	8. One who had married a foreign wife.	Ezr. 10:29
A. Jeremy	AV. and RV. form of Jeremiah.	1 Es. 1:28
Jeriah	Levite, Kohathite.	1 Ch. 23:19
	AV. and RV. form of Jerijah.	1 Ch. 26:31
Jeribai	One of David's 'Thirty'.	1 Ch. 11:46
Jeriel	Chief of Issachar.	1 Ch. 7:2
Jerijah	S. Jeriah.	1 Ch. 26:31
Jerimoth	1. Benjamite.	1 Ch. 7:7
	2. Benjamite, who joined David.	1 Ch. 12:5
	3. is Jeremoth 3.	1 Ch. 24:30
	4. is Jeremoth 4.	1 Ch. 25:4
	5. Levite who supervised temple treasuries in days of k. Hezekiah.	2 Ch. 31:13
	6. s. of David, and f. of Mahalath, w. of k. Rehoboam.	2 Ch. 11:18

Jerioth	w. of Caleb. Uncertain text in 1 Ch. 2:18 a genealogy.
Jeroboam	1. s. of Nebat, and at first a foreman for Solomon. First k. of Israel after the disruption, and founder of the northern kingdom, and of the shrines of Bethel and Dan, rivals of Jerusalem (1 K. 11:26-40, 12:1-14, 20). 2. Jeroboam II. s. and successor of Joash, reigned for 41 years. k. of Israel (790-749 B.C.). Under him N. Israel reached its peak of prosperity. Fourth k. of Jehu's dynasty, he extended his kingdom until it was as large as in Solomon's day. The social conditions of his reign are reflected in the diatribes of Amos (2 K. 14:23).
Jeroham	1. grandf. of Samuel, Ephraimite. 1 S. 1:1 2. Benjamite. 1 Ch. 8:27 3. Priest in post-exilic Jerusalem. 1 Ch. 9:12 4. 'Sons of Jeroham' were among 1 Ch. 12:7 David's 'Thirty'. 5. Danite, f. of Azarel, a tribal 1 Ch. 27:22 chief. 6. f. of captain Azariah who 2 Ch. 23:1 rebelled against Q. Athaliah. 7. Post-exilic Benjamite. 1 Ch. 9:8
Jerubbaal	Name given to Gideon. Jg. 6:32 is Jerubbesheth. 2 S. 11:21
Jerubbesheth	S. Jerubbaal.
Jerusha	m. of Jotham, k. of Judah. 2 K. 15:33 is Jerushah. 2 Ch. 27:1
Jeshaiah	1. grands. of Zerubbabel. 1 Ch. 3:21 2. s. of Jeduthuen, Levite, 1 Ch. 25:3 musician. 3. Levite supervising temple 1 Ch. 26:25 treasuries. 4. Head of family who returned Ezr. 8:7 with Ezra. 5. Chief of the Merarites in time Ezr. 8:19 of Ezra.

	6. Benjamite in post-exilic Jerusalem.	Neh. 11:7
Jesharelah	Asaphite musician.	1 Ch. 25:14
	is Asharelah.	1 Ch. 25:2
Jeshebeab	Levite.	1 Ch. 24:13
Jesher	s. of Caleb.	1 Ch. 2:18
Jeshishai	Gadite.	1 Ch. 5:14
Jeshohaiah	Simeonite prince.	1 Ch. 4:36
Jeshua	1. Another form of Joshua, s. of Nun.	Neh. 8:17
	2. Priest in David's days.	1 Ch. 24:11
	is Jeshuah AV.	
	3. Levite paymaster in time of Hezekiah.	2 Ch. 31:15
	4. Descendants returned with Zerubbabel.	Ezr. 2:6
	5. Levite, temple rebuilder.	Ezr. 3:9
	6. High Priest, returned from exile with Zerubbabel.	Ezr. 3:2
	is Joshua.	Hag. 1:1
	grands. of Seraiah, s. of Jehozadak.	
	7 and 8. Descendants returned from Babylon.	Ezr. 2:36, 40
	9. f. of a Levite.	Ezr. 8:33
	10. f. of Ezer.	Neh. 3:19
	11. Expounder of law.	Neh. 8:7
	12. Sealer of covenant.	Neh. 10:9
	13. Temple rebuilder.	Neh. 9:4
	14. is Jesus, teacher of the law.	1 Es. 5:58, 9:48
A. Jesias	returned from exile with Ezra.	1 Es. 8:33
AV. Josias	is Jeshaiah.	Ezr. 8:7
Jesimiel	Simeonite prince.	1 Ch. 4:36
Jesse	grands. of Boaz and f. of David, a Bethlehemite. He had eight sons.	Ru. 4:17; 1 S. 16:1
Jesus	Gk. form of the name Joshua or Jeshua.	

	A. 1. Joshua, s. of Nun.	1 Mac 2:55 etc.
	A. 2. High Priest in time of Zerubbabel.	1 Es. 5:5 etc.
	A. 3. Levite.	1 Es. 5:26 e
	is Jeshua.	Ezr. 2:40
	4. Anc. of Jesus Christ. AV. is Jose.	Lk. 3:29
	5. s. of Sirach, author of Ecclesiasticus.	Prologue to Sir.
	6. grandf. of Jesus, s. of Sirach.	Prologue to Sir.
	7. is Jesus Barabbas.	
	8. Called Justus, Jewish Christian resident in Rome.	Col. 4:11
Jesus Christ	The son of God.	
Jether	1. f.-in-law of Moses. probably a mistake for Jethro.	RV. Ex. 4:18
	2. s. of Gideon.	Jg. 8:20
	3. f. of Amasa, Ishmaelite.	1 K. 2:5
	4. Man of Judah, Jerahmeelite.	1 Ch. 2:32
	5. Man of Judah, s. of Ezrah.	1 Ch. 4:17
	6. Asherite.	1 Ch. 7:38
Jetheth	Head of an Edomite clan.	Gn. 36:40
Jethro	Priest of Midian, f.-in-law of Moses, and f. of Hobab. Is Reuel (Ex. 3:1ff.). Led the worship for Israel at Sinai, organised judicial life of the tribes in the wilderness (Ex. 18).	
Jetur	s. of Ishmael.	Gen. 25:15
Jeuel AV. Jeiel	1. Judahite chief.	1 Ch. 9:6
	2. Levite, contemporary of Hezekiah.	2 Ch. 29:13
AV. Jeiel	3. Contemporary of Ezra.	Ezr. 8:13
Jeush	1. s. of Esau.	Gn. 36:5
	2. Benjamite chief.	1 Ch. 7:10
	3. desc. of Saul.	1 Ch. 8:39
	4. Levitical family name, Gershonite.	1 Ch. 23:10ff.
	5. s. of Rehoboam.	2 Ch. 11:19

Jeuz	Benjamite.	1 Ch. 8:10
Jezaniah	Judahite military officer.	Jer. 40:8
	is Jaazaniah.	2 K. 25:23
Jezebel	d. of Ethbaal, w. of Ahab (1 K. 16:31), who brought the religion of her home to the court of her husband. She believed in absolute monarchy, and her vicious worship and lust brought her into conflict with Elijah the prophet (1 K. 18:17-40).	
A. Jezelus	1. Returned from exile.	1 Es. 8:32
	is Jahaziel.	Ezr. 8:5
	2. Returned from exile.	1 Es. 8:35
	is Jehiel.	Ezr. 8:9
Jezer	s. of Naphtali.	Gn. 46:24
Jeziel	Benjamite, served under David.	1 Ch. 12:3
Jezrahiah	Leader of the singers at the dedication of the walls of Jerusalem.	Neh. 12:42
	is Izrahiah.	1 Ch. 7:3
Jezreel	1. Judahite.	1 Ch. 4:3
	2. s. of Hosea—symbolic name.	Hos. 1:4
	3. A name for Israel.	Hos. 2:22
A. Jezrielus	One who took a foreign wife.	1 Es. 9:27
AV. Hierielus	is Jehiel.	Ezr. 10:26
Jidlaph	Seventh s. of Nahor.	Gn. 22:22
Joab	1. s. of Zeruiah David's sister (2 S. 2:12-32). He led David's forces to victory over the remnant of the army of Saul's son, Ishbosheth, led by Abner. He captured Jerusalem, and became David's commander-in-chief. He was faithful to David through many years, and helped the king not merely in battle (2 S. 11:6-26), but also in peace (2 S. 14:31-33).	
	2. desc. of Judahite, Seraiah, and of Kenaz.	1 Ch. 4:14
	3. His family returned from exile with Zerubbabel.	Ezr. 2:6
A. Joachaz	s. of Josiah.	1 Es. 1:34

	is Jehoahaz.	2 Ch. 36:1
A. Joadanus	s. of Jesus, s. of Josedek the priest.	1 Es. 9:19
Joah	1. s. of Asaph, Court official and royal messenger.	2 K. 18:18
	2. Levitical family name, s. of Zimnah.	1 Ch. 6:21
	3. Levite, s. of Obed-edom.	1 Ch. 26:4
	4. s. of Joahaz, and recorder under k. Josiah.	2 Ch. 34:8
Joahaz	1. f. of Joah and recorder in the reign of Josiah.	2 Ch. 34:8
	2. S. Joah 4.	
	3. S. Jehoahaz.	
A. Joakim	is Jehoiakim.	
	is Joacim or Joachim A. AV.	
	1. King, s. of Josiah.	Bar. 1:3
	2. s. of Jehoiakim. is Jehoiachin.	1 Es. 1:43
	3. Priest, s. of Hilkiah.	Bar. 1:7
	4. High Priest, who directed military affairs.	Jth. 4:6, 7
	5. Priest among the returning exiles.	1 Es. 5:5
	6. h. of Susanna.	Sus. 63
Joanan AV. Joanna	Anc. of Jesus Christ.	Lk. 3:27
Joanna	w. of Chuza, steward of Herod Antipas (Lk. 8:2ff.). She had been healed of infirmities by Jesus and ministered to Him 'of her substance'.	
A. Joannes AV. Johannes	1. s. of Akatan. is Johanan.	1 Es. 8:38 Ezr. 8:12
	2. s. of Bebai. is Jehohanan.	1 Es. 9:29 Ezr. 10:28
A. Joarib	Head of priestly family from which the Maccabees were descended. is Jehoiarib.	1 Mac. 2:1 1 Ch. 24:7

Joash	1. f. of Gideon.	Jg. 6:11
	2. s. of Ahab.	1 K. 22:26
	3. desc. of Judah.	1 Ch. 4:22
	4. Benjamite of clan of Becher.	1 Ch. 7:8
	5. Benjamite warrior, archer and slinger.	1 Ch. 12:3
	6. A comptroller of David's private estate.	1 Ch. 27:28
	7. s. of Ahaziah, and k. of Judah.	2 K. 11:2-12
	8. k. of Israel, s. and successor of Jehoahaz.	2 K. 13:10
Job	The suffering and patient hero of the Book of Job, and no doubt a historical personage.	
		Job; Ezk. 14:14
Jobab	1. Youngest s. of Joktan.	Gn. 10:29
	2. Second k. of Edom	Gn. 36:33ff.
	3. k. of town of Madon, N.W. Palestine.	Jos. 11:1
	4. Benjamite, s. of Shaharaim.	1 Ch. 8:9
	5. Benjamite, s. of Elhaal.	1 Ch. 8:18
Jochebed	m. of Aaron and Moses.	Ex. 6:20
A. Joda	1. s. of Iliadun, head of family of Levite temple repairers.	1 Es. 5:58
	is Judah.	Ezr. 3:9
	is Hodaviah.	Ezr. 2:40
	is Hodevah.	Neh. 7:43
AV. Juda	2. Anc. of Jesus.	Lk. 3:26
A. Jodan	is Gedaliah.	1 Es. 9:19
Joed	Benjamite.	Neh. 11:7
Joel	1. 'Yah is God'. s. of Pethuel. He was a prophet and the author of the second of the twelve short books of prophecy. His date is disputed, ?750 B.C. or ?400 B.C. (Joel).	
	2. Elder s. of Samuel and Kohathite.	1 S. 8:2
	Levite, and f. of Heman.	1 Ch. 6:33
	3. Kohathite, Levite and Anc. of Samuel.	1 Ch. 6:36
	is Shaul.	1 Ch. 6:24

4. Simeonite prince.	1 Ch. 4:35
5. Reubenite.	1 Ch. 5:4
6. Gadite chief.	1 Ch. 5:12
7. Chief of Issachar.	1 Ch. 7:3
8. One of David's mighty men.	1 Ch. 11:38
9. s. of Gershom chief of Levites who brought the ark to Jerusalem.	1 Ch. 15:7
10. Levite (may be 9).	1 Ch. 15:11
11. Levite, f. of Heman (may be 2).	1 Ch. 15:17
12. Manassite chief, s. of Pedaiah.	1 Ch. 27:20
13. One who married a foreign wife.	Ezr. 10:43
14. Benjamite overseer of laity.	Neh. 11:9
15. s. of Ladan, Gershonite.	1 Ch. 23:8
16. s. of Azariah, Levite, Kohathite.	2 Ch. 29:12

Joelah · s. of Jeroham. He joined David at Ziklag. — 1 Ch. 12:7

Joezer · A Benjamite who attached himself to David at Ziklag. — 1 Ch. 12:6

Jogli · f. of Danite chief, Bukki. — Nu. 34:22

Joha
1. s. of Benah, Benjamite. — 1 Ch. 8:16
2. One of David's mighty men. — 1 Ch. 11:45

Johanan
1. s. of Kareah (2 K. 25:23). After the murder of Gedaliah, he carried Jeremiah off to Egypt (Jer. 40-43).
2. Eldest s. of k. Josiah. — 1 Ch. 3:15
3. desc. of David, s. of Elioenai. — 1 Ch. 3:24
4. High Priest, s. of Azariah 5, contemporary of Solomon. — 1 Ch. 6:9
5. Benjamite who joined David. — 1 Ch. 12:4
6. Gadite who joined David. — 1 Ch. 12:12
7. One who returned with Ezra. — Ezr. 8:12
   A. is Joannes. — 1 Es. 8:38
8. Ephraimite, f. of Azariah. 17 — 2 Ch. 28:12
9. High Priest and grands. of Eliashib.
   is Jehohanan. — Ezr. 10:6 / Neh. 12:22

	is Jonathan	Neh. 12:11

A. John

1. f. of Mattathias.
   grandf. of the five Maccabaean 1 Mac. 2:1
   brothers.
   S. Joarib.   1 Ch. 24:7
2. Eldest s. of Mattathias, called 1 Mac. 2:2
   Gaddi.
3. s. of Accos and f. of Eupolemus who was
   ambassador to Rome.   1 Mac. 8:17
4. Envoy sent by Jews to treat   2 Mac. 11:17
   with Lysias.
5. s. of Simon the Maccabee appointed commander of the forces.   1 Mac. 16:2
6. A member of a priestly family mentioned
   as present at a meeting of the Sanhedrin.
                                        Ac. 4:6
7. f. of Simon Peter.   Jn. 1:42
   is Jonas.   Mt. 16:17
8. John the Baptist. This John was the s. of
   Zacharias and Elizabeth, and was mentioned
   in the Gospels and in Josephus—the Jewish
   historian. He lived in the wilderness of
   Judea, possibly among the dissident sects of
   the Jordan valley, but launched out on his
   own as an independent prophet. He lived on
   locusts and wild honey. He condemned the
   existing order, predicted the coming of the
   Messiah—the Saviour—and baptised many—
   including Jesus—in readiness for that event.
   John may also have extended his ministry into
   the highlands of Israel (Jn. 3:23). Later John
   denounced the marriage of Herod Antipas
   with his brother Philip's wife. As a result he
   was imprisoned in the fortress of Machaerus
   and finally executed. In spite of his doubts
   about the identity of Jesus Christ (Mt. 11:2-6),
   he was the forerunner of Christ, and the mission
   of John and the ministry of our Lord were
   more closely related than appears at first
   sight.
9. John Mark. S. Mark

10. John the apostle was the fisherman s. of Zebedee and of Salome (cp. Mt. 27:56 with Mk. 15:40), the younger brother of James, one of the twelve disciples, and one of the trio present at the raising of Jairus' daughter (Mk. 5:37), the transfiguration (Mk. 9:2), and in Gethsemane (Mk. 14:33). Jesus nicknamed James and John, who may have been his cousins on his mother's side, 'Boanerges', 'Sons of thunder'. He figures in several incidents (Lk. 9:49, 11:54; Mk. 10:37; Lk. 22:8). John is not mentioned by name in the fourth gospel, but he is almost certainly 'the disciple whom Jesus loved'. He lay near to Jesus at the last Supper (Jn. 13:23), was appointed guardian of Jesus' mother (19:26f.), and was first inside the empty tomb on resurrection day. He was one of seven to see the Risen Lord by the Sea of Galilee (21). In the Acts of the Apostles, John is named second after Peter (1:13), was imprisoned and released, (Ac. 3-4) and visited Samaria (8:14-25). He guided the church in Jerusalem. Paul describes him as one of the three pillars of the church (Gal. 2:9). He may have been martyred (Mk. 10:39), but it is more likely that he removed to Ephesus, and lived there as Bishop of the church until at least AD. 98. If he is the author of the Book of the Revelation, he may have been exiled to Patmos for some time. Reputedly he is the author of the Fourth Gospel, the three Epistles of John, and the Book of Revelation.

11. John the Elder is mentioned in 2 Jn. 1 and 3 Jn. 1. He may have been the same person as John the Apostle, but he may have been a younger John, who held the office of Elder at Ephesus beneath the Apostle. In this event this John the Elder would be the author of the Fourth Gospel, and the three Epistles of John.

Joiada	1. s. of Paseah and one who repaired the old gate.	Neh. 3:6
	2. High Priest, s. of Eliashib.	Neh. 12:10
Joiakim	High Priest, s. of Jeshua.	Neh. 12:10
	A. is Joakim.	1 Es. 5:5
Joiarib	1. Priest in days of David.	1 Ch. 24:7
	2. A colleague of Ezra.	Ezr. 8:16
	3. Judahite, Anc. of Maaseiah.	Neh. 11:5
	4. Priest.	Neh. 11:10
Jokim	Judahite.	1 Ch. 4:22
Jokshan	s. of Abraham, and Keturah. f. of Sheba and Dedan.	Gn. 25:2
Joktan	s. of Eber, desc. of Shem.	Gn. 10:26
Jonadab	S. Jehonadab.	
Jonah	'dove'.	
	1. s. of Amittai, the hero of the Book of Jonah, the fifth of the small books of the prophets (2 K. 14:25). He was a native of Gath Hepher in Zebulon. He predicted the restoration of the borders of Israel as achieved under Jeroboam 11, k. of Israel. Later Jonah was sent on a mission to Nineveh and this story is told in the book that bears his name.	
	A. 2. A Levite who had married a foreign wife.	1 Es. 9:23
	is Eliezer.	Ezr. 10:23
	3. is Jonas, Simon Peter's father.	Mt. 16:17
Jonam AV. Jonan	Anc. of Jesus Christ.	Lk. 3:30
Jonas AV. Joanan	A. 1. s. of Eliasib.	1 Es. 9:1
	is Jehohanan.	Ezr. 10:6
	is Johanan.	Neh. 12:23
	A. 2. Levite who had a foreign wife.	1 Es. 9:23
	is Eliezer.	Ezr. 10:23
	A. 3. The Prophet Jonah.	2 Es. 1:39
Jonathan	The LORD has given.	
	1. Levite, priest, s. of Gershom and desc. of Moses, and a native of Bethlehem (Jg. 17-18).	

Hired by Micah as a priest in his family shrine, he later became the founder of a line of priests to the tribe of Dan.

2. Eldest s. of Saul (1 S. 14:49), and self-denying and famous friend of David. Commander of a thousand men (1 S. 13:2), and hero of the exploit at Micmash, in which he and his armour bearer surprised the Philistine army. Jonathan and David made a pact of friendship (1 S. 18:1-4), and Jonathan protected David in various ways from the jealous wrath of his father (1 S. 19f.), and promised to serve David when he became king, as his first minister (1 S. 23:16-18). Jonathan lost his life in the battle of Gilboa, and was eventually buried by David in the tomb of Kish, his own grandf., in the land of Benjamin (2 S. 21:13f.). 2 Sam. 1. contained David's lament for his friend. A noble, courageous and loyal prince.

3. s. of Shimei, David's b., who killed a giant. 2 S. 21:21
1 Ch. 20:7

4. s. of Abiathar the priest. 2 S. 15:27ff.
a courier in several events. 1 K. 1:42-43

5. u. of David, Counsellor and Scribe. 1 Ch. 27:32

6. A scribe in whose house Jeremiah was imprisoned. Jer. 37:15ff.

7. High priest in fifth century, s. of Joiada, and f. of Jaddua. Neh. 12:11
is Johanan. Ezr. 10:16;
Neh. 12:22

8. s. of Shammah and one of David's warriors. 2 S. 23:32

AV. Jehona-than 9. s. of Uzziah and one of David's provincial treasurers. 1 Ch. 27:25

10. s. of Shemaiah and f. of Zechariah. A Levite and a trumpeter. Neh. 12:35

11. s. of Kareah, Judahite captain. Jer. 40:8

12. f. of Ebed, and fellow traveller with Ezra. Ezr. 8:6

13. s. of Asahel, who with Jahzeiah stood out

113

	against the idea of setting up a committee of princes to investigate mixed marriages.	
		Ezr. 10:15; 1 Es. 9:14
	14. A Priest who was head of the priestly family of Malluchi.	Neh. 12:14
	15. s. of Jada, and f. of Peleth and Zaza, and desc. of Jerahmeel of Judah.	1 Ch. 2:32-3
A.	16. s. of Mattathias, and one of the Maccabees (1 Mac. 9:23, 12:53). He succeeded Judas in leadership.	
A.	17. s. of Absalom, a messenger of Simon Maccabaeus.	1 Mac. 13:11
A.	18. Priestly leader of prayer.	2 Macc. 1:23
Jorah	Head of family that returned from exile.	Ezr. 2:18
	is Hariph.	Neh. 7:24
A.	is Arsiphurith.	1 Es. 5:16
Jorai	Gadite chief.	1 Ch. 5:13
Joram	1. s. of Toi, K. of Hamath.	2 S. 8:10
	is Hadoram.	1 Ch. 18:10
	2. Levite, desc. of Eliezer.	1 Ch. 26:25
A.	3. A captain in Josias's time.	1 Es. 1:9
	4. Chief of the Levites.	2 Ch. 35:9
	is Jozabad 4.	
	5. S. Jehoram 1.	
	6. S. Jehoram 2.	
A. Joribus AV. Joribas	1. Chief sent by Ezra to Casiphia.	1 Es. 8:44
	is Jarib.	Ezr. 8:16
	2. Priest who married a foreign wife.	1 Es. 9:19
	is Jarib.	Ezr. 10:18
Jorim	Anc. of Jesus Christ.	Lk. 3:29
Jorkeam	desc. of Judah.	1 Ch. 2:44
A. Josabdus	Levite.	1 Es. 8:63
	Jozabad no. 6.	Ezr. 8:33
A. Josaphias	Came up with Ezra from Babylon.	1 Es. 8:36
	is Josiphiah.	Ezr. 8:10
Josech AV. Joseph.	Anc. of Jesus.	Lk. 3:26

Josedek	S. Jehozadak.
Joseph	'May he add'.

1. The Patriarch (Gn. 30:23, 24, 37, 39-50). Eleventh and favourite s. of Jacob, and his elder s. by Rachel, Jacob's favourite but at first barren wife. Jacob favoured him by giving him a coat with long sleeves, and once sent him from Hebron to look for his shepherd brothers, whom he found in the plain of Dothan. Thence he was sold into Egypt, and into the household of one Potiphar. After a false accusation by Potiphar's wife, he was thrown into prison. Here Joseph's skill in interpreting dreams led not only to his release, but eventually to his appointment as the prime minister of Egypt. He saved the land of Egypt from famine, and as prime minister, but unrecognised, he received his brothers who were on a corn-buying mission to Egypt. After a second mission, he made himself known to his brothers, and interpreted his life in terms of a providential arrangement for the preservation of his father and all his family. Later Jacob and his family joined Joseph in Egypt, where he died at the age of 110 years. He gave instructions that when the Israelites left Egypt, they were to take his bones with them (Gn. 50:26 and Ex. 13:19).

2. f. of Igal, a man and a spy from Issachar. Nu. 13:7

3. A Levite. s. of Asaph. 1 Ch. 25:2

4. s. of Bani who married a foreign wife. Ezr. 10:42

A. is Josephus. 1 Es. 9:34

5. Priest, contemporary with Joiakim, a postexilic high priest. Neh. 12:14

A. 6. Anc. of Judith. Jth. 8:1

A. 7. s. of Zechariah and an officer of Judas Maccabaeus. 1 Mac. 5:18

A. 8. b. of Judas Maccabaeus. 2 Mac. 8:22
is John.

	9. Anc. of our Lord.	Lk. 3:24
	10. Anc. of our Lord.	Lk. 3:30
	11. h. of Mary (Jn. 1:45), m. of Jesus, desc. of David (Mt. 1:20). He acted as a father to Jesus (Lk. 2:22; Mt. 2; Lk. 2:41). He probably died before Jesus commenced his public work.	
	12. a b. of James the younger.	Mk. 15:40
	13. One of the Lord's brethren.	Mt. 13:55
	AV. and RV. form of Joses.	Mt. 27:56; Mk. 6:3
	14. Joseph of Arimathaea (Lk. 23:50), described as a good and just man who waited for God's kingdom. He begged Jesus' body from Pilate, and buried him in his own private tomb, providing also the linen (Mt. 27:57-60).	
AV. Barsabas	15. Joseph Barsabbas, called Justus (Ac. 1:23). He was put forward with Matthias as one suitable to take the place of Judas Iscariot.	
	16. S. Barnabas.	Ac. 4:36
AV. Joses	17. is Jaosech.	

Josephus	A. s. of Ozora. One who took a foreign wife.	1 Es. 9:34
	is Joseph 4.	Ezr. 10:42
Joses	1. Anc. of our Lord (Jesus).	Lk. 3:29
AV. Jose	2. One of the 'brethren of the Lord'.	Mk. 6:3
	is Joseph 13.	
	3. S. Joseph 12.	
	4. Joseph Barnabas.	Ac. 4:36
	is Joseph 16.	
Joshah	Simeonite chief.	1 Ch. 4:34
Joshaphat	1. One of David's warriors.	1 Ch. 11:43
	2. Priest in David's time, who blew the trumpet before the ark.	1 Ch. 15:24
Joshaviah	s. of Elnaam. One of David's 'Thirty'	1 Ch. 11:46
Joshbekashah	s. of Heman and a singer.	1 Ch. 25:4
Josheb-basshebeth	S. Jashobeam.	
Joshibiah	Simeonite.	1 Ch. 4:35

Joshua   The LORD is salvation.

1. s. of Nun, grands. of Elishama, his name was Hoshea (Nu. 13:8), until he was renamed Joshua (13:16). At first one of Moses' commanders (Ex. 17:8-16), then his liturgical assistant (33:11), then the Ephraim representative in the reconnaissance of Canaan (13f.): he became his successor (Nu. 27:18-23), and the principal figure in the conquest of Canaan about 1230 B.C. as related in the Book of Joshua. He crossed the Jordan and established his base at Gilgal. From here he conquered Jericho and penetrated the highlands. He also overcame a group of fortresses in the S.W. part of the country (Jos. 10:28-43), and made one sweep into the N.W. (Jos. 11:1-15). He is not said to have conquered the Shechem area, and it was presumably in the possession of the Israelites. Jos. 24 probably relates the formal alliance of the invading and indigenous Israelites. He subsequently retired to his own inheritance at Timnath Heres (Jg. 2:9), in Ephraim, where he died at the age of 110 years. He was depicted as a second Moses, but as Moses' successor he would inevitably have performed many of Moses' functions in addition to those of his own position.

2. Bethshemite, in whose field the Ark was set on its return from the land of the Philistines.   1 S. 6:14

3. Governor of Jerusalem at time   2 K. 23:8 of Josiah.

4. High Priest (Hag. 1:1), who returned from exile with Zerubbabel. is Jeshua.   Ezr. 3:2

Josiah   1. King of Judah, 639-609. s. of Amon. grands. of Manasseh (2 K. 21:24). He became king when only 8 years old. In the eighteenth year of his reign, a law book was found in the Temple during renovations. The religious

A. Josias

laws of this book, which comprised most of our Deuteronomy, confirmed the idealistic and reforming zeal of the young king (2 Ch. 34:3-7). On the basis of this book he purified and reformed the worship of the Jerusalem temple, ended idolatrous cults in the land, and attempted to centralise sacrifice in Jerusalem only (2 K. 22f.; 2 Ch. 34f.). He also held a national celebration of the Passover. The extent of the reform in Israel as well as in Judah shows that he also achieved some political liberty for his people. In 609 Josiah foolishly offered the passage of the Egyptian Pharaoh, Necho, through Palestine, and thereby met an early and unexpected death. One of Judah's greatest kings (2 K. 23:25).

	2. s. of Zephaniah.	Zec. 6:10
A. Josias	is Josiah, k. of Judah.	1 Es. 1:1
Josiphiah	f. of one of Ezra's companions.	Ezr. 8:10
Jotham	1. Youngest of the seventy sons of Gideon (Jg. 9:5). He proclaimed from Mt. Gerizim a curse upon Shechem and Abimelech.	
	2. k. of Judah, s. of Uzziah, in the days of Isaiah, Hosea and Micah.	2 K. 15:5ff.
	3. Judahite s. of Jahdai.	1 Ch. 2:47
Jozabad	1. Benjamite and one of David's mighty men.	1 Ch. 12:4
	2. Manassite chief and one of David's mighty men.	1 Ch. 12:20
	3. One of David's mighty men.	1 Ch. 12:20
	4. Head of Levitical family and treasurer in days of Hezekiah.	2 Ch. 31:13
	5 and 6. Priests who married a foreign wife.	Ezr. 10:22 f
	7. Levite chief in charge of work outside the temple.	Ezr. 8:33 Neh. 11:16.
	8. Chief of the Levites. is Joram 4.	2 Ch. 35:9
	9. Levite who expounded the law.	Neh. 8:7

118

	10. Levite chief in Jerusalem.	Neh. 11:16
A. Josabdus	One who had taken a foreign wife.	1 Es. 9:29
	is Zabbai.	Ezr. 10:28
Jozacar, AV. Jozacher	s. of Shimeath. Servant of Joash, k. of Judah, whom he murdered.	2 K. 12:21
Jozadak	S. Jehozadak.	
Jubal	s. of Lamech. Inventor of musical instruments.	Gn. 4:21
Jucal	S. Jehucal.	
Judah	1. Fourth s. of Jacob and Leah (Gn. 29:35), and Anc. of the tribe of Judah. In the stories about Joseph in Egypt, Judah represents his brothers (Gn. 37:26f., 43:3-10, 44:16-34). The stories about Judah in Gn. 38 are probably tribal history.	
	2. Overseer at rebuilding of temple.	Ezr. 3:9
	is Hodaviah.	Ezr. 2:40
	is Hodevah.	Neh. 4:73
	3. Levite who married foreign wife.	Ezr. 10:23; 1 Es. 9:23
	4. Levite.	Neh. 12:8
	5. Benjamite, s. of Hassenuah and overseer of Jerusalem.	Neh. 11:9
	6. Prince.	Neh. 12:34
	7. Priest and musician.	Neh. 12:36
Judas (= Judah).	A. 1. Third s. of Mattathias (1 Mac. 2:4), priest of Modein (1 Mac. 2:1). He became the leader of the Jews in their successful revolt against Antiochus. After a series of striking victories he was able to rededicate the temple from the reproach of Gentile use, and so achieved the religious liberty of his people. His victories continued until he lost his own life in battle. He was a brave, resourceful and spiritually minded soldier.	

A. 2.	s. of Chalphi, captain under Jonathan.	1 Mac. 11:70
A. 3.	Jew, unidentified (unless Judas I).	2 Mac. 1:10
A. 4.	s. of Simon the Maccabee, and neph. of Judas.	1 Mac. 16:2
A. 5.	One who took a foreign wife. is Judah 3.	1 Es. 9:23 Ezr. 10:23
6.	Anc. of Jesus Christ.	Lk. 3:30
7.	One of the brethren of the Lord.	Mt. 13:55
AV. Barsabas 8.	Barsabbas.	

Prominent member of Jerusalem Church (Ac. 15:22), and one of two messengers from Jerusalem to Antioch etc. to convey the decisions of the Jerusalem Council.

9.	Man of Damascus, with whom Paul was staying after his conversion.	Ac. 9:11
10	A Galilean who instigated an abortive rebellion against the Romans.	Ac. 5:37
11.	Iscariot. s. of Simon (Jn. 6:71) and the disciple of Jesus who betrayed him in the Garden of Gethsemane. He was probably a native of Kerioth, about twelve miles south of Judah. He was the pilfering treasurer of the group (12:6, 13:29). He was avaricious (12:3-5), and he betrayed Jesus for an agreed sum of money.	

Judas actually betrayed the rendezvous in the garden. Filled with remorse he either committed suicide (Mt. 27:3-10), or died by a fall (Ac. 1:18), and so went to his own place (Ac. 1:25).

12.	s. or b. of James, one of the twelve. May be Judas 13.	Lk. 6:16
13.	'Not Iscariot'. One of the twelve, identified with Labaeus and Thaddeus.	Jn. 14:22 Mt. 10:3
Jude	Author of Epistle of Jude. b. of James.	

Judith	1. w. of Esau.	Gn. 26:34
	A. 2. d. of Merari. Simeonite. w. of Manasses, wealthy widow and heroine of the Book of Judith.	Jth. 8:1
A. Juel	1. Jew who took a foreign wife. is Uel.	1 Es. 9:34 Ezr. 10:34
	2. One who took a foreign wife. is Joel.	1 Es. 9:35 Ezr. 10:43
Julia	One greeted by St. Paul.	Ro. 16:15
Julius	Centurion in whose custody St. Paul journeyed to Rome.	Ac. 27:1
Junias or Junia	One greeted by St. Paul.	Ro. 16:7
Jushab-Hesed	s. of Zerubbabel.	1 Ch. 3:20
Justus	1. S. Joseph 15.	Ac. 1:23
	2. Titius Justus, a worshipper of God and a Corinthian with whom St. Paul lodged.	Ac. 18:7
	3. Surname of Jew called Jesus, fellow-worker with Paul.	Col. 4:10

K

Kadmiel	Head of Levitical family, who returned with Zerubbabel.	Ezr. 2:40
Kallai	Head of priestly family in time of Joiakim.	Neh. 12:20
Kareah	f. of Johanan, Judaean, who escaped deportation to Babylon.	2 K. 25:23
Kedar	Second s. of Ishmael.	Gn. 25:13
Kedemah	s. of Ishmael.	Gn. 25:15
Kelaiah	Levite who married a foreign wife.	Ezr. 10:23
	A. is Colius.	1 Es. 9:23
	is Kelita.	Neh. 8:7
Kelita	S. Kelaiah.	

Kemuel	1. s. of Nahor.	Gn. 22:21
	f. of Aram.	
	2. Ephraimite leader.	Nu. 34:24
	3. f. of Hashabaiah ruler of	1 Ch. 27:17
	Levites in days of David.	
Kenan	s. of Enosh.	
AV. Cainan	f. of Mahalelel.	Gn. 5:9
Kenaz	1. s. of Eliphas and grands of	Gn. 36:11
	Esau.	
	2. grands. of Caleb.	1 Ch. 4:15
	3. f. of Othniel.	Jos. 15:17
A. Keras	Head of family of temple servants	1 Es. 5:29
AV. Ceras	who returned with Zerubbabel.	
	is Keros.	Ezr. 2:44
Keren-Happuch	Youngest d. of Job born in his	Job 42:14
	second state of prosperity.	
Keros	S. Keras.	
A. Ketab	Head of family of temple servants	1 Es. 5:30
	who returned with Zerubbabel.	
Keturah	w. of Abraham, who bore six sons who became	
	ancestors of Arab tribes.	Gn. 25:1f.
Keziah	Second d. born to Job after his	Job 42:14
	return to prosperity.	
A. Kilan	His s. returned with Zerubbabel.	1 Es. 5:15
A. Kiseus	Benjamite gt.-grandf. of	Ad. Est. 11:2
	Mordecai.	
	is Kish no. 4.	Est. 2:5
Kish	1. Benjamite f. of Saul, first k.	1 S. 9:1
	of Israel.	
	2. s. of Jeiel. u. of Kish 1.	1 Ch. 9:36
	3. s. of Mahli the Levite.	1 Ch. 23:21f.
	f. of Jerahmeel.	
	4. S. Kiseus.	
	5. s. of Abdi, Levite in time of	2 Ch. 29:12
	Hezekiah.	
Kishi	Merarite Levite.	1 Ch. 6:44
	is Kushaiah.	1 Ch. 15:17

Kittim	desc. of Noah.	Gn. 10:4
AV. Chittim	Name for Cyprus.	Jer. 2:10
		Ezk. 27:6
Kohath	Second s. of Levi, grandf. of Aaron, Miriam and Moses. His descendants became important branch of priesthood.	Ex. 6:16
Koheleth	Hebrew name of author of Ecclesiastes.	Ecc. 1:1
Kolaiah	1. f. of a false prophet named Ahab.	Jer. 29:21
	2. Benjamite living in Jerusalem after the exile.	Neh. 11:7
Korah	(? baldness).	
	1. s. of Esau and a duke of Edom.	Gn. 36:5, 14
	2. s. of Eliphaz, grands. of Esau, and a duke of Edom.	Gn. 36:16
	3. s. of Hebron of Calebite family.	1 Ch. 2:43
	4. Grands. of Kohath, a desc. of Izhar, and Anc. of 'sons of Korah', a choir of temple musicians (1 Ch. 6:22, 37). S. superscription above Ps. 42 and eleven other Psalms.	
	5. s. of Izhar, and leader of revolt in the wilderness against Moses and Aaron, but when preparing for worship the ground opened beneath their feet and swallowed them up.	
		Nu. 16
	(*Note:* 4 and 5 may be the same person.)	
Kore	1. desc. of Korah, his family were doorkeepers.	1 Ch. 9:19
	2. s. of Imnah. Levite in the time of Hezekiah, had charge of offerings.	2 Ch. 31:14
Koz	desc. of Judah.	1 Ch. 4:8
Kushaiah	S. Kishi.	

L

Laadah	Judahite.	1 Ch. 4:21
Laban	s. of Bethuel.	

	b. of Rebekah the w. of Isaac, Abraham's son, grands. of Nahor, f. of Leah and Rachel, u. and f.-in-law of Jacob (Gn. 24:29, 25:20, 28:5, 29-31). He was one of the leading members of that Aramean family which remained in Harran, when another part of that family headed by Abraham migrated to Palestine.	
A. Labana	His family returned from exile.	1 Es. 5:29
	is Lebanah.	Ezr. 2:45
A. Laccunus	s. of Addi.	1 Es. 9:31
AV. Lacunus	Jew who had taken foreign wife during exile.	
	is Chelal.	Ezr. 10:30
Ladan	1. Anc. of Joshua.	1 Ch. 7:26
AV. Laadan		
	2. Levite of the family of Gershom.	1 Ch. 23:7, 8
	is Libni.	1 Ch. 6:17
AV. Ladan	A. 3. Head of family who could not prove their Israelite descent.	1 Es. 5:37
Lael	Levite, f. of Eliasaph.	Nu. 3:24
Lahad	Judahite.	1 Ch. 4:2
Lahmi	Philistine giant, b. of Goliath the Gittite.	1 Ch. 20:5
Laish	f. of Palti (or Paltiel) to whom Michal, David's wife, was given by Saul.	1 S. 25:44
	is Leshem.	Jos. 19:47
Lamech	1. desc. of Cain.	Gn. 4:18ff.
	2. f. of Noah.	Gn. 5:25f.
Lappidoth	h. of Deborah the prophetess.	Jg. 4:4
A. Lasthenes	Officer of high rank under Demetrius II, Nikator.	1 Mac. 11:31f.
Lazarus of Bethany	b. of Martha and Mary (Jn. 11:1-53). The fourth Gospel tells how Jesus raised him from the dead several days after his death.	
	N.B.—Lazarus was also the name of the beggar, the imaginary character, at the gate of Dives the rich man (Lk. 16:19-31).	

Leah	Elder d. of Laban the Aramean (Gn. 29:21ff., 49:31), who became the first w. of Jacob, and mother of six sons, Reuben, Simeon, Levi, Judah, Issachar and Zebulon, and one daughter, Dinah. Leah had weak eyes and was not as attractive as her younger sister, Rachel. She went to Palestine with Jacob from her home in Harran and was eventually buried in the cave at Machpelah.	
Lebana	Head of family of returning exiles.	Neh. 7:48
	is Labanah.	Ezr. 2:45
	A. is Labana.	1 Es. 5:29
Lebbaeus	Name given to one of the Twelve. AV. of	Mt. 10:3
	S. Thaddeus.	
Lecah	desc. of Judah, and s. of Er.	1 Ch. 4:21
Lehabim	desc. of Ham.	1 Ch. 1:11
Lemuel	K. of Massa in Arabia.	Pr. 31:1-9
Leshem	S. Laish.	
Letushim	s. of Dedan.	
	desc. of Abraham.	Gn. 25:3
Leummim	desc. of Dedan, s. of Abraham.	Gn. 25:3
Levi	1. Third s. of Jacob and Leah (Gn. 29:34 and cp. Gn. 34 and 49:5-7). f. of Gershon, Kohath and Merari, gt.-grandf. of Moses, s. of Amram, s. of Kohath. Levi joined with his b. Simeon in massacring the males of the city of Shechem, the prince of which, Shechem, had raped their sister Dinah. From Levi and from the descendants of his three sons, the branches of the priestly Levites are descended.	
	2. s. of Melchi and f. of Mattat, and Anc. of Jesus Christ.	Lk. 3:24
	3. s. of Symeon and f. of Mattat, and an Anc. of Jesus Christ.	Lk. 3:29
	4. A tax collector who lived at Capernaum. He was the s. of Alphaeus (Mk. 2:14), and he	

	became a disciple of Jesus Christ, and was identified in Matt. 9:9 and 10:3 as Matthew, though Levi was not named as one of twelve disciples.
A. Levis	He opposed Ezra's action about foreign wives. 1 Es. 9:14
	'Shabbethai the Levite'. Ezr. 10:15
Libni	1. Eldest s. of Gershon the Levite. Ex. 6:17
	2. Levite descended from Merari. 1 Ch. 6:29
	3. Libnites, family of Levites. Nu. 26:58
Likhi	s. of Shemida, Manassite. 1 Ch. 7:19
Linus	Christian. Joins Paul in sending greetings to Timothy. 2 Ti. 4:21
Lo-ammi	Second s. of Gomer, w. of the prophet Hosea. Hos. 1:2f.
	Name is symbolical, 'not my people'.
A. Loddeus AV. Saddeus	Captain in the place of the Treasury, to whom Ezra sent for Levites. 1 Es. 8:45
	is Iddo. Ezr. 8:17
Lois	grandm. of Timothy, m. of Eunice, a devout and sincere Jewess at Lystra. 2 Ti. 1:5, 3:15
Lo Ruhamah	d. of Hosea, symbolical name = 'I will have no mercy'. Hos. 1:6
Lot	s. of Haran and Abraham's n., grands. of Terah. He accompanied his family in the migration from Ur to Harran (Gn. 11:26-29) and went on from there with his uncle to Canaan (12:4-5). Later his uncle gave him the right to choose the part of the land in which he wished to settle, and Lot chose the Jordan basin and went to live in Sodom (13:8-12). When this city was looted and Lot was captured, Abraham effected his rescue (14:11-16). Later still after Lot and his family had fled in face of the destruction of Sodom, Lot was

trapped into incestuous intercourse by his two daughters, and by them became the Anc. of the Moabites and the Ammonites (19:30-38) (cp. Lk. 17:28f. and 2 Pet. 2:7-8).

Lotan	s. of Seir the Horite.	Gn. 36:20f.
A. Lothasubus	Stood on Ezra's left hand. is Hashum.	1 Es. 9:44 Neh. 8:4

A. Lozon	His family returned with
	   Zerubbabel.
	is Darkon.
		1 Es. 5:33
		
		Ezr. 2:56;
		   Neh. 7:58

Lucas	AV. form of name Luke. S. Luke.	Philem 24

Lucius	A. 1. Roman Consul.
	2. Of Cyrene. Christian leader
	   at Antioch.
	3. A kinsman of Paul.
	   S. Luke.
		1 Mac. 15:16ff.
		Ac. 13:1
		
		Ro. 16:21

Lud	fourth s. of Shem.	Gn. 10:22
Ludim	s. of Mizraim, desc. of Ham.	Gn. 10:13
Luke the Evangelist	was described in Col. 4:14 as 'the beloved physician', and in Philemon (24) as one of Paul's fellow-workers, and as the solitary companion of Paul in Rome (2 Ti. 4:11). According to Christian tradition he was the author of the third Gospel and The Acts of the Apostles. The use of the first person plural in Ac. (16:10-17, 20:5, 21:18, 27:1-28:16), probably included Luke who was thus shown to be Paul's companion during the last journey to Jerusalem, the voyage to Rome, and at least during Paul's second imprisonment there. His character may thus be deduced from his writings, though nothing more is certainly known of him. If the Lucius of Cyrene of Ac. 13:1, and Lucius of Ro. 16:21 was the same person as Luke, then he was at first a leader of the Church at Antioch, and a	

	kinsman of Paul, but the identification is doubtful.	
Lydia	Purple seller from Thyatira, living in Philippi, she and her household were converted by St. Paul (Ac. 16:11-40). Paul resided in her house, and out of this company grew the Church at Philippi.	
Lysanias	Tetrarch of Abilene at beginning of John the Baptist's ministry.	Lk. 3:1
Lysias	A. 1. Syrian general, an honourable man.	1 Mac. 3:32f.
	2. S. Claudius Lysias.	
A. Lysimachus	1. s. of Ptolemy. Named as the translator of the book of Esther into Greek (Ad. Est. 11:1).	
	2. b. of High Priest Menelaus, plunderer of Temple treasures.	2 Mac. 4:29

M

Maacah	1. f. of Achish k. of Gath in beginning of Solomon's reign.	1 K. 2:39
	2. w. of David. m. of Absalom.	2 S. 3:3
	3. Favourite w. of Rehoboam. d. (or grandd.) of Absalom.	2 Ch. 11:20
	4. s. of Nahor, b. of Abraham.	Gn. 22:24
	5. One of the concubines of Caleb.	1 Ch. 2:48
	6. w. of Machir. d. of Benjamin.	1 Ch. 7:15, 16
	7. w. of Jeiel the f. of Gibeon.	1 Ch. 8:29
	8. f. of Hanan, one of David's 'Thirty'.	1 Ch. 11:43
	9. f. of Shephatiah, Simeonite.	1 Ch. 27:16
Maadai	One who had married a foreign wife.	Ezr. 10:34
	A. is Momdis.	1 Es. 9:34

Maadiah	Priest who returned with Zerubbabel.	Neh. 12:5
	is Moadiah.	Neh. 12:17
Maai	s. of Asaph, musician who took part in dedication of the walls.	Neh. 12:36
A. Maani AV. Meani	Returned with Zerubbabel. is Meunim.	1 Es. 5:31 Ezr. 2:50
Maasai, AV. Maasiai	s. of Adiel, priest who returned with Zerubbabel.	1 Ch. 9:12
	is Amashsai.	Neh. 11:13
A. Maaseas	grandf. of Baruch.	Bar. 1:1
	is Mahseiah.	Jer. 32:12
Maaseiah	1. Priest, s. of Jeshua, who married foreign wife.	Ezr. 10:18
A.	is Mathelas.	1 Es. 9:19
	2. Priest, s. of Harim, who married a foreign wife.	Ezr. 10:21
	3. Priest who married a foreign wife.	
	s. of Pashhur.	Ezr. 10:22
A.	is Massias.	1 Es. 9:22
	4. Layman who married a foreign wife.	
	s. of Pahath-moab.	Ezr. 10:30
	5. f. of Azariah who helped to rebuild the wall.	Neh. 3:23
	6. One who stood upon the right hand of Ezra.	Neh. 8:4
A.	is Baalsamus.	1 Es. 9:43
	7. One who expounded the law to the people.	Neh. 8:7
A.	is Maiannas.	1 Es. 9:48
	8. One who sealed the covenant.	Neh. 10:25
	9. Post-exilic Judahite, resident in Jerusalem.	Neh. 11:5
	is Asaiah.	1 Ch. 9:5
	10. Benjamite, whose descendants returned to Jerusalem.	Neh. 11:7
	11. Priest who took part in dedication of walls of Jerusalem.	Neh. 12:42f.

129

	12. Priest.	Neh. 12:41f.
	13. Priest. f. of Zephaniah the priest.	Jer. 21:1
	14. f. of the false prophet Zedekiah.	Jer. 29:21
	15. Levitical singer during David's reign.	1 Ch. 15:18
	16. Captain who assisted Jehoiada against Athaliah.	2 Ch. 23:1
	17. Officer of k. Uzziah.	2 Ch. 26:11
	18. s. of k. Ahaz.	2 Ch. 28:7
	19. Governor of Jerusalem under Josiah.	2 Ch. 34:8
	20. is Baaseiah, who ministered with song in the tabernacle.	1 Ch. 6:40
	21. s. of Shallum, Jerusalem temple doorkeeper.	Jer. 35:4
A. Maasmas AV. Masman	Came from Babylon with Ezra. is Shemaiah.	1 Es. 8:43 Ezr. 8:16
Maath	Anc. of Jesus.	Lk. 3:26
Maaz	Judahite desc. of Jerahmeel.	1 Ch. 2:27
Maaziah	1. Head of a priestly course. 2. Head of priestly family who returned from exile.	1 Ch. 24:18 Neh. 10:8
Maccabaeus	A. Title (meaning Hammerer) of Judas. Third s. of Mattathias (1 Mac. 2:4), a Jewish priest. Judas was the most famous of the Jewish Generals and heroes in the inter-testamental period (165-160 B.C.). He gained several victories against the Syrians, and achieved religious freedom for his people, and the renewal of worship at Jerusalem following the re-dedication of the temple. He eventually fell in battle in 160 B.C. in a vain attempt to achieve political freedom for his people.	
Machbannai	Gadite warrior.	1 Ch. 12:13
Machbena	s. of Sheva. grands. of Caleb.	1 Ch. 2:49

Machi	f. of Geuel, Gadite, one of the twelve men sent to spy out the land of Canaan. Nu. 13:15	
Machir	1. s. of Manasseh.	Gn. 50:23; Jos. 17:1
	2. s. of Ammiel, faithful to the house of Saul.	2 S. 9:1ff.
	Came to David's assistance.	2 S. 17:27-29
Machnadebai	s. of Bani, who married a foreign wife.	Ezr. 10:40
A. Macron	Surname of Ptolemy, Governor of Cyprus.	2 Mac. 10:12f. 1 Mac. 3:38
Madei	s. of Japheth.	Gn. 10:2
A. Maelus	Jew who took a foreign wife.	1 Es. 9:26
	is Mijamin.	Ezr. 10:25
Magbish	S. Niphis.	
Magdiel	'Duke' of Edom.	Gn. 36:43
Magog	s. of Japheth (Gn. 10:2). Gog and Magog were made representatives of the northern nations (Rev. 20:8).	
Magor-Missabib	Name given by Jeremiah to Pashhur ben-Immer, governor (Jer. 20:3) of the temple, who had put the prophet in the stocks. (Name means 'Terror all around'.)	
Magpiash	Leader of the people who signed the covenant.	Neh. 10:20
Mahalaleel	S. Mahalalel 1.	
Mahalalel	1. s. of Kenan.	Gn. 5:12
	is Mehujael.	Gn. 4:18
	is Mahalaleel.	Lk. 3:37 RV.
	is Maleleel.	Lk. 3:37 AV.
	2. s. of Perez, post-exilic Judahite.	Neh. 11:4
Mahalath	1. d. of Ishmael. w. of Esau.	Gn. 28:9
	2. w. of Rehoboam, her cousin.	2 Ch. 11:18
Maharai	One of David's 'Thirty'.	2 S. 23:28

Mahath	1. desc. of Levi, one of those set apart to administer temple music.	1 Ch. 6:35
	2. Levite who assisted in reforms in time of Hezekiah.	2 Ch. 31:13
Mahazioth	s. of Heman, chief of course of singers.	1 Ch. 25:4
Maher-Shalal-Hash-Baz	Symbolical name given to one of Isaiah's sons.	Is. 8:1; cp. 2 K. 15:37f.
Mahlah	1. One of the five daughters of Zelophehad.	Nu. 26:33
AV. Mahalah	2. desc. of Manasseh.	1 Ch. 7:18
Mahli	1. Levite, s. of Merari.	Ex. 6:19, Ezr. 8:18
	2. Levite, s. of Mushi, Merarite.	1 Ch. 6:47
Mahlon	s. of Naomi, married Ruth the Moabitess.	Ru. 1:2
Mahol	f. of certain sages with whom Solomon was compared.	1 K. 4:31
Mahseiah, AV. Maaseiah	Priest. grandf. of Baruch and Seraiah.	Jer. 32:12
A. is Maaseas.		Bar. 1:1
A. Maiannas AV. Maianeas	S. Maaseiah 7.	1 Es. 9:48
Malachi	which means 'my messenger' (Malachi), is the name of the last book of the O.T. (in English), and is probably the name of the author of that book. He lived in Palestine, about 450 B.C., during the Persian period, and was probably a near contemporary of Nehemiah.	
A. Malachy	is Malachi the prophet.	2 Es. 1:40
Malcam	1. Benjamite.	1 Ch. 8:9
	2. K. of Ammonites. AV. and RV. translate 'their king'.	RVm. 2 S. 12:30
Malchiah	1. Priest.	Jer. 21.1
	is Malchijah.	1 Ch. 9:12

AV. Malchijah	2. Prince who owned the cistern in which Jeremiah was gaoled.	Jer. 38:6
Malchiel	Asherite.	Gn. 46:17
Malchijah	1. Temple Musician, desc. of Gershom.	1 Ch. 6:40
	2. Priest.	1 Ch. 9:12
	is Malchiah.	Jer. 21:1
	3. Priest in David's reign.	1 Ch. 24:9
	4. One who married a foreign wife, s. of Parosh.	Ezr. 10:25
A.	is Melchias.	1 Es. 9:26
	5. One who married foreign wife, another s. of Parosh.	Ezr. 10:25
A.	is Asibias.	1 Es. 9:26
	is Hashabiah.	
	6. s. of Harim, helped to repair the wall.	Ezr. 10:31 Neh. 3:11
A.	is Melchias.	1 Es. 9:32
	7. s. of Rechab, repaired the dung-gate.	Neh. 3:14
	8. One of the guild of goldsmiths who helped to repair the wall.	Neh. 3:31
	9. One who stood at Ezra's left hand at the reading of the law.	Neh. 8:4
	10. One who sealed the covenant.	Neh. 10:3
	11. Priest.	Neh. 12:42
Malchiram	s. of Jeconiah (Jehoiachin).	1 Ch. 3:18
Malchi-Shua	s. of Saul, who was slain by the Philistines on Mt. Gilboa.	1 S. 14:49
Malchus	Personal servant of the high priest whose right ear Peter cut off when Jesus was arrested.	Jn. 18:10
Maleleel	S. Mahalalel 1.	
Mallothi	s. of Heman, priest-musician.	1 Ch. 25:4
Malluch	1. Merarite Levite	1 Ch. 6:44
	2. s. of Bani who married a foreign wife.	Ezr. 10:29

	A. is Mamuchus.	1 Es. 9:30
	3. s. of Harim who married a foreign wife.	Ezr. 10:32
	4. Sealed the covenant with Ezra.	Neh. 10:4
	is Malluchi.	Neh. 12:14
	5. Sealed the covenant.	Neh. 10:27
	6. Priest who returned from exile with Zerubbabel.	Neh. 12:2
Malluchi	Returned with Zerubbabel.	Neh. 12:14
	is Malluch 4.	Neh. 10:4
A. Maltanneus	One who agreed to put away his foreign wife.	1 Es. 9:33
AV. Altaneus	is Mattenai.	Ezr. 10:33
A. Mamdai	Had taken a foreign wife.	1 Es. 9:34
AV. Mabdai	is Benaiah.	Ezr. 10:35
A. Mamuchus	S. Malluch 2.	
A. Mamnitanemus	s. of Bani who had married a foreign woman.	1 Es. 9:34
AV. Mamnitanaimus	is Mattaniah.	Ezr. 10:37
A. Mamuchus	S. Malluch 2.	
Manaen	One of the 'prophets and teachers' in the church of Antioch (Ac. 13:1); had been an intimate friend of Herod the Tetrarch.	
Manahath	Horite, second s. of Shobal, s. of Seir.	Gn. 36:23
A. Manasseas	1. Jew who married a foreign wife.	1 Es. 9:31
	2. is Manasseh 3.	
Manasseh	1. K. of Judah, for 55 years. s. of Hezekiah (2 K. 21:1ff.). Most important feature of his reign was the blending of foreign worships with the popular religion of Israel.	
RV. Moses	2. His grands. Jonathan was first Priest at the sanctuary of Dan.	Jg. 18:30
	3. s. of Pahath-moab. Married a foreign wife.	Ezr. 10:30

	4. s. of Hashum. Married foreign wife.	Ezr. 10:33
	5. The elder son of Joseph, who really lost the privileges of the first born to his younger b. Ephraim (Gn. 41:51; Nu. 26:28-34; Jos. 22:7). He and his brother were blessed (adopted) by Jacob, and Manasseh became the eponymous Anc. of one of Israel's twelve tribes. The Manasseh tribe occupied territory on each side of the Jordan.	
Manasses	A. 1. is Manasseh 4.	1 Es. 9:33
	A. 2. h. of Judith.	Jth. 8:2
	A. 3. One who gave alms.	To. 14:10
	4. is Manasseh 1 only in Apoc. book 'Prayer of Manasses'.	
A. Manes AV. Eanes	One who put away his foreign wife.	1 Es. 9:21
	is Harim.	Ezr. 10:21m.
A. Mani	Jew who had taken foreign wife.	1 Es. 9:30
	is Bani.	Ezr. 10:29; 1 Es. 5:12
A. Manius, AV. Manlius	Roman ambassador to Jews.	2 Mac 11:34-38
Manoah	Native of Zorah, Danite. f. of Samson.	Jg. 13:2ff.
Maoch	f. of Achish k. of Gath under whom David took service.	1 S. 27:2
	is probably Maacah.	1 K. 2:39
Maon	desc. of Caleb.	1 Ch. 2:45
Mara	Name which Naomi claimed for herself: 'bitter'.	Ru. 1:20
Marcus RV. Mark	AV. form of the name of St. Mark (Col. 4:10; Philem. 24; 1 P. 5:13).	
A. Mardocheus	1. u. of Esther.	Ad. Est. 10:42
	is Mordecai.	Est. 2:5ff.
	2. Jew who returned to Jerusalem with Zerubbabel.	1 Es. 5:8
	is Mordecai.	Ezr. 2:

Mareshah	1. Eldest s. of Caleb. f. of Hebron.	1 Ch. 2:42
	2. Judahite, so of Laadah.	1 Ch. 4:21
A. Marimoth	Anc. of Ezra.	2 Es. 1:2
	is Meraioth.	Ezr. 7:3
	is Memeroth.	1 Es. 8:2

Mark (John) is the name of the second Gospel and of the man, John Mark of Jerusalem, who wrote it (Ac. 12:12, 15-37). His mother's name was Mary, and he was a relative of Barnabas (Col. 4:10). Mark was a companion of Paul and Barnabas on the first missionary journey, but later left them (Philem. 24). Afterwards he accompanied Barnabas to Cyprus, and was mentioned several times in the Epistles.

A. Marmoth	He weighed the silver and gold brought to Jerusalem by Ezra.	1 Es. 8:62
	is Meremoth.	Ezr. 8:33
A. Marsena	One of the seven princes of Media and Persia.	Est. 1:14

Martha The one Martha of the N.T. is the sister of Mary (Lk. 10:38-41), who anointed Jesus before his death, and of Lazarus resurrected by Jesus from the dead (Jn. 11:1-12:2). All three were close friends of Jesus. The family lived at Bethany two miles or so from Jerusalem. She was the mistress of the household.

Mary is the name of seven women in the N.T.

1. Mary was the virgin m. of Jesus. She gave birth to Jesus in Bethlehem when betrothed to Joseph, and later with him brought up a family in Nazareth. She was called his wife in Matt. 1:24f. She figured in several of the stories of the infancy of Jesus in Mt. and Lk. She was with Jesus at the marriage in Cana, and was once outside a house where her son was teaching (Mk. 3:31-35). She was present at the crucifixion of her son, who in his last moments committed her to the care of the

beloved John. In Ac. 1:14 she was present at a prayer meeting. There were other children in the family (Mk. 6:3; Mt. 13:55-56), and they were probably blood brothers of Jesus, rather than his step-brothers or his cousins. Mary is blessed among woman, and certainly she is the most honoured woman of our race.

2. Mary of Magdala (Mt. 28:1; Mk. 15f.; Lk. 24:10; Jn. 20). She was a native of Magdala in Galilee and from her Jesus cast out seven devils. She helped with the mission to Galilee (Lk. 8:1-3). She was present at the Crucifixion, and was first at the empty tomb on the day of resurrection. She called the disciples to the scene, and after their departure, saw two angels and then Jesus himself.

3. Sister of Martha and Lazarus of Bethany. She sat at Jesus' feet listening to his words rather than helping Martha with her household duties. For this she was rebuked by Martha but praised by Jesus (Lk. 10:38-42). Jn. 11:2 identified this Mary as the woman who anointed Jesus and wiped his feet with her hair, 12:3. One, two, or even three anointings of Jesus may have taken place, but Mary's was, by its timing, the most significant and the most commended (Mk. 14:9).

4. m. of John Mark. This Mary owned a house in Jerusalem and kept a maid Rhoda. The house was probably a rendezvous for Jerusalem Christians, for Peter went there after his escape from prison (Ac. 12). She was a relative of Barnabas.

5. The mother of James the less (the younger) and Joses, was presumably a Galilean who was a follower and financial supporter of Jesus. Mk. 15:40 and Lk. 8:3. She came with Jesus to Jerusalem for the last time, witnessing the crucifixion and the burial. She helped to procure spices to anoint Jesus' dead body,

saw the tomb was empty, heard the angel's testimony to the resurrection and told the disciples her news. She may well have been the same as the wife of Cleopas.

6. The w. of Cleopas who witnessed the crucifixion.   Jn. 19:25

7. A Mary appears in the list of twenty-four persons greeted by Paul in Ro. 16:6. She is said to have worked hard for her fellow-believers.

Mash	s. of Aram.	Gn. 10:23
	is Meshech.	1 Ch. 1:17
A. Masias	Head of family of Solomon's servants who returned with Zerubbabel.	1 Es. 5:34
Massa	Seventh s. of Ishmael.	Gn. 25:14
A. Massias	Priest who had taken a foreign wife	1 Es. 9:22
	is Maaseiah 3.	Ezr. 10:22
A. Mathelas AV. Matthelas	Priest who had foreign wife.	1 Es. 9:19
	is Maaseiah 1.	Ezr. 10:18
Mathusala	AV. form of Methuselah.	Lk. 3:37
Matred	m.-in-law of Hadar (or Hadad) k. of Edom.	Gn. 36:39
Mattan	1. Priest of the temple of Baal in Jerusalem.	2 K. 11:18
	2. f. of Shephatiah, contemporary of the prophet Jeremiah.	Jer. 38:1
Mattaniah	1. Original name of k. Zedekiah.	2 K. 24:17
	2. Asaphite, returned to Jerusalem after exile.	1 Ch. 9:15
	3. desc. of Asaph.	2 Ch. 20:14
	4. Jew who married foreign wife.	Ezr. 10:26
A.	is Matthanias.	1 Es. 9:27
	5. One who married foreign wife.	Ezr. 10:27
A.	is Othonias.	1 Es. 9:28
	6. One who married foreign wife.	Ezr. 10:30
A.	is Matthanias.	1 Es. 9:31

		7. One who married foreign wife.	Ezr. 10:37
	A.	is Mamnitanemus.	1 Es. 9:34
		8. Levite treasurer.	Neh. 13:13
		9. s. of Heman, musician in the House of the Lord.	1 Ch. 25:4
		10. Asaphite, took part in Temple reforms under k. Hezekiah.	2 Ch. 29:13
		11. Levite leader of temple choir.	Neh. 11:17
		12. Levite musician.	Neh. 12:8
		13. Levite gatekeeper.	Neh. 12:25
		14. Levite, f. of Shemaiah.	Neh. 12:35

| **Mattatha** | grands. of David, Anc of Jesus. | Lk. 3:31 |

Mattathias
AV. Matthias
AV. Mattathah

| A. 1. Jew who married foreign wife. | 1 Es. 9:33 |
| is Mattattah. | Ezr. 10:33 |

A. 2. Stood at right hand of Ezra during the reading of the law. 1 Es. 9:43
is Mattithiah. Neh. 8:4

A. 3. f. of the five Maccabaean brothers. 1 Mac. 2:1

A. 4. s. of Absalom, a captain in the army of Jonathan the Maccabaean. 1 Mac. 11:70

A. 5. s. of Simon the high priest. 1 Mac. 16:14

A. 6. Envoy sent by Nicanor to treat with Judas Maccabaeus. 2 Mac. 14:19

7. s. of Amos. Anc. of Jesus. Lk. 3:25
8. s. of Semein. Anc. of Jesus. Lk. 3:26
AV. Semei

Mattattah
s. of Hashum layman who married and divorced his foreign wife. Ezr. 10:33
A. is Mattathias 1. 1 Es. 9:33

Mattenai
1. Layman who married foreign wife. Ezr. 10:33
A. is Maltanneus. 1 Es. 9:33
2. One who married foreign wife. Ezr. 10:37
3. Priest in the days of Joiakim. Neh. 12:19

Matthan
grandf. of Joseph. Mt. 1:15
is Matthat, Anc. of Jesus. Lk. 3:24

A. Matthanias	1. s. of Elam, who took a foreign wife.	1 Es. 9:27
	is Mattaniah.	Ezr. 10:26
	2. s. of Pahath-moabi, Jew who married a foreign wife.	1 Es. 9:31
	is Mattaniah.	Ezr. 10:30
Matthat	1. S. Matthan.	
	2. Anc. of Jesus.	Lk. 3:29
Matthew, Apostle	was according to all four lists in the N.T. (Mk 3:18; Mt. 10:3; Lk. 6:15; Ac. 1:13), one of the twelve disciples of Jesus; was probably the same as Levi, and the author of the first Gospel or one of the sources underlying it. The first Gospel described him as a publican, *i.e.* tax gatherer, before he became a follower of Jesus (Mt. 9:9, 10:3). See Levi.	
Matthias	Disciple elected after the ascension to vacant apostleship owing to the death of Judas.	
		Ac. 1:15-26
Mattithiah	1. s. of Nebo who married foreign wife.	Ezr. 10:43
A.	is Mazitias.	1 Es. 9:35
	2. Levite 'over the things that were baked in pans'.	1 Ch. 9:31
	3. Levite who ministered before the ark with harps.	1 Ch. 15:18
	4. Asaphite Levite, musician.	1 Ch. 16:5
	5. One who stood at Ezra's right hand at the reading of the law.	Neh. 8:4
A.	is Mattathias.	1 Es. 9:43
A. Mazitias	S. Mattithiah 1.	
Mebunnai	One of David's 'Thirty'.	2 S. 23:27
	is Sibbecai.	1 Ch. 11:29
Medad	Israelite who prophesied in the wilderness camp.	Nu. 11:26f.
Medan	Third s. of Abraham and Keturah.	Gn. 25:2
A. Meedda AV. Meeda	His family, Temple servants, returned with Zerubbabel.	1 Es. 5:32
	is Mehida.	Ezr. 2:52

Mehetabel, AV. Mehetabeel	1. Anc. of Shemaiah, a false prophet.	Neh. 6:10
	2. w. of Hadar (or Hadad) k. of Edom.	Gn. 36:39
Mehida	S. Meeda.	
Mehir	Judahite.	1 Ch. 4:11
Mehujael	gt.-grands. of Cain.	Gn. 4:18
	is Mahalalel.	Gn. 5:12ff.
Mehuman	One of the seven eunuchs in attendance upon k. Ahasuerus.	Est. 1:10
Melatiah	Gibeonite, repaired a portion of the walls of Jerusalem.	Neh. 3:7
Melchi	1. Anc. of Jesus.	Lk. 3:24
	2. Anc. of Jesus.	Lk. 3:28
A. Melchias	1. One who took foreign wife. is Malchijah.	1 Es. 9:26 Ezr. 10:25
	2. One who took foreign wife. is Malchijah.	1 Es. 9:32 Ezr. 10:31
	3. Stood on Ezra's left hand. is Malchijah (Malchiah).	1 Es. 9:44 Neh. 8:4
A. Melchiel	f. of Charmis, magistrate to whom Judith appealed.	Jth. 6:15
Melchizedek	The name means 'Zedek (a god) is my king' and was borne by the pre-Israelite Canaanite king of Salem (Jerusalem) who was also priest of El Elyon (God most High) (Gn. 14:17-20), probably a, or the, God of Jerusalem in the days of Abraham. As the most important figure in Gn. 14 he welcomed Abraham and his friends to the city and gave them gifts of bread and wine and received a tribute of one tenth from the spoil captured by Abraham. He is mentioned again in Ps. 110:4, and Heb. 5 and 6 for theological purposes as the prototype of the Davidic king and a type of Jesus Christ.	
Melea	Anc. of Jesus.	Lk. 3:31

Melech	Benjamite, grands of Merib-Baal (Mephibosheth).	1 Ch. 8:35
Melzar	Name of Steward in charge of Daniel. RV. 'the steward'.	Dan. 1:11
A. Memeroth AV. Meremoth	Anc. of Ezra. is Meraioth. A. is Marimoth.	1 Es. 8:2 Ezr. 7:3 2 Es. 1:2
A. Memmius	Roman envoy to the Jews.	2 Mac. 11:34
Memucan	One of the seven princes of Persia, at the court of k. Ahasuerus.	Est. 1:13-22
Menahem	means 'comforter', and he was the son of Gadi and one of the military leaders in Tirzah, capital of Israel before Samaria (2 K. 15:14-22). He assassinated, and succeeded, Shallum who had himself usurped the throne. He was a cruel man but succeeded in reigning for ten years. He paid a tribute of 1,000 talents to Tiglath Pileser III whose vassal he was. He died a peaceful death being succeeded by his son Pekahiah.	
A. Menelaus	Usurping high priest in the time of Antiochus Epiphanes.	2 Mac. 4:23
A. Menestheus	f. of Apollonius, who was governor under Antiochus Epiphanes.	2 Mac. 4:21
Menna AV. Menan	Anc. of Jesus.	Lk. 3:31
Meonothai	s. of Othniel, Judahite.	1 Ch. 4:14
Mephibosheth	1. s. of Jonathan, protected by David. Transformation of the original name of Merib-Baal.	2 S. 4:4; 1 Ch. 8:34
	2. s. of Saul and Rizpah.	2 S. 21:8
Merab	Elder d. of Saul promised to the slayer of Goliath.	1 S. 17:25
Meraiah	Priest in the days of Joiakim.	Neh. 12:12
Meraioth	1. s. of Ahitub. f. of Zadok.	1 Ch. 9:11

	2. Levite, desc. from Aaron.	1 Ch. 6:6ff.
A.	is Memeroth.	1 Es. 8:2
A.	is Marimoth.	2 Es. 1:2
	3. Head of priestly family.	Neh. 12:15
	is Meremoth.	Neh. 12:3
Merari	1. Third s. of Levi, his descendants were in charge of temple music or doorkeepers.	Ex. 6:16; 1 Ch. 26:10ff.
	2. A Levite.	Ez. 8:19
A.	3. f. of Judith.	Jth. 8:1
Mered	Judahite, married Bithiah, Pharaoh's d.	1 Ch. 4:17
Meremoth	1. Priest who returned with Zerubbabel.	Neh. 12:3
	2. Temple Treasurer.	
	3. s. of Bani, married a foreign wife.	Ezr. 10:36
	4. Sealed the covenant.	Neh. 10:5
Meres	One of the counsellors of Ahasuarus.	Est. 1:14
Meribbaal	S. Mephibosheth.	
Merodach-Baladan	is Berodach-B. Ruler of the Chaldaeans (Babylon).	2 K. 20:12 Is. 39:1f.
Mesha	1. s. of Shaharaim, a Benjamite.	1 Ch. 8:9
	2. firstborn of Caleb.	1 Ch. 2:42
	3. k. of Moab, paid tribute to Ahab, but rebelled against Israel's overlordship (2 K. 3:4). He erected a famous inscribed monument called, 'The Moabite Stone'.	
Meshach	The name Mishael was changed into Meshach. One of Daniel's three friends. Dan. 1:7	
Meshech	1. s. of Japheth.	Gn. 10:2
	2. S. Mash.	
Meshelemiah	Head of family of Korahite doorkeepers.	1 Ch. 9:21
	is Shelemiah.	1 Ch. 26:14
	is Shallum.	1 Ch. 9:17
	is Meshullam.	Neh. 12:25

Meshezabel	1. His descendants assisted in repairing the wall.	Neh. 3:4
	2. One who sealed the Covenant.	Neh. 10:21
	3. f. of Pethahiah, Judahite.	Neh. 11:24
Meshillemith	Priest, s. of Immer.	1 Ch. 9:12
	is Meshillemoth.	Neh. 11:13
Meshillemoth	1. Ephraimite.	2 Ch. 28:12
	2. S. Mishillemith.	
Meshobab	Simeonite leader.	1 Ch. 4:34
Meshullam	1. Benjamite, s. of Elpaal.	1 Ch. 8:17
	2. Benjamite, f. of Sallu.	1 Ch. 9:7
	3. Benjamite, s. of Shephatiah.	1 Ch. 9:8
	4. Gadite.	1 Ch. 5:13
	5. grandf. of Shaphan the scribe.	2 K. 22:3
	6. s. of Zadok and f. of Hilkiah the priest.	1 Ch. 9:11
	7. Priest.	1 Ch. 9:12
	8. Kohathite appointed to direct the repairs on the temple by k. Josiah.	2 Ch. 34:12
	9. s. of Zerubbabel.	1 Ch. 3:19
	10. Commissioned by Ezra to procure Levites, and Temple Servants.	Ezr. 8:16
	is Mosollamus.	1 Es. 8:44
	11. Levite who opposed Ezra's way of dealing with foreign wives.	Ezr. 10:15
	is Mosollamus.	1 Es. 9:14
	12. s. of Bani who married a foreign wife.	Ezr. 10:29
	13. s. of Berechiah, one who helped to repair the walls of Jerusalem.	Neh. 3:4
	f.-in-law of Tobiah.	Neh. 6:18
	14. s. of Besodeiah, helped to repair the old gate.	Neh. 3:6
	15. One who stood at Ezra's left hand during the reading of the Law.	Neh. 8:4
	16. Priest who sealed the covenant.	Neh. 10:7
	17. Leader who sealed the covenant.	Neh. 10:20
	18. Prince of the house of Judah, at the dedication of the repaired wall.	Neh. 12:33

	19. Head of priestly house in time of Joiakim.	Neh. 12:13
	20. Head of priestly house in Joiakim.	Neh. 12:16
	21. Gatekeeper in time of Joiakim.	Neh. 12:25
Meshullemeth	w. of k. Manassaeh, k. of Judah. m. of Amon.	2 K. 21:19
Methuselah	desc. of Seth.	
	f. of Lamech.	Gn. 5:21ff.
	is Methushael.	Gn. 4:18
	The eighth patriarch; lived for 969 years—the longest lived of all figures in Genesis.	
Methushael	S. Methuselah.	
Meunim	Anc. of temple servants.	Ezr. 2:50
Mezahab	f. of Matred.	Gn. 36:39
Mibhar	One of David's warriors.	1 Ch. 11:38
Mibsam	1. s. of Ishmael.	Gn. 25:13
	2. Simeonite, f. of Mishma.	1 Ch. 4:25
Mibzar	'Duke' of Edom, desc. of Esau.	Gn. 36:42
Mica	1. s. of Merib-baal.	2 S. 9:12
	is Micah.	1 Ch. 8:34
	2. s. of Zichri, Asaphite.	1 Ch. 9:15
	is s. of Zabdi.	Neh. 11:22
	is Micaiah.	Neh. 12:35
	3. Levite who set his seal to the covenant.	Neh. 10:11
Micah	1. Resident in the highlands of Ephraim (Jg. 17), and founder of the sanctuary of Dan.	
RV. Mica	2. S. Mica 1.	
	3. Head of family of Levites at the end of David's reign.	1 Ch. 23:20
	4. Reubenite, Anc. of Beerah who was taken into captivity.	1 Ch. 5:5f.
	5. Contemporary of Josiah f. of Abdon.	2 Ch. 34:20
	is Micaiah.	2 K. 22:12
	A. 6. Simeonite, f. of Ozias, one of the three rulers of Bethulia.	Jth. 6:15

7. S. Micaiah no. 3.

8. (Micah). The name means 'who is like Yah' and belonged to a prophet from the city of Moresheth in the lowlands of Judah. He was the author of the book of Micah and was a contemporary of Isaiah. He was the author of some very famous words (*e.g.* 6:8).

Micaiah	1. m. of Abija.	2 Ch. 13:2
AV. Michaiah	Corruption of Maacah.	1 K. 15:2
AV. Michaiah	2. Prince of Judah appointed by Jehoshaphat to superintend religious instruction.	2 Ch. 17:7
RV. Micah	3. s. of Imlah, prophet in Israel in the days of Ahab (1 K. 22:8; 2 Ch. 18:14). King Ahab was planning a military expedition against the city of Ramoth Gilead, and was confirmed in his resolve by the favourable oracle of four hundred prophets attached to his court. Micaiah, at first not consulted, then confirmed this oracle, but later predicted disaster, and in fact Ahab was killed in the battle.	
RV. Micah	4. is Prophet.	Micah 1:1ff.; Jer. 26:18
	5. s. of Gemariah. Noble of Judah in the days of Jeremiah.	Jer. 36:11
AV. Michaiah AVm. Micah	6. f. of Achbor. Possibly same as no. 5 above.	2 K. 22:12
AV. Michaiah	7. s. of Zaccur. is Mica (AV. Micah). is Mica (AV. Micha), s. of Zabdi. f. of Mattaniah who took part in worship at the dedication of the walls.	Neh. 12:35 1 Ch. 9:15 Neh. 11:17
AV. Michaiah	8. Priest who took part in the dedication of the walls.	Neh. 12:41
Michael	1. f. of Asherite spy.	Nu. 13:13
	2. Gadite.	1 Ch. 5:13
	3. Gadite.	1 Ch. 5:14
	4. Levite singer.	1 Ch. 6:40

	5. s. of Izrahiah of the tribe of Issachar.	1 Ch. 7:3
	6. Benjamite.	1 Ch. 8:16
	7. Manassite who joined David.	1 Ch. 12:20
	8. s. of k. Jehoshaphat.	2 Ch. 21:2
	9. f. of Zebadiah, an exile who returned with Zerubbabel.	Ezr. 8:8
	10. f. of Omri, prince of tribe of Issachar.	1 Ch. 27:18
Michal	Younger d. of Saul. w. of David.	1 S. 14:49; 18:20f.; 25:44
A. Micheas	is prophet Micah.	2 Es. 1:39
Michri	Benjamite.	1 Ch. 9:8
Midian	s. of Abraham and Keturah, founder of Midianite nation.	Gn. 25:1-4
Mijamin	1. s. of Parosh who married a foreign wife.	Ezr. 10:25
A.	is Maelus.	1 Es. 9:26
	2. Priest in David's time whose desc. returned with Zerubbabel. is Miniamin.	1 Ch. 24:9 Neh. 12:17
	3. Priest who put his seal to the covenant under Ezra.	Neh. 10:7
	4. Priest who returned from exile with Zerubbabel.	Neh. 12:5
Mikloth	1. s. of Jeiel, Benjamite.	1 Ch. 9:37
	2. Officer of David.	1 Ch. 27:4
Mikneiah	Levite appointed to play the harp when the Ark was brought to Jerusalem. 1 Ch. 15:18	
Milalai	Priest Musician, who returned to Jerusalem after the exile.	Neh. 12:36
Milcah	1. d. of Haran. w. of Nahor. grandm. of Rebekah.	Gn. 11:29 Gn. 24:15
	2. d. of Zelophehad.	Nu. 26:33
Miniamin	1. Levite, assisted in the collection of freewill offerings.	2 Ch. 31:15
	2. S. Mijamin 2.	

	3. Priest trumpeter who took part at the dedication of the walls of Jerusalem.	Neh. 12:41
Miriam	1. d. of Amram and Jochebed (Ex. 2:4ff.). s. of Aaron and Moses (Ex. 15:20f.). She was Moses' nursemaid, and became a prophetess (Nu. 12). Later she joined Aaron in a revolt against Moses and was punished. She died at Kadesh. cp. also Micah 6:4.	
	2. A child of Ezra and relative of Shammai and Ishbah.	1 Ch. 4:17
Mirmah	Benjamite s. of Shaharaim.	1 Ch. 8:10
A. Misael	1. Stood on Ezra's left hand at the reading of the law. is Mishael.	1 Es. 9:44 Neh. 8:4
	2. S. Mishael 3.	
Misaias	S. Masias.	
Mishael	1. Levite, s. of Uzziel.	Ex. 6:22
	2. One of Daniel's three companions.	Dan. 1:6f.
A.	is Misael.	1 Mac. 2:59
Misham	Benjamite, s. of Elpaal.	1 Ch. 8:12
Mishma	1. s. of Ishmael.	Gn. 25:14
	2. Simeonite.	1 Ch. 4:25
Mishmannah	Gadite warrior who joined David at Ziklag (1 Ch. 12:10), and became an officer.	
Mispar	One of the exiles who returned with Zerubbabel.	Ezr. 2:2
	is Mispereth.	Neh. 7:7
Mispereth	S. Mispar.	
A. Mithradates AV. Mithridates	1. Treasurer of Cyrus, k. of Persia.	1 Es. 2:11
	is Mithredath.	Ezr. 1:8
	2. Persian officer in Samaria who tried to prevent the rebuilding of Jerusalem.	1 Es. 2:16
	is Mithredath.	Ezr. 4:7

Mithredath	1. is Mithradates 1.	Ezr. 1:8
	2. is Mithradates 2.	Ezr. 4:7
Mizzah	'Duke' of Edom descended from Esau.	Gn. 36:13
Mnason	With whom St. Paul and his companions lodged on the Apostle's last visit to Jerusalem (Ac. 21:16). An early disciple.	
Moab	s. of Lot (Gn. 19:37) by his incestuous union with his elder daughter. Anc. of the Moabites.	
Moadiah	Member of priestly family who returned from Exile.	Neh. 12:17
	is Maadiah.	Neh. 12:5
A. Moeth	S. Noadiah 1.	
Molid	s. of Abishur of the tribe of Judah.	1 Ch. 2:29
A. Momdis	S. Maadai.	1 Ezr. 9:34
A. Mooli	S. Mahli 1.	1 Ezr. 8:47
A. Moossias	S. Maaseiah 4.	1 Ezr. 9:31
Mordecai	1. One of the leaders of the people at the time of the return from exile under Zerubbabel.	
		Ezr. 2:2
A.	is Mardocheus.	1 Es. 5:8
	2. Hero of Bk. of Esther, u. of Esther. Jew who had been taken into captivity by Nebuchadrezzar. Later he was promoted to the highest rank and was able to obtain permission for the Jews to defend themselves and celebrate the feast of Purification. Est. 2:5ff.	
Moses	The name means either child, son or 'one who draws forth', and was given to one person in the Bible, Moses, the human agent of Israel's deliverance from Egypt, and the human transmitter of the Ten Commandments. He was the s. of Amram and Jochebed and so a member of the tribe of Levi. He was delivered from the Egyptian purge of Israelite male babies and was brought up in the Egyptian Court. Thence he fled to the desert after his	

murder of an Egyptian foreman had become known. He married Zipporah and at Mount Sinai felt himself called to return to Egypt and effect the deliverance of his people. After many disappointments he was successful, and led his compatriots to the desert scene of his own commissioning.

Here the Ten Commandments were given, and a covenant between God and the people set up. Soon the people infringed this by the worship of the golden calf, and Moses had to lead them from Sinai the mountain through the desert for many years, amidst many revolts and rebellions. Because of a certain sin (Nu. 20:10 RV.) he was not allowed to enter the promised land, but to view it from Mt. Nebo.

Moses is seen to have served as leader, adviser, lawgiver, legislator, priest and prophet. He was probably a preacher too. The Book of Exodus probably reflected his life and ministry and was remarkable for an emphasis upon what must have been Moses' own favourite phrase 'the presence of God with his people'. (cp. Ex. 3, 17:7, 33:16, etc.).

He was the founder of Israel's religious and national life, was renowned for his close fellowship with God (Dt. 34:10), and withal a meek man (Nu. 12:3). He figured very often in the later histories, prophesies and psalmody of the O.T.; and also in the four gospels and eight other books of the N.T. He was one of the four or five greatest men in the O.T.

A. Mosollamus AV. Mosoll- amon	1. S. Meshullam 10.	
AV. Mosol- lam	2. S. Meshullam 11.	
Moza	1. s. of Caleb, Judahite.	1 Ch. 2:46
	2. desc. of Saul.	1 Ch. 8:36

Muppim	s. of Benjamin.	Gn. 46:21
	is Shuppim.	1 Ch. 7:12
	is Shephupham.	Nu. 26:39
	is Shephuphan.	1 Ch. 8:5
Mushi	Second s. of Merari.	Ex. 6:19

N

Naam	s. of Caleb, Judahite.	1 Ch. 4:15
Naamah	1. Sister of Tubal-Cain.	Gn. 4:22
	2. Ammonitess, w. of Solomon. m. of Rehoboam.	1 K. 14:21
Naaman	1. Syrian general, and a leper cured by the Israelite prophet, Elisha.	2 K. 5
	2. s. or grands. of Benjamin.	Gn. 46:21; 1 Ch. 8:3
	3. s. of Ehud.	1 Ch. 8:7
Naarah	w. of Ashhur, Judahite.	1 Ch. 4:5f.
Naarai	s. of Ezbai, one of David's valiant soldiers.	1 Ch. 11:37
	is Paarai.	2 S. 23:35
A. Naathus	s. of Addi, Jew who had married a foreign wife.	1 Es. 9:31
	is Adna.	Ezr. 10:30
Nabal	h. of Abigail, who later became w. of David. Wealthy sheep farmer (1 S. 25:2ff.). His name means 'foolish', and he was true to his name, for his foolish conduct led to his death.	
A. Nabariah	Stood on Ezra's left at the reading of the law.	1 Es. 9:44
	is Hashbaddanah.	Neh. 8:4
Naboth	Native of Jezreel who in the time of Ahab owned land near that town, coveted by Ahab and his wife Jezebel (1 K. 21:1ff.). Upon Naboth's refusal to sell, Jezebel had him stoned on the false charge of blasphemy, a crime condemned by Elijah.	
A. Nabucho-donosor	Gk. form of Nebuchadnezzar.	1 Es. 1:40ff.

Nacon, AV. Nachon	The threshing floor of Nacon was the place where Uzzah the priest died after touching the Ark on its journey from Kirieth-jearim. 2 S. 6:6
	is Chidon. 1 Ch. 13:9
Nadab	1. Eldest s. of Aaron, who went up on Mt. Sinai with Moses (Ex. 6:23). He was made a priest, but died suddenly (Nu. 3:2).
	2. s. of Shammai, of the tribe of 1 Ch. 2:28 Judah.
	3. Benjamite, s. of Jeiel, u. of 1 Ch. 8:30 Saul.
	4. k. of Israel for two years. s. of Jeroboam I. 1 K. 14:20
	A. 5. Came with his u. Ahikar to To. 11:18 the marriage feast of Tobias.
Naggai AV. Nagge	Anc. of Jesus. Lk. 3:25 Greek form of Nogah.
Naham	s. (or b.-in-law) of Hodiah. 1 Ch. 4:19
Nahamani	One of the twelve heads of the Jewish community that returned from exile (Neh. 7:7).
	A. is Eneneus. 1 Es. 5:8
Naharai	One of the 'Thirty' and armour 1 Ch. 11:39 bearer of Joab.
	is Nahari. 2 S. 23:37
Nahash	1. k. of the Ammonites through- 2 S. 10:1; out Saul's reign. 1 Ch. 19:1
	2. f. of Abigail or sister of 2 S. 17:25 Zeruiah.
Nahath	1. Clan chief of Edom. Gn. 36:13
	2. Levite, grands. of Elkariah. 1 Ch. 6:26
	is Toah. 1 Ch. 6:34
	is Tohu. 1 S. 1:1
	3. Levite overseer in the time 2 Ch. 31:13 of Hezekiah.
Nahbi	One of the twelve men sent by Moses to spy out the land. Nu. 13:14 Naphtalite, s. of Vophsi.

Nahor	1. desc. of Shem, s. of Serug, f. of Terah and grandf. of Abraham. Gn. 11:22 is Nachor. Jos. 24:2 AV. 2. s. of Terah and h. of Milcah, b. of Abraham. (Gn. 11:26). Abraham was the Anc. of the Israelites, and Nahor of the Aramaean tribes.
Nahshon	s. of Amminadab and a Judahite chief who assisted Moses at taking of census (Nu. 1:7), b.-in-law of Aaron (Ex. 6:23), and Anc. of David and Jesus (1 Ch. 2:10f.; Mt. 1:4).
Nahum	1. is the name of a prophet from Elkosh (? in Judah), who wrote a short book of prophecy, the seventh of the 'minor prophets', directed against the imperial power of Assyria. He lived in the latter half of the seventh century B.C. Neh. 1:1 2. Anc. of Jesus Christ. Lk. 3:25
A. Naidus	Jew who took a foreign wife 1 Es. 9:31 during the exile. is Benaiah. Ezr. 10:30
Naomi	'Pleasant', cp. Mara 'bitter'. w. of Elimelech of Bethlehem (Ru. 1:2), m.-in-law of Ruth. Ruth's s. Obed, by Boaz, was grandf. of k. David (Ru. 4:16f.).
Naphish	eleventh s. of Ishmael. Gn. 25:15
Naphtali	second s. of Jacob by Bilhah, Rachel's handmaid (Gn. 30:7f.). Anc. of the tribe of Naphtali which settled on the eastern side of Upper Galilee (Jos. 19:32-39).
Naphtuhim	s. of Mizraim, and grands. of 1 Ch. 1:11 Ham.
Narcissus	St. Paul saluted, among other Roman Christians, those of the household of Narcissus. Ro. 16:11
A. Nasbas	Guest at wedding of Tobias. To. 11:18 S. Nadab 5.

A. Nasi

A. Nasi	Returned from exile with	1 Es. 5:32
AV. Nasith	Zerubbabel.	
	is Neziah.	Ezr. 2:54

Nathan 'God has given'.

1. Nathan was a prophet at the court of David and played a prominent part in David's personal and dynastic life. He denounced David to his face for arranging the death of Uriah, husband of Bathsheba, with whom David had committed adultery (2 S. 12). In 2 S. 7 Nathan corrected David's building plans, but confirms under divine instruction the perpetual character of David's dynasty.

2. Third s. of David, elder b. of Solomon. — 2 S. 5:14
Anc. of Jesus Christ. — Lk. 3:31

3. f. of Igal, and a native of Zobah.
b. of Joel, one of David's Thirty mighty men. — 1 Ch. 11:38

4. Judahite, grands. of Sheshan. Jerahmeelite. — 1 Ch. 2:36

5. One of the deputation sent by Ezra to Iddo. — Ezr. 8:16

6. One who had taken a foreign wife. — Ezr. 10:39
A. is Nathanias. — 1 Es. 9:34

7. f. of two sons who were high in rank under Solomon. — 1 K. 4:5

Nathanael A. 1. One of the captains over thousands at Josiah's passover. — 1 Es. 1:9
A. 2. Priest who had married a foreign wife. — 1 Es. 9:22
is Nethanel. — Ezr. 10:22
A. 3. Anc. of Judith. — Jth. 8:1
4. Of Cana of Galilee, this Nathanael was an Israelite without guile (Jn. 1:45-51, 21:2), who was deeply impressed by Jesus and was promised that he should see the future glory of the Son of man.

A. Nathanias	S. Nathan 6.	
Nathan-Melech	Official under Josiah.	2 K. 23:11
A. Nave	Gk. form of Heb. Nun.	Sir. 46:1 AV.
Neariah	1. s. of Shemaiah, desc. of David.	1 Ch. 3:22f.

Neariah
2. Simeonite captain in the army of Hezekiah, who fought against the Amalekites.

1 Ch. 4:42

Nebai AV.	Chief who signed the covenant of Ezra. S. Nobai.	Neh. 10:19
Nebaioth	Eldest s. of Ishmael.	Gn. 25:13
Nebat	f. of Jeroboam 1.	1 K. 11:26
Nebo	S. Nooma.	
Nebuchad-nezzar	S. Nebuchadrezzar.	

Nebuchad-rezzar
was king of Babylon 605-562 B.C., and was mentioned in Jeremiah, Ezekiel and Daniel. s. of Nabopolassar. In 605 B.C. he defeated Necho, Pharaoh of Egypt in the battle of Carchemish, and became king in Sept. 605 B.C. After varying fortunes he captured Jerusalem in March 597 (2 K. 24:10-17). In 587 B.C. he again captured Jerusalem (Jer. 39:5f.). In 582 B.C. he ordered a third deportation of Jews to Babylon (Jer. 52:30). According to Dan. 4:23-33 he suffered fits of madness. He was a pious ruler rebuilding many temples in many of his cities, but paying special attention to his capital, Babylon. Here he built great defensive walls, the Ishtar Gateway, the seven stage tower of the Ziggurat and a Pall Mall—a processional way. He died in the autumn of 562 B.C.

Nebushazban	Chief of the captains at the time of Nebuchad-rezzar's capture of Jerusalem.	Jer. 39:13
Nebuzaradan	Commanded Nebuchadrezzar's bodyguard.	2 K. 25:8-20
Necho, Nechoh	S. Neco.	

Neco
  or Nechoh,
  or Necoh
	Pharaoh, second k. of the 26th dynasty. He played a not insignificant part in the fortunes of the last years of the kingdom of Judah (610-594 B.C.) (2 K. 23:29ff.).

Nedabiah	s. of Jeconiah (Jehoiachin), 1 Ch. 3:18 desc. of David.
Neemias	S. Nehemiah.
Nehemiah	1. A Jew who was taken into captivity by Nebuchadrezzar and returned with Zerubbabel. Ezr. 2:2 is Nehemias. Neh. 7:7 2. s. of Azbuk who helped to repair the wall of Jerusalem. Neh. 3:16 3. s. of Hacaliah and cup bearer to the Persian ruler Artaxerxes 1. He paid two visits to Jerusalem. During the first in 445, he rebuilt or repaired the walls of Jerusalem in 52 days (Neh. 6:15). He helped to repeople the city, and to establish the Law as the norm. He arranged for a service of dedication of the walls (Neh. 12). On his second visit, twelve years later, he carried out further reforms, and enforced the laws (13:30f.).
A. Nehemias	1. is Nehemiah 1. 2. Contemporary of Ezra. 1 Es. 5:40 S. Nehemiah 3.
Nehum	One of the leaders of the Jewish community who returned with Zerubbabel. Neh. 7:7 A. is Roimus. 1 Es. 5:8 is Rehum. Ezr. 2:2
Nehushta	w. of k. Jehoiakim. She and her s. Jehoiachin were taken to Babylon. 2 K. 24:8, 12
Nekoda	1. Head of a family of Nethinim. Ezr. 2:48 A. is Noeba. 1 Es. 5:31 2. His descendants could not Ezr. 2:60 prove their Jewish descent. A. is Nekodan. 1 Es. 5:37
A. Nekodan AV. Necodan	S. Nekoda 2.

Nemuel	1. S. Jemuel.	
	2. Reubenite, b. of Dathan.	Nu. 26:9
Nepheg	1. s. of Izhar, Levite.	Ex. 6:21
	2. s. of David.	2 S. 5:15
Nephushesim AV. Nephishesim	Head of family of temple servants who returned from exile.	Neh. 7:52
Ner	u. or grandf. of Saul, f. of Abner.	1 S. 14:50; 1 Ch. 8:33
Nereus	Roman Christian greeted by St. Paul.	Ro. 16:15
Nergal-Sharezer	One of the Babylonian leaders who entered Jerusalem after its capture. He released Jeremiach from prison.	Jer. 39:3
Neri	Anc. of Jesus.	Lk. 3:27
Neriah	f. of Baruch the scribe.	Jer. 32:12
	A. is Nerias.	Bar. 1:1
A. Nerias	S. Neriah.	Bar. 1:1
Nethanel, AV. Nethaneel	1. s. of Zuar of the tribe of Issachar and a commander.	Nu. 1:8, 2:5
	2. Fourth s. of Jesse and b. of David.	1 Ch. 2:14
	3. One of the priests who blew trumpets before the ark.	1 Ch. 15:24
	4. Levite, f. of Shemaiah.	1 Ch. 24:6
	5. s. of Obed-edom, Levite gatekeeper.	1 Ch. 26:4
	6. Sent by k. Jehoshaphat to teach in the cities of Judah.	2 Ch. 17:7-9
	7. Chief of the Levites in the reign of Josiah. b. of Conaniah.	2 Ch. 35:9
	8. Priest who married a foreign wife. s. of Pashhur.	Ezr. 10:22
	A. is Nathanael.	1 Es. 9:22
	9. Priest who returned from captivity in Babylon.	Neh. 12:21

	10. Levite Musician at the dedication of the new walls of Jerusalem.	Neh. 12:36
Nethaniah	1. f. of Ishmael who murdered Gedaliah at Mizpah.	2 K. 25:23
	2. Asaphite, a leader of the temple choir.	1 Ch. 25:2
	3. Levite sent by k. Jehoshaphat to teach the law in the cities of Judah.	2 Ch. 17:8
	4. f. of Jehudi.	Jer. 36:14
Neziah	His descendants, Temple servants, returned with Zerubbabel.	Ezr. 2:54
	A. is Nasi or Nasith.	1 Es. 5:32
Nicanor	A. 1. s. of Patroclus appointed governor of Judaea because of his hatred of the Jews (2 Mac. 8:9, 14:12).	
	2. One of the seven chosen to relieve the apostles of their more secular duties (Ac. 6:5).	
Nicodemus	The name means 'conqueror of the people'. Nicodemus was mentioned in three places in the Fourth Gospel. He was a Pharisee and a master in Israel. He was described as 'the teacher'. He visited Jesus by night but found himself quite confused after an interview (Jn. 3:1-21). In Jn. 7 Nicodemus challenged the right of the Jews to condemn Jesus unheard. In 19:39 Nicodemus provided spices for the body of Jesus.	
Nicolas	A proselyte to Judaism of Antioch. One of the seven men selected to serve the poor at meal times.	Ac. 6:5
Niger	Nickname or assumed name of Symeon, a teacher at Antioch, with Barnabas and Saul.	Ac. 13:1
Nimrod	s. of Cush, a great hunter and Mesopotamian king.	Gn. 10:8-11; Mic. 5:6
Nimshi	grandf. of K. Jehu.	2 K. 9:2; cp. 1 K. 19:16

A. Niphis	His family returned with Zerubbabel.	1 Es. 5:21
	is Magbish.	Ezr. 2:30
Noadiah	1. s. of Binnui, one of the four Levites to whom was entrusted the silver and gold brought back from Babylon.	Ezr. 8:33
A.	is Moeth.	1 Es. 8:63
	2. Prophetess who tried to intimidate Nehemiah at the time of the re-building of the walls of Jerusalem.	Neh. 6:14
Noah AV. Noe	1. s. of Lamech, and the tenth patriarch before the flood (Gn. 6-10). He died at the age of 950. He was born 126 years later than the death of Adam, and when 500 became the father of Shem, Ham and Japheth. The flood of waters came in his 600th year, but Noah and his sons and the wives survived to become the founders of the second humanity in the earth. After the flood he became a husbandman. Noah thus became a figure of the remnant, of salvation and of the sign of the rainbow. He was mentioned in Isaiah and Ezekiel and in Matthew and Luke and three epistles.	
	2. d. of Zelophehad the Manassite; the five daughters claimed the inheritance as they had no brother (Nu. 26:33, 27:7-11).	
Nobah	Manassite chieftain who settled in Kenath.	Nu. 32:42
Nobai	One who set seal to the covenant with Nehemiah.	Neh. 10:19
Nodab	Founder or leader of one of the tribes defeated by the tribes of Reuben, Gad and Manassaeh.	1 Ch. 5:19
Noe	S. Noah 1.	
A. Noeba	His family returned from captivity with Zerubbabel.	1 Es. 5:31
	is Nekodan.	1 Es. 5:37
	is Nekoda.	Ezr. 2:48

Nogah	s. of David.	1 Ch. 3:7
Nohah	desc. of Benjamin.	1 Ch. 8:2
Non	S. Nun.	
A. Nooma	His sons had taken foreign wives.	1 Es. 9:35
	is Nebo.	Ezr. 10:43
A. Numenius	s. of Antiochus.	1 Mac. 12:16
	Ambassador to Rome 141 B.C.	
Nun	Ephraimite, f. of Joshua, Moses' assistant and successor.	Ex. 33:11
	is Non.	1 Ch. 7:27
Nympha or Nymphas	A prominent member of the Church at Laodicea which met together at her house (Col. 4:15).	

O

A. Oabdius	s. of Ela who had married a foreign wife in Babylon.	1 Es. 9:27
	is Abdi.	Ezr. 10:26
Obadiah	The name means 'Servant of Yah'.	

1. Steward of Ahab who protected Yahweh's prophets when they were being persecuted by Jezebel. 1 K. 18:3ff.
2. Levite returned from exile. 1 Ch. 9:16
   is Abda. Neh. 11:17
3. Judahite, desc. of David. 1 Ch. 3:21
4. A man of valour of the tribe of Issachar. 1 Ch. 7:3
   s. of Izrahiah.
5. desc. of Saul, Benjamite s. of Azel. 1 Ch. 8:38
6. Gadite leader who joined David's army. 1 Ch. 12:9
7. f. of Ishmaiah of the tribe of Zebulun. 1 Ch. 27:19
8. One of the princes sent by k. Jehoshaphat to teach in the cities of Judah. 2 Ch. 17:7f.
9. Levite, one of Josiah's overseers of the

workmen who were repairing the Temple.
2 Ch. 34:12

		10. Head of a family that returned with Ezra.	Ezr. 8:9
A.		is Abadias.	1 Es. 8:35
		11. Priest who sealed the covenant.	Neh. 10:5
		12. Porter who guarded the storehouses.	Neh. 12:25

13. The prophet Obadiah was responsible for the book of that name (Obad.), the shortest in the O.T., and was the fourth 'minor' prophet. He lived probably in the period following the Fall of Jerusalem in 587, or a century later.

Obal
s. of Joktan, desc. of Shem.   Gn. 10:28
is Ebal.   1 Ch. 1:22

A. Obdia
A priest, whose sons could not prove their Jewish descent.   1 Es. 5:38
is Habaiah.   Ezr. 2:61
is Hobaiah.   Neh. 7:63

Obed
1. s. of Boaz and Ruth and grandf. of k. David.   Ru. 4:17
2. s. of Ephlal, Judahite, desc. of Sheshan.   1 Ch. 2:37f.
3. 'Mighty man' of David's armies.   1 Ch. 11:47
4. s. of Shemiah, who belonged to a family of gatekeepers.   1 Ch. 26:1-7
5. f. of Azariah who was one of Jehoiada's captains when Athaliah was deposed (2 Ch. 23:1).

Obed-Edom
1. Philistine, a native of Gath in whose house David deposited the ark after the death of Uzzah.   2 S. 6:10f.
2. Head of family of keepers of the S. gates of the temple.   1 Ch. 15:18
(1 and 2 may be identical.)
3. Levitical musicians who played the harp when the ark was brought from the house of Obed-edom.   1 Ch. 15:21

	4. Guardian of sacred vessels in the Temple.	2 Ch. 25:24
A. Obeth	Head of family that returned from exile in Babylon.	1 Es. 8:32
	is Ebed.	Ezr 8:6
Obil	Ishmaelite, overseer of David's camels.	1 Ch. 27:30
A. Ochielus AV. Ochiel	Priest under k. Josiah. is Jeiel.	1 Es. 1:9 2 Ch. 35:9
Ochran	f. of Pagiel, Asherite leader.	Nu. 1:13
A. Ocidelus	Jew who took a foreign wife. is Jozabad.	1 Es. 9:22 Ezr. 10:22
Oded	1. f. of prophet Azariah.	2 Ch. 15:1
	2. Prophet who succeeded in obtaining kindly treatment and release for the men of Judah who were taken prisoners during Pekah's invasion of the S. kingdom.	2 Ch. 28:9ff.
A. Odomera AV. Odo- narkes	Nomad chief.	1 Mac. 9:66
Og	Amorite k. of Bashan (Jos. 13:12). The conquest of Og by Moses was one of the great events of Israel's conquest of the promised land (Jos. 9:10). He had a very special bed of black basalt (Deut. 3:11).	
Ohad	s. of Simeon.	Gn. 46:10
Ohel	s. or grands. of Zerubbabel.	1 Ch. 3:20
Oholah and Oholibah	Two feminine names figurative of Samaria and Jerusalem.	Ezek. 23:4
Oholiab AV. Aholiab	s. of Ahisamach, of the tribe of Dan, chief assistant of Bezalel.	Ex. 31:6
Oholibah	S. Oholah.	
Oholibamah	1. w. of Esau, d. of Anah. 2. Edomite 'duke', desc. of Esau.	Gn. 36:2 Gn. 36:41
A. Olamus	desc. of Bani who married a foreign woman.	1 Es. 9:30
	is Meshullam.	Ezr. 10:29
	A. is Mosollamus.	1 Es. 8:44

Olympas	Member of the Church at Rome. Ro. 16:15
Omar	grands. of Esau, clan chief of Gn. 36:11, 15 Edom.
Omri	1. k. of Israel for twelve years (1 K. 16:16ff.). During the anarchy following the end of the dynasty of Jeroboam 1 of Israel, the Israelite army elected its general Omri as king. He captured the capital Tirzah, but after six years moved to a new capital on the hill of Samaria. He had to cede cities to the Syrians of Damas- cus; made an alliance with Phoenicia, by marrying his son Ahab to Jezebel, daughter of the king of Tyre, and subdued Moab. He founded the dynasty of Omri. He is some- times described as the northern David and was a powerful king. The Assyrians described Israel as 'the land of Omri' for more than a century after his death. 2. desc. of Benjamin, s. of Becher. 1 Ch. 7:8 3. Judahite living in Jerusalem. 1 Ch. 9:4 s. of Imri. 4. Prince of the tribe of Issachar in David's time. s. of Michael. 1 Ch. 27:18
On	Reubenite, who joined in Nu. 16:1 rebellion against Moses.
Onam	1. Fifth s. of Shobal, desc. of Gn. 36:23 Esau. 2. s. of Jerahmeel, of the tribe 1 Ch. 2:26 of Judah.
Onan	Second s. of Judah. Gn. 38:4
Onesimus	Means 'useful'. He was a runaway slave of Philemon (Philem. 16), a Christian of Colossae, to whom Paul had him returned.
Onesiphorus	Friend of St. Paul at Rome. 2 Ti. 1:16-18
A. Onias	1. Onias I. High Priest. f. of 1 Mac. 12:7 Simon the Just. 2. Onias III. High priest. Sir. 50:1 3. Onias III. s. of Simon II, High priest who

	attached himself to the Ptolomies and built temple in Heliopolis.	2 Mac. 3:3f.
Ophir	Eleventh of the thirteen sons of Joktan.	Gn. 10:29
Ophrah	Judahite, s. of Meonothai.	1 Ch. 4:14
Oreb	Midianite Prince.	Jg. 7:25
Oren	Judahite, s. of Jerahmeel.	1 Ch. 2:25
Ornan	Form of the name Araunah. S. Araunah.	1 Ch. 21:15
Orpah	Moabitess sister of Ruth, and d.-in-law of Naomi.	Ru. 1:4-14
A. Osaias	Priest who returned from exile. is Jeshaiah.	1 Es. 8:48 Ezr. 8:19
A. Osea	The last k. of the Northern kingdom. S. Hoshea.	2 Es. 13:40
A. Oseas	is prophet Hosea.	2 Es. 1:39
Oshea AV.	is Joshua.	Nu. 13:8
Osnappar	K. of Assyria, is Assurbanipal.	Ezr. 4:10
Othni	s. of Shemaiah. Levite gatekeeper in the Temple.	1 Ch. 26:7
Othniel	Nephew of Caleb, first 'judge' and deliverer of the people.	Jg. 1:13, 3:9ff.
A. Othonias	Priest who had married a foreign wife in Babylon. is Mattaniah 5.	1 Es. 9:28 Ezr. 10:27
A. Ox	f. of Merari, and grandf. of Judith.	Jth. 8:1
Ozem	1. Sixth s. of Jesse, b. of David. 2. s. of Jerahmeel, Judahite.	1 Ch. 2:15 1 Ch. 2:25
A. Ozias	1. Anc. of Ezra. is Uzzi. 2. Head of family which returned with Zerubbabel. is Uzza.	2 Es. 1:2 Ezr. 7:4 1 Es. 5:31 Ezr. 2:49

	3. s. of Micah. Simeonite. Ruler of Bethulia.	Jth. 6:15
Oziel	Anc. of Judith.	Jth. 8:1
Ozni	s. of Gad.	Nu. 26:16
	is Ezbon.	Gn. 46:16

P

Paarai	One of David's Thirty picked soldiers.	2 S. 23:35
	is Naarai.	1 Ch. 11:37
Padon	His family of Temple servants returned with Zerubbabel.	Ezr. 2:44
A. is Phaleas.		1 Es. 5:29

Pagiel   s. of Ochran and leader of the tribe of Asher, assisted Moses in taking the census (Nu. 1:13).

Pahath-Moab	Lit. 'Governor of Moab.'	
	1. Founder of Israelite family.	Ezr. 2:6
	2. Father of repairers of wall.	Neh. 3:11
	3. Chief who sealed the covenant.	Neh. 10:14
A. is Phaath-Moab.		1 Es. 5:11

Palal	s. of Uzai, helped to rebuild the walls of Jerusalem.	Neh. 3:25
Pallu AV. Phallu	Second s. of Reuben.	Gn. 46:9

Palti   1. Benjamite leader, s. of Raphu and one of the twelve men sent by Moses to spy out the land of Canaan.   Nu. 13:9

AV. Phalti	2. s. of Laish. Saul gave him Michal, David's wife.	1 S. 25:44
	is Paltiel.	2 S. 3:15
Paltiel	1. Prince of tribe of Issachar.	Nu. 34:26
	2. S. Palti 2.	
Parmashta	s. of Haman put to death by the Jews.	Est. 9:9
Parmenas	One of the seven men appointed to serve at table, to help the Apostles.	Ac. 6:5

Parnach	f. of Elizaphan.	Nu. 34:25
Parosh AV. Pharosh	1. Israelite whose family returned with Zerubbabel and Ezra.	Ezr. 2:3 Neh. 3:25
A.	is Phoros.	1 Es. 5:9
	2. Chief who set his seal to the covenant.	Neh. 10:14
Parshandatha	s. of Haman put to death by the Jews in Shushan.	Est. 9:7
Paruah	f. of Jehoshaphat, Solomon's commissariat officer in Issachar.	1 K. 4:17
Pasach	s. of Japhlet, desc. of Asher.	1 Ch. 7:33
Paseah	1. desc. of Judah.	1 Ch. 4:12
	2. f. of Joiada who repaired the old gate.	Neh. 3:6
	3. Head of family of Nethinim who returned with Zerubbabel.	Ezr. 2:49
A.	is Phinoe.	1 Es. 5:31
Pashhur	1. s. of Malchiah sent by Zedekiah to Jeremiah to seek an oracle from God (Jer. 21:1; Neh. 11:12).	
	2. s. of Immer, governor of the temple, and priest, who imprisoned Jeremiah (Jer. 20:1).	
	3. f. of Gedaliah, prince during Zedekiah's reign.	Jer. 38:1
	4. Chief of family which returned with Ezra.	Ezr. 2:38
	is Phaisur.	1 Es. 5:25
	5. A priest who sealed the covenant with Nehemiah.	Neh. 10:3
A. Patheus	Levite.	1 Es. 9:23
	is Pethahiah.	Ezr. 10:23
Patrobas	Christian man greeted by Paul.	Ro. 16:14
A. Patroclus	f. of the Syrian general Nicanor.	2 Mac. 8:9
Paul the Apostle	Paul was a Benjamite, a tent maker, a Pharisee, who was born in Tarsus. Educated under Gamaliel, he was appointed to repress the Christian church. He was converted by a vision of Jesus on the road leading to Damas-	

cus. Paul spent long periods in the desert, in Damascus and in Tarsus. After a year at Antioch Paul went to Jerusalem, and then undertook three extended missionary journeys for evangelistic work. At the end of these journeys, he was arrested in Jerusalem, and appealing to Caesar, was taken to Rome in the spring of A.D. 62. He was under house arrest for two years. Nothing more after this is certainly known of him. He was a missionary, teacher, theologian, correspondent and author, and was the apostle of the mission to the Gentiles (Ro. 11:13). He is the second person in al Christendom.

Paulus, Sergius Proconsul in Cyprus when Paul and Barnabas visited the island. A man of understanding who believed Paul's teaching. Ac. 13:7

Pedahel Prince of the tribe of Naphtali. Nu. 34:28 s. of Ammihud.

Pedahzur f. of Gamaliel. Representative of the tribe of Manasseh, when Moses and Aaron counted the men of Israel (Nu. 1:10).

Pedaiah
1. f. of Joel, ruler over the tribe of Manasseh. 1 Ch. 27:20
2. f. of Zebidah, one of the wives of k. Josiah. 2 K. 23:36
3. s. of Jehoiachin who was taken captive to Babylon. 1 Ch. 3:18
4. One who repaired the wall of Jerusalem. Neh. 3:25
5. One of those who stood on Ezra's left hand when he read the law to the people (Neh. 8:4). A. is Phaldeus. 1 Es. 9:44
6. Levite appointed by Nehemiah to receive and distribute the tithes and offerings. Neh. 13:13
7. f. of Joed, Benjamite. Neh. 11:7

A. Pedias One who had a foreign wife. 1 Es. 9:34
AV. Pelias is Bedeiah. Ezr. 10:35

Pekah s. of Remaliah (2 K. 15:27-31). Captain of

	Pekahiah's Gileadite bodyguard who slew the king and seized the throne in Samaria for himself.	
Pekahiah	s. and successor of k. Menahem, k. of Israel for 2 years. Assassinated by Pekah (2 K. 15:22-26).	
Pelaiah	1. s. of Elioenai, desc. of David.	1 Ch. 3:24
	2. Levite who helped Ezra to interpret the law to the people, and sealed the covenant with Nehemiah.	Neh. 8:7; 10:10
Pelaliah	Priest living in Jerusalem in the time of Nehemiah.	Neh. 11:12
Pelatiah	1. s. of Benaiah and pro-Egyptian prince of the people, seen by Ezekiel in a vision (Ezk. 11:1).	
	2. s. of Hananiah, grands. of Zerubbabel.	1 Ch. 3:21
	3. s. of Ishi, captain of Simeonite band who followed and destroyed the Amalekites at Mt. Seir.	1 Ch. 4:42
	4. Jew who sealed Nehemiah's covenant.	Neh. 10:22
Peleg	s. of Eber, desc. of Shem.	1 Ch. 1:19
Pelet	1. Judahite. s. of Jahdai.	1 Ch. 2:47
	2. s. of Azmaveth, Benjamite chief, who joined David.	1 Ch. 12:3
Peleth	1. Reubenite. f. of On.	Nu. 16:1
	2. s. of Jonathan, Judahite desc. of Jerahmeel.	1 Ch. 2:33
Pelias	S. Pedias.	
Peninnah	w. of Elkanah, f. of Samuel.	1 S. 1:2f.
Penuel	1. grands. of Judah, s. of Hur.	1 Ch. 4:4
	2. Benjamite, s. of Shashak.	1 Ch. 8:25
Peresh	s. of Machir, and grands. of Manasseh.	1 Ch. 7:16
Perez AV. Pharez	One of twin sons of Judah and Tamar.	Gn. 38:29
	A. is Phares.	1 Es. 5:5

Perida	Head of family of 'Solomon's servants'.	Neh. 7:57
	is Peruda.	Ezr. 2:55
	A. is Pharida.	1 Es. 5:33
A. Perseus	k. of Macedonia. s. and successor Philip III.	1 Mac. 8:5
Persis	Christian freedwoman who 'laboured much in the Lord', greeted by Paul. Ro. 16:12	
Peruda	S. Perida.	

Peter (Simon) s. of Jona, married and of Bethsaida (Jn. 1:44), with a house in Capernaum (Mk. 1:21). He was thus a Galilean fisherman called to be a disciple of Jesus, and always occurred first in the lists of disciples. He was generally the spokesman of the disciples, and played a leading role in the Caesarea Confession, the Transfiguration, the denial the night before the crucifixion, and the new commission after the resurrection (Mk. 16 and Jn. 21). He was the first witness to the Resurrection. Became the principal preacher and leader in the early parts of the Book of the Acts, *i.e.* for 15 years. He undertook missionary work in various places in Palestine, accompanied by his wife (1 Cor. 9:5), was imprisoned in Jerusalem (Ac. 12), and urged the admission of the Gentiles (Ac. 15). Probably martyred and buried in Rome. He was the outstanding personality among the twelve disciples, and the acknowledged leader of the early church for its first 15 years. He was gradually overshadowed by James and Paul, but remained a missionary apostle and author. His words 'Thou are the Christ' at Caesarea Philippi have remained basic to and formative of the church ever since.

Pethahiah	1. Priest of David's days.	1 Ch. 24:16
	2. Levite who married a foreign wife.	Ezr. 10:23
	3. Levite.	Neh. 9:5

	4. Judahite, Jewish adviser in Jerusalem to k. Artaxerxes.	Neh. 11:24
Pethuel	f. of the prophet Joel.	Jl. 1:1
Peullethai	s. of Obed-Edom. Levite gatekeeper.	1 Ch. 26:5
A. Phaath Moab	S. Pahath-Moab.	
A. Phacareth	S. Pochereth-Hazzebaim.	
A. Phaisur	S. Pashhur.	
A. Phaldeus AV. Phaldais	S. Pedaiah 5.	
A. Phaleas	S. Padon	1 Es. 5:29
A. Phalias AV. Biatas	S. Pelaiah 2.	1 Es. 9:48
Phallu	S. Pallu.	
Phaltiel	Captain of the people.	3 Es. 5:16
Phanuel	f. of Anna the prophetess.	Lk. 2:36
A. Pharakim AV. Pharacim	His sons were amongst the temple servants who returned with Zerubbabel (1 Es. 5:31).	
Pharaoh	Title (not name) of Egyptian Rulers, e.g. Ex. 1-15. S. Neco.	
Phares	S. Perez.	
A. Pharita	S. Perida.	
A. Phasiron	His descendants were defeated by Jonathan (Maccabaeus).	1 Mac. 9:66
A. Phassurus AV. Phassaron	S. Pashhur 4.	
Phicol	Captain under Abimelech against Abraham.	Gn. 21:22ff.
Philemon	A convert and a dear and intimate friend of St. Paul (Philem. 1). He was a wealthy Christian of Colossae and the owner of the runaway slave, Onesimus.	

Philetus	He and Hymenaeus shared the same heresy regarding the resurrection.	2 Ti. 2:17

Philip
The name means 'lover of horses'.

A. 1. k. of Macedonia 359-336 B.C.   1 Mac. 1:1
f. of Alexander the Great.

A. 2. Phrygian who was governor   2 Mac. 5:22
of Jerusalem.

A. 3. Foster brother and friend of   1 Mac. 6:14-18
Antiochus Epiphanes.

A. 4. k. of Macedonia 220-179 B.C.   1 Mac. 8:5

5. The Apostle. Philip lived at Bethsaida, and became a disciple of Jesus the day after Andrew and Peter were called. Philip brought Nathanael to Jesus, and figured in the fourth gospel (6:5, 12:21f. and 14:8). He probably died at Hierapolis.

6. Evangelist. One of the seven ordained as deacons by the apostles. Hebrew, with conspicuously liberal sympathies. Departed from Jerusalem for missionary ministry in Samaria, then south of Jerusalem, where he baptised the Ethiopian eunuch (Ac. 8:26-34), then in Ashdod and Caesarea. He had four daughters who were prophetesses (Ac. 6; 21:9).

7 and 8. S. Herod 4 and 5.

Philologus	Christian greeted by St. Paul.	Ro. 16:15
A. Phinees	1. grands. of Aaron.	1 Es. 5:5
	is Phinehas 1.	Ex. 6:25
	2. s. of Heli, Anc. of Ezra.	2 Es. 1:2a
	is Phinehas 2.	1 S. 1:3
	3. Priest of the time of Ezra.	1 Es. 8:63
	is Phinehas 3.	Ezr. 8:33
Phinehas	1. Succeeded his f. Eleazar in office of High Priest.	Nu. 25:7f.; cf. Ps. 106:30
	2. Younger s. of Eli.	1 S. 2:12-17
	3. f. of Eleazar, priest in Jerusalem at the time of the return from exile.	Ezr. 8:33

A. Phinoe AV. Phinees	S. Paseah.	
Phlegon	Christian at Rome greeted by St. Paul.	Ro. 16:14
Phoebe	Christian at Cenchreae who had greatly helped St. Paul and others (Ro. 16:1f.). She seems to have carried Paul's letter to Rome and he charged the Roman Christians to receive her worthily.	
A. Phoros	S. Parosh.	
Phygelos	With Hermogenes refused to help St. Paul during his last imprisonment in Rome.	2 Ti. 1:15
Pilate	Pontius Pilate (Mk. 15:1-15, etc.), a middle class Roman who became in A.D. 26 the fifth procurator of Judaea with military, judicial and some ecclesiastical control. He did many things to offend the Jews of his province. He authorised the death of Jesus and the words inscribed on the cross.	
Pildash	Sixth s. of Nahor.	Gn. 22:22
Pilha	Jewish leader who sealed the covenant with Nehemiah.	Neh. 10:24
Piltai	Post-exilic representative of priestly house of Moadiah in the time of Joiakim	Neh. 12:17
Pinon	Edomite duke.	Gn. 36:41
Piram	k. of Jarmuth defeated by Joshua.	Jos. 10:3ff.
Pispa AV. Pispah	Asherite, s. of Jether.	1 Ch. 7:88
Pithon	Benjamite. s. of Micah who was grands. of k. Saul.	1 Ch. 8:35
Pochereth-Hazzebaim	Head of family of 'Solomon's servants' who returned with Zerubbabel.	Ezr. 2:57
	A. S. Phacareth.	

Pontius Pilate	S. Pilate.	
Poratha	s. of Haman put to death by the Jews.	Est. 9:8
Porcius Festus	S. Festus.	
A. Posidonius	Envoy sent by Nicanor to Judas Maccabaeus.	2 Mac. 14:19
Potiphar	Important official of Pharaoh's bodyguard, to whom Joseph was sold by the Midianites (Gn. 37:36, 39:1ff.).	
Potiphera	Chief Priest of On. f.-in-law of Joseph.	Gn. 41:45
Prisca or Priscilla	w. of Aquila. is Priscilla. is Prisca always in St. Paul's epistles.	Ac. 18:2, 18, 26 Ro. 16:3
Prochorus	One of the seven servants appointed to relieve apostles	Ac. 6:5
A. Psaltiel	S. Phaltiel.	

Ptolemy   A. 1. Sotor, s. of Lagos and founder of the dynasty
Succeeded Alexander to Satrapy of Egypt,
and became king 305-283 B.C. Dan. 11:5
2. Philadelphus, Ptolemy II 283- cp. Dan. 11:6
247 B.C. s. of Soter.
3. Euergetes, Ptolemy III 245-221 B.C. s. of
Philadelphus and grands. of Soter (cp. Dan.
11:7-9).
4. Philopator, Ptolemy IV 221- Dan. 11:11
204 B.C. s. of Euergetes.
5. Ptolemy V (Epiphanes) 204- Dan. 11:13-18
180 B.C. s. of Philopator.
6. Ptolemy VI Philometer 180- 1 Mac. 10:51-57
145 B.C.
h. of Cleopatra.
f. of Cleopatra.
7. Ptolemy VIII Euergetes II 1 Mac. 1:18
170/1-117 B.C.
8. A General of Antiochus IV 1 Mac. 3:38
Epiphanes.

	9. s. of Abubus and s.-in-law of Simon Maccabaeus.	1 Mac. 16:11
	10. s. of Dositheus, priest and Levite.	Ad. Est. 11:1
Puah	1. Hebrew Midwife.	Ex. 1:15
	2. f. of Tola of the tribe of Issachar.	Jg. 10:1
	3. s. of Issachar, went to Egypt with Jacob.	Gn. 46:13
	is Puvah.	Nu. 26:23
Publius or Poplius	Rich and hospitable magistrate in Malta when St. Paul was shipwrecked on the island (Ac. 28:7).	
Pudens	A Christian in Rome at the time of St. Paul's last imprisonment there	2 Ti. 4:21
Pul	1. Original name of Tiglath-Pileser, k. of Assyria.	2 K. 15:19
	2. S. Put.	
Purah	Servant to Gideon.	Jg. 7:10f.
Put AV. Phut	s. of Ham, Anc. of an African nation.	Gn. 10:6; Is. 66:19
Putiel	f.-in-law of Eleazar, Aaron's s.	Ex. 6:25
Puvah	S. Puah 3.	
Pyrrhus	f. of Sopater, one of St. Paul's companions on his last journey to Jerusalem from Philippi.	Ac. 20:4

Q

Quartus	With St. Paul sent greetings to the Christians in Rome.	Ro. 16:23
Quintus Memmius	S. Memmius.	
Quirinius	Governor of Syria at the time of the birth of Jesus.	Lk. 2:2

R

Raamah	s. of Cush.	Gn. 10:7
	f. of Sheba and Dedan.	
	is Raama.	1 Ch. 1:9
Raamiah	One of the twelve chiefs who returned with Zerubbabel.	Neh. 7:7
	is Reelaiah.	Ezr. 2:2
A.	is Resaias.	1 Es. 5:8
Rab-mag	Officer or prince with Nebuchadnezzar at the siege of Jerusalem.	Jer. 39:3
Rab-Saris	Assyrian officer sent by Sennacherib to demand the surrender of Jerusalem.	2 K. 18:17
Rab-Shakeh	Sent with Rab-Saris.	2 K. 18:17
Rachel	'ewe'.	
	Younger d. of Laban and favourite w. of Jacob, m. of Joseph and Benjamin (Gn. 29:1). She was a very beautiful woman for whom Jacob waited seven years before (29:17) being able to marry her. Rachel went with Jacob when he returned to Palestine. She died giving birth to her second son, Benjamin. Jer. 31:15 shows that she must have been buried a few miles N. of Jerusalem (Gn. 35:16-20).	
	is Rahel.	Jer. 31:15 AV.
Raddai	Fifth s. of Jesse.	1 Ch. 2:14
Raguel	1. f.-in-law of Moses.	Nu. 10:29
RV. Reuel	is Jethro.	Nu. 3:1
A.	2. f. of Sarah, the w. of Tobias.	To. 3:7
Rahab	1. Harlot of Jericho who hid the spies of Joshua.	Jos. 2
	2. Anc. of Jesus Christ. w. of Salmon and m. of Boaz.	Mt. 1:5
Raham	desc. of Caleb.	1 Ch. 2:44
	S. of Shema.	
Rahel	S. Rachel.	
Rakem	S. Rekem 3.	

Ram	1. Anc. of David.	Ru. 4:19
	2. Head of Elihu's family, Job's friend.	Job. 32:2
	3. Eldest s. of Jerahmeel.	1 Ch. 2:25
Ramiah	s. of Parosh who had married a foreign wife.	Ezr. 10:25
	A. is Hiermas.	1 Es. 9:26
Ramoth RV. Jeremoth	s. of Bani who married a foreign wife.	Ezr. 10:29
	A. is Hieremoth.	1 Es. 9:30
Rapha	fifth s. of Benjamin.	1 Ch. 8:2
Raphah AV. Rapha	desc. of Saul. S. Rephaiah 4.	1 Ch. 8:37
Raphaim	Anc. of Judith.	Jth. 8:1
Raphu	f. of Palti, the Benjamite spy.	Nu. 13:9
Rathumus	S. Rehum 2.	
A. Raziz	Elder of Jerusalem who escaped arrest by committing suicide	2 Mac. 14:37ff.
Reaiah	1. grands. of Judah	1 Ch. 4:2
	is Haroeh.	1 Ch. 2:52
AV. Reaia	2. desc. of Reuben.	1 Ch. 5:5
	3. Head of family of gatekeepers who returned from exile.	Ezr. 2:47
	A. is Jairus.	1 Es. 5:31
Reba	Prince of Midian slain by Israelites under Moses.	Jos. 13:21
Rebecca	S. Rebekah.	
Rebekah	is Rebecca. d. of Bethuel. grandd. of Nahor and Milcah (Gn. 22:20). gt.-niece of Abraham. Sister of Laban. w. of Isaac (Ro. 9:10). Her love story was related in Gn. 24. She was at first barren, like Sarah and Rachel, but later gave birth to twins, Esau and Jacob. She was always attached to her home in Harran (27:42, 28:9). She was buried with her husband in the cave of Machpelah (49:31).	
Rechab	1. s. of Rimmon and a Benjamite. A captain	

following Ishbosheth who with Baanah murdered k. Ishbosheth, carried the news to David and was put to death by his order (2 S. 4:5ff.).

2. desc. of Caleb and f. of Jonadab and founder of the order of Rechabites (1 Ch. 2:55), who drank no wine as a protest against drunken orgies of Canaanites (2 K. 10:15ff.; Jer. 35).

3. f. of Malchiah who helped to rebuild the walls of Jerusalem (Neh. 3:14).

Reelaiah	S. Raamiah.	
A. Reelias AV. Reelius	A leader of the returning exiles.	1 Es. 5:8
Regem	Judahite, desc. of Caleb.	1 Ch. 2:47
Regem-Melech	One sent to consult the priests (Zec. 7:2) as to whether the fast-days observed during the exile were still to be observed after the return to Jerusalem.	
Rehabiah	Levite, desc. of Moses.	1 Ch. 23:17
Rehob	1. f. of Hadadezer, k. of Zobah.	2 S. 8:3
	2. Jew who sealed Nehemiah's covenant.	Neh. 10:11
Rehoboam	Rehoboam (1 K. 14:21), s. of Solomon and Naamah, was the last k. of the united kingdom bequeathed by David and Solomon, and the first k. of the southern kingdom, Judah. At the beginning of his reign he went to the city of Shechem, and here, rejecting the advice of his counsellors, he refused to ameliorate the conditions of his subjects, whereupon the northern tribes under Jeroboam revolted and formed the northern kingdom. His kingdom was later invaded by Shishak the Egyptian Pharaoh. Rehoboam died after a reign of about 17 years.	
Rehum	1. One of the leaders who brought back the Jewish exiles with Zerubbabel.	Ezr. 2:2
	is Nehum.	Neh 7:7
A.	is Roimus.	1 Es. 5:8

	2. Representative in Judah of k. Artaxerxes who tried to prevent the rebuilding of Jerusalem.	Ezr. 4:8ff.
	A. is Rathumus.	1 Es. 2:16
	3. s. of Bani and a Levite who helped to repair the wall	Neh. 3:17
	4. One who sealed Nehemiah's covenant.	Neh. 10:25
	5. Priest whose family returned with Zerubbabel.	Neh. 12:3
Rei	Judean officer and one of Solomon's supporters.	1 K. 1:8
Rekem	1. Midianite prince slain by Israelites under Moses.	Jos. 13:21
	2. s. of Hebron, desc. of Caleb.	1 Ch. 2:43
	3. is Rakem, desc. of Manasseh.	1 Ch. 7:16
Remaliah	f. of Pekah.	2 K. 15:25
Rephael	Second s. of Shemaiah, gatekeeper.	1 Ch. 26:7
Rephah	Ephraimite.	1 Ch. 7:25
Rephaiah	1. Judahite, desc. of k. David.	1 Ch. 3:21
	2. Simeonite chief.	1 Ch. 4:42
	3. desc. of Issachar. s. of Tola. A mighty warrior.	1 Ch. 7:2
	4. desc. of Saul, f. of Eleasah. is Raphah.	1 Ch. 9:43 1 Ch. 8:37
	5. s. of Hur who helped to repair the wall.	Neh. 3:9
A. Resaias	S. Raamiah.	
Resheph	Ephraimite, f. of Telah.	1 Ch. 7:25
Reu	s. of Peleg, desc. of Shem.	Gn. 11:18
Reuben	Firstborn s. of Jacob and Leah (Gn. 29:32), who figured several times in the story of Joseph as his friend (Gn. 37:21, 29 and 42:37). He was the Anc. of the tribe of Reuben (Nu. 16:1), which settled east of Jordan but rapidly died out of the story.	

Reuel	1. s. of Esau.	Gn. 36:4
	2. Midianite priest.	Ex. 2:18
	S. Raguel.	
	is Hobab.	
	is Jethro.	
	3. f. of Eliasaph, Gadite.	Nu. 2:14
	4. Benjamite, grandf. of Meshullam.	1 Ch. 9:8
Reumah	Concubine of Nahor.	Gn. 22:24
Rezin	1. k. of Damascus, in the time of k. Ahaz of Judah.	2 K. 16:5
	2. His family were among the returning exiles.	Ezr. 2:48
Rezon	s. of Eliada. General under Hadadezer (2 S. 8:3). k. of Zobah whom David overthrew.	
Rhesa	s. of Zerubbabel. Anc. of Jesus.	Lk. 3:27
Rhoda	Servant of Mary, m. of Mark.	Ac. 12:13ff.
Rhodocus	A. Jew who was imprisoned for betraying political secrets to Antiochus Eupator. 2 Mac. 13:21	
Ribai	Benjamite f. of Ittai, one of David's 'Thirty'.	2 S. 23:29
Rimmon	f. of Baanah and Rechab who murdered Ishbosheth.	2 S. 4:2ff.
Rinnah	Judahite, s. of Shimon.	1 Ch. 4:20
Riphath	s. of Gomer. grands. of Japheth.	Gn. 10:3
Rizia	Asherite chief, s. of Ulla.	1 Ch. 7:39
Rizpah	Concubine of k. Saul. d. of Aiah (2 S. 21:8). Abner took her as his own after Saul's death (2 S. 3:7), thereby claiming either the throne, or the power behind the throne. By Saul she had had two sons, Mephibosheth and Armoni. These were surrendered to the Gibeonites by David, and were hanged and their bodies were watched over by Rizpah for several months (2 S. 21:1-14).	

Rodanim	desc. of Noah.	1 Ch. 1:7
	is Dodanim.	Gn. 10:4
Rohgah	Asherite, s. of Shemer.	1 Ch. 7:34
A. Roimus	S. Rehum 1.	
Romamti-ezer	s. of Heman (1 Ch. 25:4), skilful with the horn in the House of the Lord.	
Rosh	Seventh s. of Benjamin.	Gn. 46:21
Rufus	1. 'Chosen in the Lord', greeted by Paul.	Ro. 16:13
	2. s. of Simon of Cyrene.	Mk. 15:21
Ruth	Heroine of the Book of Ruth. She was a woman of the land of Moab who married an immigrant, Mahlon. She was left a childless widow, but accompanied her widowed m.-in-law, Naomi, to her home at Bethlehem (Ru. 1:17 for some famous words of loyalty). At Bethlehem she met and married Boaz, a wealthy relative of her f.-in-law. Their first s. was Obed, who was k. David's grandf. (1 Ch. 2:12).	

S

A. Sabanneus	One who took a foreign wife.	1 Es. 9:33
AV. Bannaia	is Zabad.	Ezr. 10:33
A. Sabannus	Levite.	1 Es. 8:63
AV. Sabban	is Binnui.	Ezr. 8:33
A. Sabateus	Teacher of the law under Ezra.	1 Es. 9:48
AV. Sabateas	is Shabbetha.	Neh. 8:7
A. Sabathus	One who took a foreign wife.	1 Es. 9:28
AV. Sabatus	is Zabad.	Ezr. 10:27
A. Sabbanis	S. Sabbeus.	
A. Sabbateus	Levite.	1 Es. 9:14
AV. Sabba-theus	is Shabbethai.	Ezr. 10:15
A. Sabbeus	Jew who took a foreign wife.	1 Es. 9:32
	is Shemaiah.	Ezr. 10:31

A. Sabi AV. Sami	His family were porters who returned from exile with Zerubbabel. is Shobai.	1 Es. 5:28 Ezr. 2:42
A. Sabias	Levite chief in time of Josiah. is Hashabiah. is Assabias.	1 Es. 1:9 2 Ch. 35:9
A. Sabie AV. Sabi	Returned from exile with Zerubbabel.	1 Es. 5:34, Ezr. 2:57
Sabta or Sabtah	s. of Cush. is Sabta.	Gh. 10:7 1 Ch. 1:9
Sabteca	s. of Cush.	Gn. 10:7
Sacar	1. f. of Ahiam, one of David's 'Thirty'. is Sharar. 2. Korahite. His family were gatekeepers.	1 Ch. 11:35 2 S. 23:33 1 Ch. 26:4
Sachia	Benjamite.	1 Ch. 8:10
A. Sadduk AV. Sadduc	High priest, Anc. of Ezra. is Zadok.	1 Es. 8:2 Ezr. 7:2
A. Sadoc	1. Anc. of Esdras. is Zadok. 2. desc. of Zerubbabel and Anc. of Jesus.	2 Es. 1:1 Ezr. 7:2 Mt. 1:14
A. Salamiel	Anc. of Judith. is Shelumiel. is Shemuel.	Jth. 8:1 Nu. 1:6 Nu. 34:20
A. Salasadai	Anc. of Judith.	Jth. 8:1
A. Salathiel	1. f. of Zerubbabel. is Shealtiel. 2. is Esdras (wrongly).	1 Es. 5:5 Ezr. 3:2 2 Es. 3:1
A. Salem AV. Salum	S. Shallum 6.	
A. Salemas	S. Shallum 6.	
A. Salimoth AV. Assali- moth	His family returned with Ezra. from Babylon. is Shelomith.	1 Es. 8:36 Ezr. 8:10

Sallai

Sallai	1. Benjamite whose family settled at Jerusalem after the return from exile.	Neh. 11:8
	2. Priest in post-exilic period.	Neh. 12:20
	is Sallu.	Neh. 12:7
Sallu	1. Benjamite, s. of Meshullam.	1 Ch. 9:7; Neh. 11:7
	2. is Sallai 2.	Neh. 12:20
A. Salum	S. Sallumus.	
A. Sallumus	S. Shallum 11.	
Salma	S. Salmon.	
Salmai	Head of family of Nethinim.	Neh. 7:48
AV. Shalmai.	is Shamlai.	Ezr. 2:46
A.	is Subai.	1 Es. 5:30
A. Salmanasar	k. of Assyria.	2 Es. 13:40
	S. Shalmaneser.	
Salmon	1. Judahite.	Ru. 4:20
or Salma	f. of Boaz.	
	s. of Nahshon.	
	h. of Rahab.	Mt. 1:5
	Anc. of k. David and Jesus.	
	2. grands. of Caleb, s. of Hur.	1 Ch. 2:51
A. Saloas	s. of Pashur who took a foreign wife.	1 Es. 9:22
AV. Talsas	is Elasah.	Ezr. 10:22
A. Salom	f. of Hilkiah.	Bar. 1:7
Salome	1. d. of Herodias. Unnamed in N.T.	Mt. 14:3
	2. w. of Zebedee present at the crucifixion and visitor at the Sepulchre (Mk. 15:40). m. of James and John (Mk. 16:1).	
Salu	f. of Zimri, Simeonite chief slain by Phinehas.	Nu. 25:14
A. Salum	Porter.	1 Es. 5:28
	is Shallum.	Ezr. 2:42
	is Sallumus.	1 Es. 9:25
A. Samaias	1. Levite chief in Josiah's reign.	1 Es. 1:9
	is Shemaiah.	2 Ch. 35:9

	2. Head of family who returned with Ezra.	1 Es. 8:39
	is Shemaiah.	Ezr. 8:13
A. Samatus	s. of Ezora.	1 Es. 9:34
	is Shemariah or Shallum.	Ezr. 10:41, 42
A. Samellius AV. Semel- lius	Scribe.	1 Es. 2:16
	is Shimshai.	Ezr. 4:8
A. Sameus AV. Sameius	s. of Emmer who married a foreign wife.	1 Es. 9:21
	is Shemaiah.	Ezr. 10:21
Samgar-Nebo	Officer of Nebuchadnezzar.	Jer. 39:3
Samlah	Edomite king.	Gn. 36:36
A. Sammus	Stood beside Ezra at reading of the law.	1 Es. 9:43
	is Shema.	Neh. 8:4

Samson — The name means 'little sun', and Samson was a judge who harrassed the Philistines in the last days of the Judges (Jg. 13-16). He was the son of a Danite man, Manoah, whose wife was at first barren, who lived in Zorah. Before he was born he was dedicated to be a Nazirite (long-haired teetotaller specially devoted to Israel's God). He was very strong, coarse, witty and virile. He was subject to visitations of the Spirit, by which he did many mighty deeds. He evaded capture by the Philistines, and once ran off with the gates of the Philistine city of Gaza. He was eventually captured and perished with many Philistines in the collapse of a temple at Gaza.

Samuel — was the s. of Elkanah of the tribe of Ephraim, and Hannah. His mother, long childless, vowed that if she was granted a son, she would dedicate him to God. When she had weaned Samuel, she brought him to Eli, head of the priests at Shiloh, and gave him over to the service of the sanctuary, visiting him

with a new outfit of clothes once a year
(1 S. 1-2). Samuel, the last of the Judges,
presumably succeeded Eli as the chief religious
leader, and as a prophet (3:20). After an
interval of many years Samuel appeared as a
national leader in worship (7:16f.) and politics
(10:25). He became the kingmaker, anointing
first Saul and then later, David, as king. The
entire nation lamented his death (28:3). He
was obviously a considerable figure, and the
most notable between Moses and David.

A. Sanaas	His sons returned with Zerubbabel.	1 Es. 5:23
	is Senaah.	Ezr. 2:35
	is Annaas (AV.).	1 Es. 5:23
	is Hassenaah.	Neh. 3:3
Sanabassar	S. Sheshbazzar.	
A. Sanasib AV. Anasib	Head of family of priests who returned with Zerubbabel.	1 Es. 5:24
Sanballat	Assyrian officer in Samaria who opposed Nehemiah's building plans in Jerusalem.	Neh. 2:10
Saph	s. of Goliath, Philistine giant slain by David's 'Thirty'.	2 S. 21:18
	is Sippai.	1 Ch. 20:4
A. Saphat AV. Sabat	1. Head of family of Solomon's servants, who returned with Zerubbabel	1 Es. 5:34
	2. Returned with Zerubbabel.	1 Es. 5:9
	is Shephatiah 2.	Ezr. 2:4
A. Saphatias	Returned from exile with Ezra.	1 Es. 8:34
	is Shephatiah.	Ezr. 8:8
A. Saphuthi AV. Sapheth	Head of family of Solomon's servants.	1 Es. 5:33
	is Shephatiah.	Ezr. 2:57
Sapphira	w. of Ananias, member of Church in Jerusalem.	Ac. 5:1-10
A. Sarabias	Teacher of the law.	1 Es. 9:48
	is Sherebiah.	Neh. 8:7

Sarah or Sarai	The name means 'Princess'.	Gn. 11:29

Sarah or Sarai — The name means 'Princess'. Gn. 11:29
1. She was the beautiful w. of Abraham, and accompanied him from Harran to Canaan. She was twice passed off by her husband as his sister. She was long barren, but eventually gave birth to Isaac, the second of the great trilogy, Abraham, Isaac and Jacob. She died at the age of 127 years and was buried in the cave of Machpelah, bought by her husband for the purpose. Mentioned in Is. 51:2, and in Heb. 11:11, and other places in the N.T.
2. d. of Raguel.
A. w. of Tobias. To. 3:7
Heroine of Book of Tobit.

A. Saraias — 1. High priest, f. of Jehozadak, 1 Es. 5:5 grandf. of Jeshua.
is Seraiah. 1 Ch. 6:14
2. f. of Ezra. 2 Es. 1:1

Saraph — desc. of Shelah, Judahite, 1 Ch. 4:22 Potter.

Sarasadai — Anc. of Judith. Jth. 8:1

A. Sarchedonus — Gk. name of Esar-haddon. To. 1:21f.

A. Sarea — Scribe of Ezra. 2 Es. 14:24

Sargon — k. of Assyria. Is 20:1 is Sargon III.

A. Sarothie — f. of 'Solomon's servants' who 1 Es. 5:34 returned under Zerubbabel.

Sarsechim — Prince of Babylon present at the taking of Jerusalem by Nebuchadnezzar. Jer. 39:3

A. Sathrabuzanes — Syrian Governor in Judah who tried to prevent the rebuilding of Jerusalem. 1 Es. 6:3 is Shethar-Bozenai. Ezr. 5:3

Saul — lit. asked (of God).
1. Saul was the s. of Kish, of the tribe of Benjamin, and first k. of Israel. He was very tall, head and shoulders above his fellows, courageous, generous, deeply religious and yet doomed to fail, to become the victim of melancholia

G 185

and to believe himself rejected by the God who had chosen him to be king. Secretly anointed (1 S. 10:1), publicly confirmed (10:17-25), he was also signally established as k. by his famous relief of the city of Jabesh Gilead (11:1-11), and then made king at Gilgal (11-14f.). It is uncertain how old Saul was at his succession and whether he reigned for the stated two years (13:1). He was thrice rebuked by Samuel (13:7-10, 15:22, 28:1-25), and saw his lieutenant, David, gradually become the leading figure among the people. Saul spent his life vainly struggling against the Philistines (1 S. 14:52), finally losing his life in a battle against them at Gilboa (21:1-13). Saul's palace was a notable building on the hill Gibeah, but he was eventually buried in Zela (2 S. 21:14).

2. Saul of Tarsus.
S. Paul.

A. Savias	Anc. of Ezra.	1 Es. 8:2
	is Uzzi.	Ezr. 7:4
Sceva	Jewish exorcist.	Ac. 19:14
Seba	s. of Cush.	Gn. 10:7
A. Sechenias	1. Companion of Ezra who returned from exile.	1 Es. 8:29
	is Shecaniah.	Ezr. 8:3
	2. Companion of Ezra who returned from exile.	1 Es. 8:32
	is Shecaniah.	Ezr. 8:5
Secundus	Thessalonian who accompanied St. Paul from Philippi to Europe.	Ac. 20:4
A. Sedekias AV. Zedechias	is Zedekiah. k. of Judah.	1 Es. 1:46
Segub	1. s. of Hiel who rebuilt Jericho.	1 K. 16:34; Jos. 6:26
	2. s. of Hezron, and f. of Jair. Judahite.	1 Ch. 2:21

Seled	Firstborn of Nadab, a Jerahmeelite.	1 Ch. 2:30
A. Selemia	Scribe of Ezra.	2 Es. 14:24
A. Selemias	Jew who took a foreign wife. is Shelemiah.	1 Es. 9:34 Ezr. 10:39
A. Seleucus	k. of Asia, s. of Antiochus the Great (2 Mac. 3:3). After reigning for twelve years, he was murdered. Three other Seleucid rulers are mentioned in Dan. 8:8; 11;7f; 11:10.	
Semachiah	s. of Shemaiah, gatekeeper.	1 Ch. 26:7
A. Semei	Jew who took a foreign wife. is Shimei.	1 Es. 9:33 Ezr. 10:33
A. Semeias AV. Semei	Benjamite Anc. of Mordecai. is Shimei.	Ad. Est. 11:2 Est. 2:5
Semein	Anc. of Jesus.	Lk. 3:26
A. Semeis AV. Semis	Levite. is Shimei.	1 Es. 9:23 Ezr. 10:23
Senaah	S. Sanaas.	
Sennacherib	k. of Assyria, s. of Sargon II and f. of Esar-haddon.	2 K. 19:36-37
Seorim	Priest.	1 Ch. 24:8
Serah AV. Sarah	d. of Asher.	Gn. 46:17
Seraiah	1. Scribe in reign of David. is Sheva is Shisha.	2 S. 8:17 2 S. 20:25 1 K. 4:3
	2. High Priest in reign of Zedekiah put to death by Nebuchadnezzar. Anc. of Ezra.	2 K. 25:18 Ezr. 7:1
A.	is Azaraias.	1 Es. 8:1
A.	is Saraias.	2 Es. 1:1
	3. Captain who joined Gedaliah.	2 K. 25:23
	4. Second s. of Kenaz. b. of Othniel. f. of Joab.	1 Ch. 4:13
	5. grandf. of Jehu, Simeonite.	1 Ch. 4:35

	6. Leader of the people who returned with Zerubbabel.	Ezr. 2:2
	is Azariah.	Neh. 7:7
A.	is Zaraias.	1 Es. 5:8
	7. Priest who returned from exile with Zerubbabel, and settled in Jerusalem.	Neh. 12:1, 11:11
	8. Prince whom Jehoiakim sent to put Jeremiah and Baruch in prison.	Jer. 36:26
	9. s. of Neriah. b. of Baruch. Chief chamberlain of Zedekiah and friend of Jeremiah.	Jer. 51:59
	10. One who sealed the covenant.	Neh. 10:2
A. Serar AV. Aserer	He returned to Jerusalem. is Sisera.	1 Es. 5:32 Ezr. 2:53
Sered	Oldest s. of Zebulun.	Gn. 46:14
A. Seron	Commander in the Syrian army defeated by Judas Maccabaeus.	1 Mac. 3:13
Serug	s. of Reu. f. of Nahor.	Gn. 11:20-23
A. Sesis	Jew who married a foreign wife. is Shashai.	1 Es. 9:34 Ezr. 10:40
A. Sesthel	Jew who married a foreign wife. is Bezalel.	1 Es. 9:31 Ezr. 10:30
Seth	1. Third s. of Adam and Eve, born after Cain had murdered his b. Abel (Gn. 4:25). His s. was Enosh, and he died at the age of 912 years.	
	2. Anc. of enemies of Israel (AV. and RV. 'tumult'. RSV. Sheth).	Nu. 24:17
Sethur	Asherite spy. s. of Michael.	Nu. 13:13
Shaaph	1. Youngest s. of Jahdai, Calebite.	1 Ch. 2:47
	2. s. of Caleb by Maacah.	1 Ch. 2:49
Shaashgaz	Chamberlain of k. Ahasuerus.	Est. 2:14
Shabbethai	1. Levite.	Ezr. 10:15
A.	is Sabbateus.	1 Es. 9:14

	2. One of the 'chiefs of the Levites'.	Neh. 11:16
Shachia	Benjamite. s. of Shaharaim.	1 Ch. 8:10
Shadrach	Name given to Hananiah, one of Daniel's companions. S. Hananiah 2.	Dan. 3
Shage	f. of Jonathan, one of David's heroes.	1 Ch. 11:34
Shaharaim	Benjamite.	1 Ch. 8:8

Shallum

1. s. Jabesh and k. of Israel, who murdered Zechariah and usurped his throne (2 K. 15:10), but reigned for one month only.

2. fourth s. of k. Josiah, and his successor in 608 B.C. Usually called Jehoahaz (1 Ch. 3:15).

3. s. of Tikvah and h. of Huldah 2 K. 22:14 the prophetess.

4. s. of Sismai and f. of   1 Ch. 2:40 Jekamiah. Judahite.

5. s. of Shaul and f. of Mibsam. 1 Ch. 4:25 desc. of Simeon.

6. f. of Hilkiah, s. of Zadok and 1 Ch. 6:12 High Priest.

A.   is Salem.   1 Es. 8:1
A.   is Salemas.   2 Es. 1:1

7. fourth s. of Naphtali.   1 Ch. 7:13
   is Shillem.   Gn. 46:24;
                             Nu. 26:49

8. Head of family of gatekeepers. 1 Ch. 9:17
A.   is Salum.   1 Es. 5:28
   is Meshullam.   Neh. 12:25

9. s. of Kore, chief of the porters 1 Ch. 9:19 at the East Gate. Probably is 8.
   is Meshelemiah.   1 Ch. 26:1
   is Shelemiah.   1 Ch. 26:14

10. f. of Jehizkiah, Ephraimite 2 Ch. 28:12 chief.

11. Porter who married a foreign Ezr. 10:24 wife.

A.	is Sallumus.	1 Es. 9:25
	12. s. of Bani who married a foreign wife.	Ezr. 10:42
	13. s. of Hallohesh who assisted at repairing the wall.	Neh. 3:12
	14. u. of Jeremiah.	Jer. 32:7
	15. f. of Maaseiah, doorkeeper.	Jer. 35:4
	16. s. of Col-hozeh. Repaired the wall and gates of Jerusalem.	Neh. 3:15

Shalman — Spoiler of Beth-arbel. May be the following. Hos. 10:14

Shalmaneser — Five Kings of Assyria bore this name.

1. is Shalmanezer III (859-824) against whom a Syrian coalition including Ahab, k. of Israel, fought at the battle of Karkar in 853 B.C., not mentioned in O.T. This Shalmanezer also claimed to have defeated in 841 Hazael (1 K. 16:29, 20:20, 22:1) of Syria mentioned in 1 K. 19:15.

2. The reference is to Shalmanezer V., s. of Tiglath Pileser III, and overlord of Hoshea, Israel's last king. Shalmanezer reigned (727-722 B.C.), and largely reduced, even if he did not actually capture, the city of Samaria, 2 K. 17:3.

Shama — One of David's heroes. 1 Ch. 11:44

Shamgar — s. of Anath and judge in South Israel who slew 600 Philistines with an oxgoad. Jg. 3:31

Shamhuth — Captain in David's army. 1 Ch. 27:8
is Shammoth. 1 Ch. 11:27
is Shammah. 2 S. 23:25

Shamir — Levite, s. of Micah. 1 Ch. 24:24

Shamlai — S. Salmai.

Shamma — Asherite, eighth s. of Zophah. 1 Ch. 7:37

Shammah —
1. s. of Reuel. grands. of Esau. Tribal chief of Edom. Gn. 36:13, 17
2. Third s. of Jesse, b. of David. 1 Ch. 2:13

	f. of Jonadab.	2 S. 13:3f.
	is Shimeah.	2 S. 13:3
	is Shimei.	2 S. 21:21
	is Shimea.	1 Ch. 2:13
	3. s. of Agee, one of the three who brought water from the well of Bethlehem to David in the cave of Adullam.	2 S. 23:11
	4. Harodite, one of 'the Thirty'.	2 S. 23:25
	is Shammoth.	1 Ch. 11:27
	is Shamhuth.	1 Ch. 27:8
Shammai	1. Jerahmeelite. s. of Onam.	1 Ch. 2:28
	2. s. of Rekem and desc. of Caleb.	1 Ch. 2:44
	3. Judahite, s. of Mered.	1 Ch. 4:17
Shammoth	S. Shamhuth and Shammah 4.	
Shammua	1. Reubenite spy. s. of Zaccur.	Nu. 13:4
	2. s. of David.	2 S. 5:14
	is Shimea.	1 Ch. 3:5
	3. Levite, f. of Abda.	Neh. 11:17
	is Shemaiah 6.	
	4. Head of priestly family. s. of Bilgah.	Neh. 12:18
Shamsherai	Benjamite. Eldest s. of Jeroham.	1 Ch. 8:26
Shapham	Gadite.	1 Ch. 5:12
Shaphan	1. Scribe in reign of Josiah (2 K. 22:3). King Josiah's secretary who read to the king the law book newly found in the Temple.	
	2. f. of Jaazaniah, leader of idolatrous sect.	Ezk. 8:11
Shaphat	1. Simeonite spy. s. of Hori.	Nu. 13:5
	2. f. of Elisha.	1 K. 19:16
	3. Judahite desc. of David, grands. of Zerubbabel and youngest s. of Shemaiah.	1 Ch. 3:22
	4. Gadite chief.	1 Ch. 5:12
	5. Herdsman of David. s. of Adlai.	1 Ch. 27:29

Sharai	s. of Bani who married a foreign wife.	Ezr. 10:40
Sharar	S. Sacar 1.	
Sharezer	1. b. of Adrammelech, assassins of k. Sennacherib.	2 K. 19:37
	2. One sent to consult Zechariah and the priests about the commemoration of the destruction of the temple by the Chaldaeans.	Zec. 7:2
Shashai	s. of Bani who married a foreign wife.	Ezr. 10:40
	A. is Sesis.	1 Es. 9:34
Shashak	s. of Elpaal. Benjamite. f. of eleven sons.	1 Ch. 8:14
Shaul	1. k. of Edom.	Gn. 36:37
	2. s. of Simeon.	Gn. 46:10
	3. Levite. Anc. of Samuel.	1 Ch. 6:24
	is Joel no. 3.	1 Ch. 6:36
Shavsha	Secretary of State in David's reign.	1 Ch. 18:16
Sheal	s. of Bani who married a foreign wife.	Ezr. 10:29
	A. is Jasaelus.	1 Es. 9:30
Shealtiel	f. of Zerubbabel.	Ezr. 3:2
	s. of k. Jeconiah.	1 Ch. 3:17
	A. is Salathiel.	1 Es. 5:5 etc.
	A. is Ezra (wrongly) in	2 Es. 3:1
Sheariah	s. of Azel of Benjamin and desc. of Saul.	1 Ch. 8:38
Shear-Jashub	s. of Isaiah, symbolical name 'Remnant shall return'.	Is. 7:3
Sheba	1. s. of Raamah, desc. of Ham.	Gn. 10:7
	2. s. of Joktan, desc. of Shem.	Gn. 10:28
	3. s. of Yokshan.	Gn. 25:3
	4. Benjamite who headed a revolt against David immediately after the suppression of Absalom's rebellion.	2 S. 20:1f.
	5. Gadite and desc. of Abihail.	1 Ch. 5:13

	6. Q. of Sheba (name unknown) (1 K. 10:1-10). She visited Solomon for commerce or possibly marriage.	
Shebaniah	1. Levite who led the worship at Ezra's fast.	Neh. 9:4
	2. Levite priest who sealed the covenant.	Neh. 10:4
	is Shecaniah 8.	
	3. Levite who sealed the covenant.	Neh. 10:10
	4. Levite who sealed the covenant.	Neh. 10:12
	5. Priest in David's time.	1 Ch. 15:24
Sheber	s. of Caleb.	1 Ch. 2:48
Shebna	Governor or Secretary of the Palace of k. Hezekiah against whom Isaiah predicted 'the fall of the mighty.'	Is. 22:15ff.
Shebuel	1. s. of Gershom. grands. of Moses.	1 Ch. 23:16
	is Shubael.	1 Ch. 24:20
	2. s. of Heman and a temple musician.	1 Ch. 25:4
	is Shubael.	1 Ch. 25:20
Shecaniah	1. desc. of Zerubbabel.	1 Ch. 3:21
	2. s. of Jehaziel. His sons returned with Ezra.	Ezr. 8:5
	A. is Sechenias.	1 Es. 8:32
	3. Chief of 10th course of priests.	1 Ch. 24:11
	4. Priest in reign of Hezekiah.	2 Ch. 31:15
	5. s. of Jehiel and contemporary of Ezra. One who had married a foreign wife (Ezr. 10:2).	
	6. f. of Shemaiah, a gatekeeper.	Neh. 3:29
	7. f.-in-law of Tobiah the Ammonite.	Neh. 6:18
	8. Head of family who returned with Zerubbabel.	Neh. 12:3
	is Shebaniah 2.	Neh. 10:4
	9. f. of Hattush, Attus.	Ezr. 8:2
	Returned from exile with Ezra.	1 Es. 8:29

Shechem	1. s. of Hamor.	Gn. 33:19
	2. Manassite.	Nu. 26:31
	3. s. of Shemida, Manassite.	1 Ch. 7:19
Shedeur	f. of Elizur, Reubenite chief.	Nu. 1:5
Sheerah	d. of Ephraim.	1 Ch. 7:24
Shehariah	Benjamite chief.	1 Ch. 8:26
Shelah	1. Third s. of Judah.	Gn. 38:5
	2. f. of Eber, desc. of Noah.	Gn. 10:24
Shelemiah	1. s. of Bani who married a foreign wife.	Ezr. 10:39
	A. is Selemias.	1 Es. 9:34
	2. f. of Hananiah who restored part of the wall of Jerusalem.	Neh. 3:30
	3. Priest appointed by Nehemiah as treasurer to distribute Levitical tithes.	Neh. 13:13
	4. f. of Jehucal in time of Zedekiah.	Jer. 38:1
	5. f. of Irijah, the captain who arrested Jeremiah.	Jer. 37:13
	6. Head of family of porters.	1 Ch. 26:14
	is Meshelemiah.	1 Ch. 26:1
	7. s. of Bani who married a foreign wife.	Ezr. 10:41
	8. s. of Cushi and Anc. of Jehudi who lived in the time of Jehoiakim.	Jer. 36:14
	9. s. of Abdeel. Sent by Jehoiakim to arrest Baruch and Jeremiah	Jer. 36:26.
Sheleph	s. of Joktan.	Gn. 10:26
Shelesh	Asherite.	1 Ch. 7:35
Shelomi	f. of Asherite prince.	Nu. 34:27
Shelomith	1. m. of Danite man stoned to death for blasphemy.	Lv. 24:11
	2. d. of Zerubbabel.	1 Ch. 3:19
	3. Levite, s. of Izhar.	1 Ch. 23:18
	is Shelomoth.	1 Ch. 24:22
	4. Child of Rehoboam.	2 Ch. 11:20
	5. s. of Josiphiah. His family returned with Ezra.	Ezr. 8:10
	A. is Salimoth.	1 Es. 8:36
Shelomoth	1. S. Shelomith 3.	

	2. desc. of Moses and a treasurer.	1 Ch. 26:25-6
	3. Gershonite, Levite.	1 Ch. 23:9
Shelumiel	Simeonite prince.	Nu. 1:6
	is Shemuel.	Nu 34:20
Shem	Eldest s. of Noah (Gn. 5:32), and one of the eight people saved by his father's ark. He was the anc. of the Shemites, *i.e.* the Semitic part of the human family.	Gn. 10:21-31
Shema	1. s. of Hebron, desc. of Caleb.	1 Ch. 2:43-4
	2. Reubenite, s. of Joel	1 Ch. 5:8
	is Shimei 8.	1 Ch. 5:4
	3. Benjamite.	1 Ch. 8:13
	is Shimei 11.	1 Ch. 8:21
	4. Stood at Ezra's right hand at the reading of the law.	Neh. 8:4
A.	is Sammus.	1 Es. 9:43
Shemaah	f. of disaffected Benjamite warrior.	1 Ch. 12:3
Shemaiah	1. Prophet, helped the revolution against Rehoboam.	2 Ch. 12:5
	2. s. of Shecaniah. desc. of Zerubbabel.	1 Ch. 3:22
	3. Simeonite chief.	1 Ch. 4:37
	4. Reubenite.	1 Ch. 5:4
	5. Merarite Levite.	1 Ch. 9:14
	6. Levite. f. of Obadiah.	1 Ch. 9:16
	is Shammua.	1 Ch. 11:17
	7. Levitical Kohathite in time of David.	1 Ch. 15:8
	8. Levite scribe. s. of Nethanel.	1 Ch. 24:6
	9. Korahite Levite. s. of Obed-Edom.	1 Ch. 26:4
	10. A Levite teacher of law under Jehoshaphat.	2 Ch. 17:8
	11. Levite in reign of Hezekiah.	2 Ch. 29:14
	12. Priest in reign of Hezekiah.	2 Ch. 31:15
	13. Levite chief.	2 Ch. 35:9
A.	is Samaias.	1 Es. 1:9
	14. Leader sent by Ezra to fetch Levites and Nethinim.	Ezr. 8:16
A.	is Samaias.	1 Es. 8:43

	15. s. of Adonikam. Companion of Ezra who returned from Babylon.	Ezr. 8:13
A.	is Samaias.	1 Es. 8:39
	16. Priest who married a foreign wife.	Ezr. 10:21
A.	is Sameus.	1 Es. 9:21
	17. Layman who married foreign wife.	Ezr. 10:31
A.	is Sabbeus.	1 Es. 9:32
A.	18. s. of Ezora—layman with foreign wife.	1 Es. 9:34
	19. Levite—keeper of East Gate.	Neh. 3:29
	20. Prophet in time of Nehemiah. s. of Delaiah.	Neh. 6:10
	21. Priest who sealed the covenant.	Neh. 10:8
	22. Priest under Zerubbabbel.	Neh. 12:6
	23. Processional Priest.	Neh. 12:34
	24. Levite, desc. of Asaph.	Neh. 12:35
	25. Levite singer at dedication of wall.	Neh. 12:36
	26. Processional musical Levite.	Neh. 12:42
	27. f. of prophet Urijah.	Jer. 26:20
	28. Prophet at Babylon brought into captivity with Jehoiakim (Jer. 29). Opposed Jeremiah.	
	29. f. of Delaiah, a prince in the reign of Zedekiah.	Jer. 36:12
	30. Kinsman of Tobias.	Tob. 5:13
Shemariah	1. Benjamite who joined David.	1 Ch. 12:5
	2. s. of Rehoboam.	2 Ch. 11:19
	3. s. of Harim who married a foreign wife.	Ezr. 10:32
	4. s. of Bani who married a foreign wife.	Ezr. 10:41
Shemeber	k. of Zeboiim.	Gn. 14:2
Shemed	S. Shemer 4.	
Shemer	1. Owner of hill on which Omri built Samaria.	1 K. 16:24
	2. Merarite.	1 Ch. 6:46
	3. Asherite.	1 Ch. 7:34
	is Shomer.	1 Ch. 7:32

	4. Benjamite who built Ono.	1 Ch. 8:12
AV. Shamed	RV. Shemed	
Shemida	desc. of Manasseh.	1 Ch. 7:19
Shemiramoth	1. Levite harpist.	1 Ch. 15:18
	2. Levite teacher of law.	2 Ch. 17:8
Shemuel	1. Simeonite s. of Ammihud.	Nu. 34:20
	is Shelumiel.	Nu. 1:6
	2. grands. of Issachar.	1 Ch. 7:2
Shenazzar	s. of Jeconiah (Jehoiachin) and u. of Zerubbabel.	
	(May be Sheshbazzar.)	1 Ch. 3:18
Shephatiah	1. s. of David.	2 S. 3:4
	2. His family returned with Zerubbabel.	Ezr. 2:4
A.	is Saphat.	1 Es. 5:9
A.	is Saphatias.	1 Es. 8:34
	3. His sons returned with Zerubbabel.	Ezr. 2:57
	4. Judahite.	Neh. 11:4
	5. Benjamite.	1 Ch. 9:8
	6. A Prince, contemporary of Jeremiah.	Jer. 38:1
	7. Benjamite who joined David.	1 Ch. 12:5
	8. Simeonite prince.	1 Ch. 27:16
	9. s. of Jehoshaphat.	2 Ch. 21:2
Shephi	Horite chief.	1 Ch. 1:40
	is Shepho.	Gn. 36:23
Shepho	S. Shephi.	
Shephupham or Shephuphan	Benjamite.	Nu. 26:39; 1 Ch. 8:5
	is Muppim.	Gn. 46:21
	is Shuppim.	1 Ch. 7:12
Sherebiah	1. s. of Mahli.	Ez. 8:18
	2. Levite who assisted Ezra.	Neh. 8:7
A.	is Asebebias.	1 Es. 8:47
A.	is Eserebias.	1 Es. 8:54
A.	is Sarabias.	1 Es. 9:48
	3. One who sealed the covenant.	Neh. 10:12

	4. Levite who came with Zerubbabel from exile.	Neh. 12:8
	5. Levite.	Neh. 12:24
Sheresh	Manassite.	1 Ch. 7:16
Sheshai	s. of Anak, dwelling in Hebron.	Nu. 13:22
Sheshan	Jerahmeelite.	1 Ch. 2:31
Sheshbazzar	Cyrus, the persian ruler, made Sheshbazzar, governor of Judah (Ezr. 1:8). As such he both brought back the Temple vessels to Jerusalem (Ezr. 5:14f.) and laid the foundation of the new Temple (5:16). Probably is Tirshatha of Ezr. 2:63.	
Sheth	S. Seth 2.	
Shethar	Prince of Persia.	Est. 1:14
Shethar-Bozenai	One who corresponded with Darius regarding the rebuilding of the temple.	Ezr. 5:3ff.
	A. is Sathrabuzanes.	1 Es. 6:3ff.
Sheva	1. s. of Caleb.	1 Ch. 2:49
	2. S. Shavsha, Seraiah and Shisha.	
Shilhi	f. of k. Asa's w., Azubah.	1 K. 22:42
Shillem	Fourth s. of Naphtali.	Gn. 46:24
Shilshah	Asherite.	1 Ch. 7:37
Shimea	1. S. Shammua 2.	
	2. Merarite, Levite.	1 Ch. 6:30
	3. Gershonite Levite.	1 Ch. 6:39
	4. S. Shammah 2.	
	S. Shimei 4.	
Shimeah	1. desc. of Jehiel, f. of Gibeon.	1 Ch. 8:32
	is Shimeam.	1 Ch. 9:38
	2. S. Shimei 4.	
Shimeam	S. Shimeah 1.	
Shimeath	f. of one of murderers of k. Joash of Judah.	2 K. 12:21
Shimei	1. grands. of Levi. s. of Gershon.	Ex. 6:17
	2. s. of Gera. Benjamite who cursed David.	2 S. 16:5ff.
	3. Friend of David.	1 K. 1:8

	4. b. of David.	2 S. 21:21
	is Shammah.	1 S. 16:9
	is Shimeah.	2 S. 13:3
	is Shimea.	1 Ch. 2:13
	5. s. of Ela one of Solomon's commissariat officers.	1 K. 4:18
	6. b. of Zerubbabel.	1 Ch. 3:19
	7. grands. of Simeon.	1 Ch. 4:26
	8. Reubenite, s. of Joel.	1 Ch. 5:4
	9. Levite, s. of Merari.	1 Ch. 6:29
	10. Levite of family of Gershom.	1 Ch. 6:42
	11. Benjamite chief.	1 Ch. 8:21
	is Shema 2.	
	12. Levite singer.	1 Ch. 25:17
	13. Officer of David, in charge of vineyards.	1 Ch. 27:27
	14. Levite in reign of Hezekiah.	2 Ch. 29:14
	15. Another Levite in Hezekiah's reform.	2 Ch. 31:12-13
	16. Levite who took a foreign wife.	Ezr. 10:23
A.	is Semeis.	1 Es. 9:23
	17. Layman who took a foreign wife.	Ezr. 10:33
A.	is Semei.	1 Es. 9:33
	18. Layman who took a foreign wife.	Ezr. 10:38
A.	is Semeis.	1 Es. 9:34
	19. Benjamite, desc. of Kish.	Est. 2:5
A.	is Semeias.	Est. 11:2

Shimeon	s. of Harim who married a foreign wife.	Ezr. 10:31
Shimon	Judahite.	1 Ch. 4:20
Shimrath	Benjamite, s. of Shimei	1 Ch. 8:21
Shimri	1. Simeonite.	1 Ch. 4:37
	2. f. of one of David's 'Thirty'.	1 Ch. 11:45
	3. Head of family of gatekeepers.	1 Ch. 26:10
	4. Levite, leading cleaner.	2 Ch. 29:13
Shimrith	S. Shimeath.	

Shimron	Fourth s. of Issachar.	Gn. 46:13
Shimshai	Scribe of Rehum.	Ezr. 4:8
	A. is Samellius.	1 Es. 2:16
Shinab	k. of Admah attacked by Chedorlaomer and his allies.	Gn. 14:2
Shiphi	Simeonite prince.	1 Ch. 4:37
Shiphrah	Hebrew midwife.	Ex. 1:15
Shiphtan	Ephraimite prince.	Nu 34:24
Shisha	S. Shavsha.	
Shishak	k. of Egypt in time of Rehoboam (1 K. 14:25). (He was Sheshonk I, the first k. of the twenty-second Egyptian Dynasty.)	
Shitrai	He kept David's herds in Sharon.	1 Ch. 27:29
Shiza	Reubenite.	1 Ch. 11:42
Shobab	1. s. of David and Bathsheba.	2 S. 5:14
	2. Calebite.	1 Ch. 2:18
Shobach	General in army of Hadadezer. k. of Syria.	2 S. 10:16
	is Shophach.	1 Ch. 19:16f.
Shobai	His family were gatekeepers.	Ezr. 2:42
Shobal	1. Second s. of Seir the Horite.	Gn. 36:20
	2. Judahite.	1 Ch. 2:50
Shobek	Chief who sealed the covenant.	Neh. 10:24
Shobi	s. of Nahash, Ammonite.	2. S. 17:27
Shoham	Merarite priest.	1 Ch. 24:27
Shomer	1. S. Shemer 3.	1 Ch. 7:32
	2. S. Shimeath.	2 K. 12:21
Shophach	S. Shoback.	
Shua	1. f. of Judah's Canaanite wife.	Gn. 38:2
	2. Asherite woman.	1 Ch. 7:32
Shuah	s. of Abraham and Keturah.	Gn. 25:2
Shual	Asherite.	1 Ch. 7:36
Shubael	S. Shebuel.	

Shuhah	b. of Caleb (Chelub).	1 Ch. 4:11
Shuham	s. of Dan.	Nu. 26:42
	is Hushim.	Gn. 46:23
Shuni	Third s. of Gad.	Gn. 46:16
Shupham	S. Muppim and Shephupham.	
Shuppim.	S. Muppim.	
Shuthelah	1. First s. of Ephraim.	1 Ch. 7:20;
	2. Descendant of Ephraim.	1 Ch. 7:21
Sia	His family returned with Zerubbabel.	Neh. 7:47
	A. is Sua.	1 Es. 5:29
	is Siaha.	Ezr. 2:44
Sibbecai, AV. Sibbechai	A Zerahite who slew the Philistine giant Saph.	2 S. 21:18
	is Mibbecai.	
Sidon.	Descendant of Ham.	Gen. 10:15
Sihon	k. of Amorites defeated by Israelites at Jahaz.	Nu. 21:21ff.

Silas   was a prominent member of the church at Jerusalem. He was both a Roman citizen and gifted in prophetic ministry (Ac. 15:22f.). He accompanied Paul on the latter's second missionary journey, and helped Paul with letters from Corinth (15:36-41; 1 Thess. 1:1, 2:1). He was almost certainly Silvanus (2 Cor. 1:19; 1 P. 5:12).

Silvanus	S. Silas.	
Simeon	1. Second s. of Jacob and Leah and anc. of the tribe of Simeon.	Gn. 29:33
	A. 2. grandf. of Judas Maccabaeus.	1 Mac. 2:1
	3. Anc. of Jesus.	Lk. 3:30
	4. Blessed the infant Jesus at his presentation in the temple (Lk. 2:25ff.). Author of *Nunc Dimittis*.	
	AV. 5. Prophet and teacher at Antioch, called Niger.	Ac. 13:1
	6. S. Peter.	

Simon	A. 1.	Simon II successor to Onias II.	Sir. 50:1; 50:1ff.

A. 2. Temple official.   2 Mac. 3:4
S. Heliodorus.

A. 3. This Simon was the second s. of Mattathias, whose five sons are the Maccabees (1 Mac. 2:3). With his father and brothers, Judas and Jonathan, he fought successfully against Antiochus Epiphanes of Syria. He eventually succeeded to the leadership and was so successful, both in war (1 Mac. 13:41), and diplomacy, that he was elected leader and high priest (1 Mac. 14:27-48). He was eventually slain by his s.-in-law in 135 B.C.

A. 4. Jew who had taken a foreign   1 Es. 9:32
wife.
S. Chosamaeus.
is Shimeon.   Ezr. 10:31

5. S. Peter the apostle.

6. is Magus, a sorcerer from Samaria (Ac. 8:9-24). He seduced his fellow citizens with his magical acts, was then converted under the preaching of Philip the evangelist, and tried to buy the power of the Holy Spirit from Peter and John.

7. is the Cananaean, *i.e.* member of the party of Zealots.   Lk. 6:15; Mt. 10:4

8. b. of Jesus.   Mt. 13:55

9. The leper at whose house in Bethany a woman anointed Jesus.   Mt. 26:6

10. Pharisee who entertained   Lk. 7:36
Jesus to dinner.

11. f. of Judas Iscariot.   Jn. 6:71

12. Cyrenian who carried the cross of Jesus; f. of Alexander and Rufus.   Mk. 15-21

13. Tanner with whom Peter   Ac. 9:43
lodged at Joppa.

Sippei	S. Saph.

A. Sirach	f. of the author of the Book Ecclesiasticus-Jesus ben Sirach.

Sisera	1. Captain of Jabin, k. of Hazor, killed by Jael.	Jg. 4:2ff.
	2. Family of Nethinim, returned with Zerubbabel.	Ezr. 2:53
Sisinnes	A. Governor of Coele-Syria and Phoenicia under Darius (1 Es. 6:3). Contemporary of Zerubbabel.	
	is Tattenai (Tatnai).	Ezr. 5:3
Sismai	Jerahmeelite.	1 Ch. 2:40
Sithri	grands. of Kohath, s. of Uzziel and cousin of Moses.	Ex. 6:22
So	k. of Egypt.	2 K. 17:4
Soco	Probably a place name in 1 Ch. 4:8.	
Sodi	f. of Gaddiel, Zebulunite spy.	Nu. 13:10
Solomon	k. of Israel, s. of David and Bathsheba. He was the third k. of Israel (1 K. 2-11). He emerged from the court intrigues during the last days of David as k. of united Israel, and he reigned for 40 years. He was famed for his great wisdom, though events in his reign conflict with this. He established and maintained an empire by peaceful means, organised it for taxation, conscript labour and defence purposes, was a great builder and merchant. He built Israel's first temple at Jerusalem, and directed many leading enterprises on sea and land. Among his many wives was a d. of Pharaoh (1 K. 11:1-3). Deut. 17:16-17 probably reflects a judgement on his reign. He was also called Jedidah (2 S. 12:25).	
A. Someis AV. Samis	One who had taken a foreign wife.	1 Es. 9:34
	is Shimei.	Ezr. 10:38
Sopater	Accompanied St. Paul on his third missionary journey.	
	s. of Pyrrhus.	Ac. 20:4
	is Sosipater.	Ro. 16:21

Sophereth	His family of Nethinim returned with Zerubbabel.	Neh. 7:57
	is Hassophereth.	Ezr. 2:55
A.	is Assaphion.	1 Es. 5:33
A. Sophonias	is Zephaniah, 1.	2 Es. 1:40
Sosipater	Jewish Christian, kinsman of St. Paul.	Ro. 16:21
Sosthenes	1. Ruler of synagogue at Corinth.	Ac. 18:17
	2. Designated b. of St. Paul in the inscription of the 1st letter to the Corinthians (1 Cor. 1:1)	
A. Sostratus	Governor of citadel at Jerusalem in time of Antiochus Epiphanes.	2 Mac. 4:27
Sotai	His family were 'servants of Solomon' who returned with Zerubbabel.	Ezr. 2:55
Stachys	Christian greeted by St. Paul.	Ro. 16:9
Stephanas	Christian of Corinth, baptised by Paul.	1 Co. 1:16
Stephen	The apostles chose 7 men (Ac. 6, 8:2), prob. Hellenistic Jewish Christians, to care for the widows of the church (Ac. 6:1-6). The greatest was Stephen, for he became also a great preacher and worker of miracles. He was soon arrested and stoned to death. His speech testified to the church's mission to the world, and his martyrdom affected Paul.	
A. Sua	Returned with Zerubbabel.	1 Es. 5:29
	is Siaha.	Ezr. 2:44
	is Sia.	Neh. 7:47
Suah	Asherite.	1 Ch. 7:36
A. Subai	Returned with Zerubbabel.	1 Es. 5:30
	is Shamlai.	Ezr. 2:46
	is Salmai.	Neh. 7:48
A. Subas	His descendants returned with Zerubbabel, as 'Solomon's Servants'.	1 Es. 5:34
A. Sudias	Levite whose family returned with Zerubbabel.	1 Es. 5:25
	is Hodaviah.	Ezr. 2:40

	is Hodevah.	Neh. 7:43
A. Susanna	1. Susanna was the beautiful d. of a priest, married to a wealthy h., Joakim (Susanna). Falsely accused of adultery, she was at first declared guilty but later found to be innocent through the advocacy of the youthful Daniel.	
	2. Woman benefactor of Jesus.	Lk. 8:3
Susi	f. of Gaddi. Manassite.	Nu. 13:12
Symeon	RV. form of Simeon in N.T.	
Syntyche	Member of the Church at Philippi, possibly deaconess.	Ph. 4:2
Synzygus	'Yoke-fellow' (Ph. 4:3). A member of Church in Philippi to whom St. Paul addressed a request to reconcile two members of the Church who were at variance.	

T

A. Tabaoth	His family of Nethinim returned with Zerubbabel.	1 Es. 5:29
	is Tabbaoth.	Ezr. 2:43
Tabeel	1. f. of Rezin, k. of Damascus.	2 K. 16:5; Is. 7:1ff.
	2. Persian official in Samaria	Ezr. 4:7
	A. is Tabellius.	1 Es. 2:16
A. Tabellius	S. Tabeel 2.	
Tabitha	S. Dorcas.	
Tabrimmon	f. of Benhadad 1, k. of Syria.	1 K. 15:18
Tahan	1. Head of Ephraimite clan.	Nu. 26:35
	2. Another Ephraimite.	1 Ch 7:25
Tahash	Third s. of Nahor.	Gn. 22:24
Tahath	1. Kohathite Levite.	1 Ch. 6:24
	2. Ephraimite, s. of Bered.	1 Ch. 7:20
	3. Ephraimite, s. of Eleadah.	1 Ch. 7:20
Tahpenes	w. of Pharaoh in David's time. s.-in-law of Hadad of Edom.	1 K. 11:19

Tahrea	grands. of Mephibosheth.	1 Ch. 9:41
	is Tarea.	1 Ch. 8:35
Talmai	1. s. of Anak whose city was Hebron before the Israelites took possession. Jos 15:14	
	2. s. of Ammihur, k. of Geshur. f. of Maacah, David's w., grandf. of Absalom.	
		2 S. 3:3, 13:37
Talmon	1. His family were temple gatekeepers.	1 Ch. 9:17
	2. Another gatekeeper.	Neh. 11:19
Tamar	1. Canaanite, w. of Er and then w. of his b. Onan. d.-in-law of Judah; bore him two sons, Pharez (Perez) and Zerah.	1 Ch. 2:4
	2. d. of David. Sister of Absalom, who was violated by her half-b. Amnon (2 S. 13:1).	
	3. d. of Absalom.	2 S. 14:27
Tanhumeth	f. of Seraiah.	2 K. 25:23
Taphath	d. of Solomon. w. of Benabinadab.	1 K. 4:11
Tappuah	s. of Hebron.	1 Ch. 2:43
Tarea	S. Tahrea.	
Tarshish	1. Benjamite, s. of Bilkan.	1 Ch. 7:10
	2. A prince of Persia and Media who had access to the royal presence.	Est. 1:14
Tartan	Assyrian officer (title).	Is. 20:1
Tattenai	Governor of Coele-Syria and Phoenicia under Darius Hystaspis.	Ezr. 5:3
	A. is Sisinnes.	1 Es. 6:3
Tebah	First s. of Nahor.	Gn. 22:24
Tebaliah	Merarite gatekeeper.	1 Ch. 26:11
Tehinnah	Judahite, s. of Eshton.	1 Ch. 4:12
Telah	Ephraimite, s. of Resheph.	1 Ch. 7:25
Telem	Gatekeeper who married a foreign wife.	Ezr. 10:24
	A. is Tolbanes.	1 Es. 9:25
Tema	s. of Ishmael.	Gn. 25:15

Temah AV. Tamah	His family of Nethinim returned with Zerubbabel.	Ezr. 2:53
Teman	Edomite chief.	Gen. 36:11
Temeni	s. of Ashhur, a s. of Caleb.	1 Ch. 4:6
Terah	f. of Abraham, Nahor and Haran, migrated from Ur to Harran.	Gn. 11:24
Teresh	Chamberlain of Ahasuerus who with Bigthan plotted against the king and was foiled by Mordecai.	Est. 2:21
	A. is Tharra.	Ad. Est. 12:1
Tertius	Amanuensis who wrote the Ep. to the Romans for St. Paul.	Ro. 16:22
Tertullus	Advocate or orator who accused St. Paul before Felix at Caeserea.	Ac. 24:1
Thaddaeus AV. Lebbaeus	is probably Lebbaeus (AV.). is Judas, b. of James (Lk. 6:16). The name Thaddaeus is only found in the lists of names of the twelve disciples.	
A. Tharra	Chamberlain of k. Ahasuerus. is Teresh.	Ad. Est. 12:1 Est. 2:21
A. Thassi	Surname or nickname of Simon the Maccabee.	1 Mac. 2:3
A. Theodotus	1. Messenger sent by Nicanor to Judas Maccabaeus. 2. Plotted assassination of k. Ptolemy Philopator, foiled by Dositheus.	2 Mac. 14:19 3 Mac. 1:2
Theophilus	The person to whom the Third Gospel and the Acts of the Apostles were addressed. Lk. 1:3; Ac. 1:1	
Theudas	Mentioned by Gamaliel as attracting a large number of people to himself.	Ac. 5:36
Thocanus AV. Theo- canus	f. of Ezechias who examined the problem of foreign wives with Ezra. is Tikvah, f. of Jahzeiah.	1 Es. 9:14 Ezr. 10:15
Thomas	is Didymus, means 'twin'. one of the twelve disciples. He risked death for and with Jesus (Jn. 11:16). He is known as 'doubting	

	Thomas' because he first denied the resurrection of Jesus, and then in the famous words, 'My Lord and my God' (20:28) affirmed it. The stories about Thomas are in the Fourth Gospel only.	
A. Thomei AV. Thomoi	He returned with Zerubbabel. is Temah.	1 Es. 5:32 Ezr. 2:53
A. Thrasaeus	f. of Apollonius.	2 Mac. 3:5
Tiberius	Second Roman Emperor, during whose rule Jesus Christ lived and died, and the earliest Christians suffered persecution. Lk. 3:1 is Caesar of the Four Gospels.	
Tibni	s. of Ginath—disputed the throne of Israel for four years with Omri (1 K. 16:15ff.), and on his death Omri reigned.	
Tidal	k. of Goiim.	Gn. 14:1
Tiglath-Pileser	is Pul, k. of Assyria.	2 K. 15:19; 1 Ch. 5:26
Tikvah	1. f.-in-law of Huldah the prophetess. is Tokhath.	2 K. 22:14 2 Ch. 34:22
	2. f. of Jahzeiah, a contemporary of Ezra.	Ezr. 10:15
A.	is Thocanus.	1 Es. 9:14
Tilgath-Pilneser	S. Tiglath-Pileser.	
Tilon	s. of Shimon, desc. of Judah.	1 Ch. 4:20
Timaeus	f. of the blind beggar Bartimaeus.	Mk. 10:46
Timna, AV. Timnah	1. Concubine of Eliphaz, Esau's son, and m. of Amalek.	Gn. 36:12
	2. s. of Eliphaz.	1 Ch. 1:36
	3. Duke of Edom.	Gn. 36:40
	4. Grands. of Esau.	1 Ch. 1:36
Timon	One of seven elected to assist the apostles.	Ac. 6:5
Timotheus A.	1. Leader of Ammonites defeated by Judas Maccabaeus.	1 Mac. 5:6ff.
	2. AV. form of Timothy, in N.T.	

Timothy	A native of Lystra, of a Greek father and a Jewish mother. He became a Christian and a companion of Paul on his second journey (Ac. 16:1-3). He was mentioned in Paul's correspondence, 1 and 2 Thess.; 2 Cor. 1:19, 4:17; Ro. 16:21. He accompanied Paul to Jerusalem (Ac. 20:4f.), and figures again in Philippians, Colossians and Philemon. Paul wrote two letters to him (1 and 2 Ti.). He was later imprisoned and freed (Heb. 13:23).	
Tiras	s. of Japheth.	Gn. 10:2
Tirhakah	k. of Cush (Ethiopia) marched against Sennacherib.	2 K. 19:9
Tirhanah	s. of Caleb and Maacah.	1 Ch. 2:48
Tiria	s. of Jehallelel, Judahite.	1 Ch. 4:16
Tirshatha	is viceroy Sheshbazzar (title). (title).	Ezr. 2:63 Neh. 7:65, 70
Tirzah	One of five d. of Zelophehad whose case decided women's rights in property among Jews.	Nu. 26:33
Titus	Companion of Paul (Tit. 1:4), and Barnabas (Gal. 2:1). He figured prominently in 2 Cor. 7, 8 and 12, serving as the representative and partner of Paul. The Epistle of Paul to Titus was written to him. Paul ordered him to organise the Church in Crete and then later to rejoin him in Nicopolis (Epirus).	
Titus Justus	S. Justus no. 2.	
Titus Manius	S. Manius.	
Toah	Levite. is Nahath.	1 Ch. 6:34 1 Ch. 6:26
Tob	is Tabeel.	Is. 7:6
Tob-Adonijah	Levite sent by Jehoshaphat to teach in Judah.	2 Ch. 17:8
Tobiah	1. Returned with Zerubbabel. 2. Ammonite who opposed Nehemiah.	Ezr. 2:60 Neh. 2:10

A. Tobias

| A. Tobias | 1. s. of Tobit. | To. 1:9 |
| | 2. f. of Hyrcanus and a prominent man. | 2 Mac. 3:11 |

| A. Tobiel | f. of Tobit. | To. 1:1 |

| Tobijah | 1. Levite sent by Jehoshaphat to teach in Judah. | 2 Ch. 17:8 |
| | 2. Member of deputation from Babylon to Jerusalem with gold and silver for a crown for Zerubbabel and Joshua. | Zec. 6:10 |

| A. Tobit | He figured in the Book of Tobit as a deeply religious Jew who by his devotion to his religion gained a miraculous deliverance for himself, his s. Tobias, and his d.-in-law Sarah. | |

| Togarmah | s. of Gomer, b. of Ashkenaz and Riphath. | Gn. 10:3 |

| Tohu | Anc. of prophet Samuel. is Nahath. | 1 S. 1:1 / 1 Ch. 6:26 |

| Toi | S. Tou. | |

| Tokhath | S. Tikvah. | |

| Tola | 1. Minor Judge following Abimelech. | Jg. 10:1 |
| | 2. s. of Issachar. | Gn. 46:13 |

| A. Tolbanes | Porter in time of Ezra. is Telem. | 1 Es. 9:25 / Ezr. 10:24 |

| Tou | k. of Hamath. is Toi. | 1 Ch. 18:9 / 2 S. 8:9 |

| Trophimus | Companion of St. Paul (Ac. 20:4). He was an Ephesian (Ac. 21:29). and he went with Paul on his last journey to Jerusalem (20:4-5). His alleged entry to the Temple court was the occasion of Paul's arrest (21:29f.). | |

| Tryphaena | Christian woman saluted by St. Paul. | Ro. 16:12 |

| A. Tryphon | Officer of Alexander Balas who supported Antiochus for the throne. | 1 Mac. 11:39 |

Tryphosa	Saluted by St. Paul, together with Tryphaena.	Ro. 16:12
Tubal	s. of Japheth and a trader in copper.	Gn. 10:2
Tubal-Cain	s. of Lamech, b. of Jabal and Jubal.	Gn. 4:22
Tychicus	Companion of St. Paul (Ac. 20:4), he carried several of Paul's letters to their destinations (Eph. 6:21).	
Tyrannus	St. Paul preached and debated daily in his School.	Ac. 19:9

U

Ucal	One of the two people whom Agur addressed (Pr. 30:1). (AV. and RV. treated as proper name but see RVm.).	
Uel	s. of Bani who married a foreign wife.	Ezr. 10:34
	A. is Juel.	1 Es. 9:34
Uknaz	desc. of Caleb. AVm.	1 Ch. 4:15
Ulam	1. Manassite.	1 Ch. 7:16f.
	2. Head of family of archers. Benjamite.	1 Ch. 8:39f.
Ulla	Asherite.	1 Ch. 7:39
Unni	1. Levite musician.	1 Ch. 15:18
	2. Post-exilic Levite.	Neh. 12:9
RV. Unno		
Unno AV. Unni	is Unni 2.	
Ur	f. of Eliphal, one of David's 'Thirty'.	1 Ch. 11:35
	cp. Ahasbai.	2 S. 23:34
Urbanus	Christian greeted by St. Paul.	Ro. 16:9
Uri	1. Judahite, f. of Bezalel.	Ex. 31:2

		2. f. of Geber, one of Solomon's commissariat officers.	1 K. 4:19
		3. Porter or gatekeeper in the restored Temple.	Ezr. 10:24
Uriah		1. One of David's 'Thirty'. mighty men. Hittite. is Urijah.	2 S. 23:39
		2. High priest in reign of Ahaz.	2 K. 16:10
		3. Prophet, s. of Shemaiah. contemporary of Jeremiah.	Jer. 26:20ff.
		4. Priest, desc. of Hakkoz.	Neh. 3:4
		5. One who stood by Ezra's right hand when he read the law.	Neh. 8:4
	A.	is Urias.	1 Es. 9:43
A. Urias AV. Iri		1. Priest. S. Uriah 4.	1 Es. 8:62
		2. One who stood by Ezra's right hand when he read the law. S. Uriah 5.	1 Es. 9:43
Uriel		1. Levite, chief of Kohathites in time of David.	1 Ch. 6:24
		2. Maternal grandf. of Abijah, k. of Judah.	2 Ch. 13:2
A. Uta		His sons returned under Zerubbabel.	1 Es. 5:30
Uthai		1. Judahite at Jerusalem after exile. is Athaiah.	1 Ch. 9:4 Neh. 11:4
		2. s. of Bigvai who returned with Ezra.	Ezr. 8:14
A. Uthi		He returned with Ezra. is Uthai 2.	1 Es. 8:40 Ezr. 8:14
Uz		1. Head of Aramaean tribe, eldest s. of Aram. grands. of Shem.	Gn. 10:23
		2. s. of Nahor.	Gn. 22:21
AV. Huz		3. s. of Dishan, Horite.	Gn. 36:28

Uzai	f. of Palal who helped Nehemiah to rebuild the wall of Jerusalem. Neh. 3:25
Uzal	s. of Joktan. Gn. 10:27
Uzza	1. Benjamite. 1 Ch. 8:7
	2. Head of family of Temple servants that returned with Zerubbabel. Ezr. 2:49
	3. Driver of cart on which the ark was removed from Kiriath-jearim (2 S. 6:3). He died after putting his hand on the ark to steady it (1 Ch. 13:7).
	4. Owner of garden in which kings Manasseh and Amon were buried. 2 K. 21:18, 26
Uzzah	1. Levite, s. of Shimei. 1 Ch. 6:29
	2. S. Uzza 3.
Uzzi	1. Priest. desc. of Aaron. 1 Ch. 6:5f.
	2. desc. of Tola, of tribe of 1 Ch. 7:2 Issachar.
	3. Benjamite. 1 Ch. 7:7
	4. Benjamite, f. of Elah. 1 Ch. 9:8
	5. Levite overseer of the Levites Neh. 11:22 dwelling in Jerusalem.
	6. Head of a priestly family. Neh. 12:19
	7. Levite musician at dedication Neh. 12:42 of walls of Jerusalem.
Uzzia	One of David's 'Thirty'. 1 Ch. 11:44
Uzziah	1. k. of Judah, s. of Amaziah (2 K. 14:2). He reigned for 52 years, and became a leper (2 Ch. 26:11ff.). cp. Is. 6:1. is Azariah. 2 K. 14:21
	2. Levite, Kohathite, s. of Uriel. 1 Ch. 6:24
	3. f. of Jonathan, one of David's 1 Ch. 27:25 stewards.
	4. Priest, s. of Harim, who Ezr. 10:21 married a foreign wife.
	5. Judahite, f. of Athaiah, in Neh. 11:4 time of Nehemiah.
Uzziel	1. s. of Kohath. Ex. 6:18
	2. Simeonite captain successful 1 Ch. 1:42 against Amalekites.

	3. Benjamite.	1 Ch. 7:7
	4. Levite musician.	1 Ch. 25:4
	is Azarel.	1 Ch. 25:18
	5. Levite of family of Jeduthun.	2 Ch. 29:14
	6. One of the goldsmiths who helped to repair the wall of Jerusalem.	Neh. 3:8

V

Vaizatha, AV. Vajezatha	s. of Haman, slain by Jews	Est. 9:9
Vaniah	s. of Bani who married a foreign wife.	Ezr. 10:36
	A. is Anos.	1 Es. 9:34
Vashni	Samuel's firstborn s. AV. cp. RV.	1 Ch. 6:28
Vashti	Q. and w. of Ahasuerus (Xerxes) who was deposed because of disobedience prompted by modesty.	Est. 1:9
Vophsi	f. of Nahbi, Naphtalite spy.	Nu. 13:14

X

Xerxes	k. of Persia.	Ezr. 4:6
	is Ahasuerus of the Book of Esther.	

Z

Zaavan AV. Zavan	Second s. of Ezer. desc. of Seir.	Gn. 36:27 1 Ch. 1:42
Zabad	1. Judahite, desc. of Jerahmeel.	1 Ch. 2:36
	2. Ephraimite.	1 Ch. 7:21
	3. One of the murderers of k. Joash.	2 Ch. 24:26
	4. Layman of time of Ezra, who married a foreign wife.	Ezr. 10:27

	5. Layman of time of Ezra who married a foreign wife.	Ezr. 10:33
	6. Layman of time of Ezra, who married a foreign wife.	Ezr. 10:43
	7. s. of Ahlai, one of David's Thirty mighty men.	1 Ch. 11:41
A. Zabadeas AV. Zabadaias	Layman who took a foreign wife. is Zabad 6.	1 Es. 9:35 Ezr. 10:43
Zabbai	1. desc. of Beba who married a foreign wife.	Ezr. 10:28
	A. is Jozabdus.	1 Es. 9:29
	2. f. of Baruch who assisted in the rebuilding of the wall.	Neh. 3:20
	is Zaccai.	Ezr. 2:9
Zabbud	Exile who returned with Ezra.	Ezr. 8:14
	A. is Istalcurus.	1 Es. 8:40
Zabdeus	A. Priest who had taken a non-Jewish wife.	1 Es. 9:21
	is Zebadiah.	Ezr. 10:20
Zabdi	1. grandf. of Achan.	Jos. 7:1
	is Zimri.	1 Ch. 2:6
	2. Benjamite.	1 Ch. 8:19
	3. Official of David. Wine steward.	1 Ch. 27:27
	4. Levite, desc. of Asaph.	Neh. 11:17
	is Zichri.	1 Ch. 9:15
Zabdiel	1. Judahite, desc. of Perez, f. of one of David's officers.	1 Ch. 27:2
	2. Prominent official in Nehemiah's time.	Neh. 11:14
	A. 3. Arabian who put Alexander Balas to death.	1 Mac. 11:17
Zabud	s. of Nathan, priest under Solomon.	1 K. 4:5
Zaccai	S. Zabbai.	
Zacchaeus	1. Tax Collector in Jericho, whose life was	

			changed through contact with Jesus.	
				Lk. 19:1ff.
	A.	2.	Officer of Judas Maccabaeus.	2 Mac. 10:19
Zaccur		1.	Reubenite.	Nu. 13:4
		2.	Simeonite.	1 Ch. 4:26
		3.	Merarite, s. of Jaaziah.	1 Ch. 24:27
		4.	Asaphite, post-exilic singer.	1 Ch. 25:2
		5.	Assisted Nehemiah to rebuild the wall. s. of Imri.	Neh. 3:2
		6.	One who sealed the covenant.	Neh. 10:12
		7.	S. Zabbud.	
	A.	8.	Post-exilic temple singer who had married a foreign wife.	1 Es. 9:24
		9.	f. of Hanan one of Nehemiah's treasurers.	Neh. 13:13

Zachariah, AV. Zacharias	In his denunciation of the Pharisees our Lord declared that the innocent blood of the prophets is to be requited of them (Mt. 23:35), a reference to the murder of Zechariah (2 Ch. 24:20).

Zacharias		1.	Priest in Josiah's reign.	2 Ch. 35:8
	A.		is Zechariah.	1 Es. 1:8
	A.	2.	Singer in David's time.	1 Es. 1:15
			is Heman.	2 Ch. 35:15
	A.	3.	is Prophet Zechariah.	1 Es. 6:1
	A.	4.	is Zechariah of the sons of Parosh.	1 Es. 8:30; Ezr. 8:3
	A.	5.	is Zechariah of the sons of Bebai.	1 Es. 8:37; Ezr. 8:11
	A.	6.	is Zechariah with whom Ezra consulted.	1 Es. 8:44; Ezr. 8:16
	A.	7.	is Zechariah of the sons of Elam.	1 Es. 9:27; Ezr. 10:26
	A.	8.	is Zechariah who stood at Ezra's left hand at the reading of the law (1 Es. 9:44; Neh. 8:4).	
	A.	9.	f. of Joseph a leader under Judas Maccabaeus.	1 Mac. 5:18
		10.	f. of John the Baptist, a priest of the course of Abijah.	Lk. 1:5ff.

A. Zachary   S. Zechariah 20.

Zadok	1. Founder of the leading branch of the priesthood in Jerusalem (2 S. 8:17). The descendants of Zadok continued during many centuries to take the lead among the priests of the temple.	
	2. Leader of armed men who fought for David at Hebron.	1 Ch. 12:28
	3. grandf. of k. Jotham.	2 K. 15:33
	4. s. of Baana, and one of Nehemiah's willing helpers in rebuilding the city wall (Neh. 3:4).	
	5. s. of Immer, repaired the wall on the east side of the city.	Neh. 3:29
	6. One of the chiefs of the people who sealed the covenant.	Neh. 10:21
	7. High Priest.	1 Ch. 6:12
	8. Scribe whom Nehemiah appointed treasurer.	Neh. 13:13
	9. Anc. of Jesus Christ.	Mt. 1:14
Zaham	s. of k. Rehoboam.	2 Ch. 11:19
Zalaph	f. of Hanun who assisted in repairing the wall.	Neh. 3:30
Zalmon	One of David's 'Thirty'.	2 S. 23:28
	is Ilai.	1 Ch. 11:29
Zalmunna	k. of Midian.	Jg. 8:4
A. Zambri AV. Zambis	s. of Maani (Bani) who took a foreign wife.	1 Es. 9:34
	is Amariah.	Ezr. 10:42
A. Zamoth	His sons had taken foreign wives.	1 Es. 9:28
	is Zattu.	Ezr. 10:27
Zaphenath-Paneah	Name given by Pharaoh to Joseph.	Gn. 41:45
A. Zaraias, AV. Zacharias	1. Returned from captivity.	1 Es. 5:8
	is Seraiah.	Ezr. 2:2
	is Azariah.	Neh. 7:7
	2. Anc. of Ezra.	1 Es. 8:2
	is Zerahiah.	Ezr. 7:4
	is Arna.	2 Es. 1:2
	3. f. of Eliehoenai returned from captivity with Ezra.	1 Es. 8:31
	is Zerahiah.	Ezr. 8:4

	4. s. of Michael returned with Ezra.	1 Es. 8:34
	is Zebadiah.	Ezr. 8:8
A. Zarakes AV. Zaraces	b. of Joakim or Jehoiakim, k. of Judah.	1 Es. 1:38
A. Zardeus, AV. Sardeus	Had taken a foreign wife. is Aziza.	1 Es. 9:28 Ezr. 10:27
A. Zathoes AV. Zathoe	Returned with Zerubbabel. is Zattu.	1 Es. 8:32 Ezr. 8:5
A. Zathui	Returned with Zerubbabel. is Zattu. is Zathoes.	1 Es. 5:12 Ezr. 2:8 1 Es. 8:32
Zattu	Head of family of exiles who sealed Nehemiah's covenant.	returned, who Ezr. 2:8
Zaza	Jerahmeelite.	1 Ch. 2:33
Zebadiah	1. Benjamite, desc. of Beriah.	1 Ch. 8:15
	2. Benjamite, desc. of Elpaal.	1 Ch. 8:17
	3. s. of Jeroham. Joined David at Ziklag.	1 Ch. 12:7
	4. One of David's officers. s. of Asahel.	1 Ch. 27:7
	5. Exile who returned with Ezra's second caravan.	Ezr. 8:8
A.	is Zaraias.	1 Es. 8:34
	6. Priest who married and divorced a foreign wife.	Ezr. 10:20
A.	is Zabdeus.	1 Es. 9:21
	7. Korahite gatekeeper.	1 Ch. 26:2
	8. Levite sent by Jehoshaphat to teach in the cities of Judah.	2 Ch. 17:8
	9. Official in local courts set up by k. Jehoshaphat.	2 Ch. 19:11
Zebah	Midianite k. captured by Gideon.	Jg. 8:4-21
Zebedee	f. of apostles James and John, fisherman on the sea of Galilee.	Mt. 4:21
Zebidah, AV. Zebudah	m. of k. Jehoiakim.	2 K. 23:36

Zebina	s. of Nebo who married a foreign wife. S. Zabad 6.	Ezr. 10:43
Zebul	Abimelech's officer and governor of Shechem.	Jg. 9:28ff.
Zebulun	Sixth s. of Jacob and Leah.	Gn. 30:19

Zechariah

1. Benjamite, b. of Ner. u. of Saul. s. of Jeiel, patriarch of Gibeon in Benjamin. 1 Ch. 9:37 is Zecher. 1 Ch. 8:31
2. Levite gatekeeper, s. of Meshelemiah. 1 Ch. 9:21
3. Levite musician. 1 Ch. 15:18
4. Priest in time of David. 1 Ch. 15:24
5. Levite desc. of Uzziel. 1 Ch. 24:25
6. Levite gatekeeper of family of Merari. 1 Ch. 26:11
7. f. of Iddo, Manassite. 1 Ch. 27:21
8. Official of Judah sent to teach the law in days of Jehoshaphat. 2 Ch. 17:7
9. Levite, desc. of Asaph. 2 Ch. 20:14
10. s. of K. Jehoshaphat, killed by his eldest brother. 2 Ch. 21:2
11. s. of Priest Jehoiada, stoned by the people when he called them to repentance. 2 Ch. 24:20
S. Zachariah.
12. Prophet of Uzziah's reign. Exercised a powerful influence for good upon the king. 2 Ch. 26:5
13. s. of Jeroboam II, k. of Israel. 2 K. 14:29 With him ended the dynasty of Jehu.
14. s. of Jeberechiah. Man of high repute who witnessed to Isaiah's prophecy written upon a tablet. Is. 8:2
15. f. of Abi (Abijah) the m. of k. Hezekiah. 2 K. 18:2
16. Reforming Asaphite under Hezekiah, who took part in the cleansing of the house of the Lord. 2 Ch. 29:13
17. Head of a house of Reubenites. 1 Ch. 5:7

18. Kohathite Levite in the days   2 Ch. 34:12
    of Josiah.

19. Priest who gave animals for celebration of
    the Passover by Josiah.   2 Ch. 35:8
    S. Zacharias 1.

20. The Prophet (Zec. 1:1), contemporary of
    Haggai and of a priestly family who returned
    from the exile.   Neh. 12:4
    He was the s. of Berechiah and grands. of
    Iddo. His ministry lasted less than two
    years. He sought to revive the hopes of his
    depressed contemporaries by persuading them
    to rebuild the ruined Temple. He comforted
    them with his visions received in the night,
    which are largely messianic. His genuine
    prophecies were probably limited to chapters
    1-8 of the book that bears his name.

A.   is Zachary.   2 Es. 1:40

21. desc. of Parosh who accompanied Ezra from
    Babylon in 458 B.C.   Ezr. 8:3

22. s. of Bebai who returned to   Ezr. 8:11
    Jerusalem with Ezra.

23. One of the delegation Ezra   Ezr. 8:16
    sent to Iddo.

24. desc. of Elam who put away his foreign wife
    according to Ezra's reform.   Ezr. 10:26

25. desc. of Perez who settled in Jerusalem
    after the return from Babylon.   Neh. 11:4

26. Judahite whose desc. settled in Jerusalem
    after the return from exile.   Neh. 11:5

27. Priest whose desc. settled in   Neh. 11:12
    Jerusalem under Nehemiah.

28. Head of priestly family.   Neh. 12:16

29. Asaphite at the dedication of the wall of
    Jerusalem.   Neh. 12:35

30. Priest, trumpeter who took part in the
    thanksgiving service.   Neh. 12:41

31. Stood with Ezra at the public   Neh. 8:4
    reading of the Law.

A. 32. f. of Joseph, a captain in the   1 Mac. 5:18
    Maccabaean army.

A. 33.	Levitical singer.	1 Es. 1:15
	is Heman.	2 Ch. 35:15

Zecher	s. of Jehiel.	1 Ch. 8:31
	S. Zechariah 1.	

A. Zechrias	Priest in the line of Ezra.	1 Es. 8:1
AV. Ezerias	is Azariah.	Ezr. 7:1

Zedekiah

1. s. of Chenaanah. One of Ahab's 400 court prophets (1 K. 22:11ff.), who promised Ahab victory against the Syrians.

2. Prophet deported to Babylon, Jer. 29:21f. denounced by Jeremiah.

3. s. of Hananiah, one of the princes of Judah in the reign of Jehoiakim. Jer. 36:12

4. Last k. of Judah. Youngest s. of Josiah. 2 K. 23:31

A.	is Sedekias.	1 Es. 1:46
	is Mattaniah.	2 K. 24:17

AV. Zidkijah 5. 'Prince', official, who sealed the covenant at Nehemiah's reformation. Neh. 10:1

Zeeb	Midianite Prince slain by Gideon.	Jg. 6-7

Zelek	Ammonite, one of David's 'Thirty'.	2 S. 23:37

Zelophehad Manassite who died during the wilderness wanderings (Nu. 26:33). His five daughters successfully asserted their claim to his estate (Nu. 26:33).

Zemirah	s. of Becher.	1 Ch. 7:8

Zenas	Lawyer, probably skilled in Jewish law.	Tit. 3:13

Zephaniah

1. The Prophet (Zeph. 1:1), and author of the ninth of the books of the Minor Prophets. He was the gt.-gt.-grands. of Hezekiah, probably K. Hezekiah of Judah, and was a contemporary of Josiah, gt.-grands. of Hezekiah.

2. Kohathite anc. of Heman the singer. 1 Ch. 6:36

	3. s. of Maaseiah, priest in Jerusalem at time of Jeremiah.	Jer. 29:25
	4. f. of Josiah, a returned exile, into whose house the messengers from the Jews went.	Zec. 6:10
Zephi	S. Zepho.	
Zepho	s. of Eliphaz. Edomite.	Gn. 36:11
	is Zephi.	1 Ch. 1:36
Zephon	Eldest s. of Gad.	Nu. 26:15
Zerah	1. s. of Reuel, the s. of Esau.	Gn. 36:13
	2. f. of early Edomite k., Jobab.	Gn. 36:33
	3. Younger of the twin sons of Judah.	Gn. 38:30
	4. s. of Simeon.	Nu. 26:13
	is Zohar.	Gn. 46:10
	5. Levite of the family of Gershom.	1 Ch. 6:21
	6. Kohathite musician.	1 Ch. 6:41
	7. Ethiopian who invaded Judah in the reign of Asa, and was defeated.	2 Ch. 14:9
Zerahiah	1. Priest, an anc. of Ezra.	1 Ch. 6:6
A.	is Zaraias.	1 Es. 8:2
	2. f. of Eliehoenai.	Ezr. 8:4
A.	is Zaraias.	1 Es. 8:31
A. Zerdaiah AV. Sardeus	Jew who had married a foreign woman.	1 Es. 9:28
	is Aziza.	Ezr. 10:27
Zeresh	w. of Haman.	Est. 5:10
Zereth	Judahite, s. of Helah.	1 Ch. 4:7
Zeri	Head of family of singers.	1 Ch. 25:3
	is Izri.	1 Ch. 25:11
Zeror	Anc. of Saul.	1 S. 9:1
Zeruah	m. of Jeroboam.	1 K. 11:26
Zerubbabel	s. of Shealtiel (Salathiel), and grands. of k. Jehoiachin. In 1 Ch. 3:19 he was erroneously called the s. of Pedaiah, Shealtiel's b. Of Davidic descent (Ezr. 3:2), he played an	

important part in connexion with the return of the Jews from exile in 537 B.C. Soon after their arrival in Jerusalem he set up an altar and took steps for the rebuilding of the temple. In the beginning of the reign of Darius he was governor of Judah (Hag. 1:1).

Zeruiah	Sister of David, m. of David's officers, Abishai, Joab and Asahel (1 Ch. 2:16; 2 S. 2:18).	
Zetham	Levite, of the family of Gershon.	1 Ch. 23:8
Zethan	Benjamite.	1 Ch. 7:10
Zethar	Eunuch of k. Ahasuerus.	Est. 1:10
Zia	Head of Gadite family.	1 Ch. 5:13
Ziba	Servant of the house of Saul, appointed steward to Mephibosheth by k. David.	2 S. 9:2
Zibeon	s. of Seir, Edomite chief and grandf. of Aholibamah who was one of Esau's wives.	Gn. 36:20, 24
Zibia	Benjamite, s. of Shaharaim.	1 Ch. 8:9
Zibiah	m. of Joash, k. of Judah.	2 Ch. 24:1
Zichri	1. grands. of Kohath.	Ex. 6:21
	2. Benjamite, desc. of Shimei.	1 Ch. 8:19
	3. Benjamite, desc. of Shashak.	1 Ch. 8:23
	4. Benjamite, desc. of Jeroham.	1 Ch. 8:27
	5. Benjamite, f. of Joel.	Neh. 11:9
	6. Asaphite.	1 Ch. 9:15
	7. Levite, s. of Joram, f. of Shelomoth who was appointed treasurer by David.	1 Ch. 26:25
	8. Reubenite, f. of Eliezer.	1 Ch. 27:16
	9. Judahite, f. of Amasiah.	2 Ch. 17:16
	10. f. of Elishaphat a captain in Jehoiada's time.	2 Ch. 23:1
	11. Might man of Ephraim.	2 Ch. 28:7
	12. Post-exilic priest in the days of Joiakim.	Neh. 12:17
Zidkijah	S. Zedekiah 5.	
Ziha	1. Head of family of Nethinim.	Ezr. 2:43
	2. Overseer of Temple servants.	Neh. 11:21

Zillah	w. of Lamech, m. of Tubal-cain.	Gn. 4:19
Zillethai	1. Benjamite.	1 Ch. 8:20
AV. Zilthai	2. Manassite, who joined David.	1 Ch. 12:20
Zilpah	m. of Gad and Asher, concubine of Jacob.	Gn. 30:9
Zilthai	S. Zillethai.	
Zimmah	1. Levite, desc. of Gershom.	1 Ch. 6:20
	2. Levite, desc. of Gershom.	1 Ch. 6:42
Zimram	s. of Abraham and Keturah.	Gn. 25:9
Zimri	1. Simeonite. Prince. s. of Salu.	Nu. 25:6f.
	2. Grands. of Judah, s. of Zerah, anc. of Achan.	1 Ch. 2:6
	is Zabdi.	Jos. 7:1
	3. Benjamite desc. of Saul's s. Jonathan.	1 Ch. 8:36
	4. Usurper k. of Israel, himself displaced by Omri.	1 K. 16:9
Zina	S. Zizah.	
Ziph	1. Calebite.	1 Ch. 2:42
	2. Judahite, s. of Jehallelel.	1 Ch. 4:16
Ziphah	Judahite, s. of Jerahmeel.	1 Ch. 4:16
Ziphion	Eldest s. of Gad.	Gn. 46:16
Zippor	f. of Balak, k. of Moab.	Nu. 22:2
Zipporah	d. of priest of Midian, w. of Moses and m. of Gershom.	Ex. 2:21
Ziza	1. Simeonite chief.	1 Ch. 4:37
	2. s. of Rehoboam.	2 Ch. 11:20
Zizah	Levite, of the family of Gershom.	1 Ch. 23:11
	is Zina.	1 Ch. 23:10
Zobebah	Judahite.	1 Ch. 4:8
Zohar	1. f. of Ephron the Hittite.	Gn. 23:8
	2. Simeonite.	Gn. 46:10
	is Zerah.	Nu. 26:13
	3. Judahite.	1 Ch. 4:7
	is Izhar.	
Zoheth	desc. of Judah.	1 Ch. 4:20

Zophah	Asherite.	1 Ch. 7:35
Zophai	Anc. of Samuel (Levite).	1 Ch. 6:26
	is Zuph (Ephraimite).	1 S. 1:1
Zophar	Third in order of Job's three friends.	Job 2:11
Zorobabel	A. form of Zerubbabel.	
Zorzelleus	f. of Augia who married Addus, the anc. of a priestly family who could not trace their genealogy at the return under Zerubbabel.	
		1 Es. 5:38
Zuar	f. of Nethanel, Simeonite head.	Nu. 1:8
Zuph	Anc. of Samuel (Ephraimite).	1 S. 1:1
	is Ziph.	1 Ch. 6:35
	is Zophai (Levite).	1 Ch. 6:26
Zur	1. Midianite leader slain by the Israelites.	Nu. 31:8
	2. (Benjamite) Gibeonite. s. of Jeiel.	1 Ch. 8:30
Zuriel	Levite. Merarite chief of carpenters in the wilderness.	Nu. 3:35
Zurishaddai	f. of Shelumiel, Simeonite leader in the wilderness.	Nu. 1:6

APPENDIX

Genealogies

Further help is available to the reader in the excellent article entitled 'Genealogy' by E. L. Curtis in Hasting's *Dictionary of the Bible*, Vol. 2, pp. 121a-137b. He shows that genealogies are in descending (*e.g.* Gn. 5; Ru. 4:18-23) or ascending order (1 Ch. 6:33-43; Ezr. 7:1-5, etc.). He discusses various types of lists and genealogies, and gives in detail the family trees of the twelve sons of Jacob.

Gn. 5 gives ten generations from the first man—Adam—to Noah, the hero of the flood. From his three sons, Shem, Ham and Japheth, the world was repeopled, as is illustrated in the table of nations in Gn. 10. Gn. 11 traces the line from Shem to Terah, the father of Abraham. From these two and Abraham's sons, Ishmael and Isaac, further families and tribes are descended (Gn. 22, 25:19 and 36). From Isaac's son Jacob sprang the twelve sons who became the ancestors of the twelve tribes of Israel. These twelve, by his two wives and his two concubines, were:

by Leah: Reuben, Simeon, Levi, Judah, Issachar and Zebulon.
by Rachel: Joseph (Ephraim and Manasseh), Benjamin.
by Bilhah: Dan and Naphtali.
by Zilpah: Gad and Asher.

The family lists of these twelve ancestors are to be found in Gn. 46:8-27; Ex. 6:14-26; Nu. 26:5-62 and 1 Ch. 1-9. The lists reveal that Levi (43), Judah (61) and Benjamin (25) produced the greatest number of families or clans. None of the rest reach double figures. Interest centres in Levi because of the priesthood, in Judah because of David, and in Benjamin, to a lesser extent, because of Saul the first king of Israel.

The Christian reader of this book will also know of the two genealogies of Jesus Christ in Mt. 1:1-17 and Lk. 3:23-28 through his earthly father, Joseph, with special reference to the descent through David. Matthew's interest is shown in his first verse 'The book of the generation of Jesus Christ, the son of David, the son of Abraham'. whereas Luke goes backwards through David, and through Abraham, to Seth who was the son of Adam, who was the son of God (Lk. 3:38). Matthew shows the Jewish descent, Luke the universal descent of Jesus, the Son of Man.

Certain other embryonic lists of a different kind are also found in Scripture, such as the list of examples in the Psalms (105, 106, 136) and the heroes of faith in the Epistle to the Hebrews 11. References are also found to the Book of the Lord (Ex. 32:32; Ps. 56:8, 139:16), and to the Book of Life (Ps. 69:28 and Dan. 12:1). These last references point to the Book of Life in Rev. 3:5, 20:12, 15, the Book which was only opened by the Lamb (Rev. 5:9-10). In turn this reminds us of the injunction of Jesus Christ in Lk. 10:20; 'Howbeit in this rejoice not, that the spirits are subject unto you; but rejoice that your names are written in heaven.'